Roland Lang

A Decision Unit for Autonomous Agents Based on Psychoanalytical Theory

Roland Lang

A Decision Unit for Autonomous Agents Based on Psychoanalytical Theory

Probing Models of Psychoanalytical Metapsychology in the Computational Framework ARSi09

Südwestdeutscher Verlag für Hochschulschriften

Impressum/Imprint (nur für Deutschland/ only for Germany)

Bibliografische Information der Deutschen Nationalbibliothek: Die Deutsche Nationalbibliothek verzeichnet diese Publikation in der Deutschen Nationalbibliografie; detaillierte bibliografische Daten sind im Internet über http://dnb.d-nb.de abrufbar.

Alle in diesem Buch genannten Marken und Produktnamen unterliegen warenzeichen-, marken- oder patentrechtlichem Schutz bzw. sind Warenzeichen oder eingetragene Warenzeichen der jeweiligen Inhaber. Die Wiedergabe von Marken, Produktnamen, Gebrauchsnamen, Handelsnamen, Warenbezeichnungen u.s.w. in diesem Werk berechtigt auch ohne besondere Kennzeichnung nicht zu der Annahme, dass solche Namen im Sinne der Warenzeichen- und Markenschutzgesetzgebung als frei zu betrachten wären und daher von jedermann benutzt werden dürften.

Verlag: Südwestdeutscher Verlag für Hochschulschriften Aktiengesellschaft & Co. KG
Dudweiler Landstr. 99, 66123 Saarbrücken, Deutschland
Telefon +49 681 37 20 271-1, Telefax +49 681 37 20 271-0
Email: info@svh-verlag.de
Zugl.: Wien, TU, Diss., 2010

Herstellung in Deutschland:
Schaltungsdienst Lange o.H.G., Berlin
Books on Demand GmbH, Norderstedt
Reha GmbH, Saarbrücken
Amazon Distribution GmbH, Leipzig
ISBN: 978-3-8381-1875-8

Imprint (only for USA, GB)

Bibliographic information published by the Deutsche Nationalbibliothek: The Deutsche Nationalbibliothek lists this publication in the Deutsche Nationalbibliografie; detailed bibliographic data are available in the Internet at http://dnb.d-nb.de.

Any brand names and product names mentioned in this book are subject to trademark, brand or patent protection and are trademarks or registered trademarks of their respective holders. The use of brand names, product names, common names, trade names, product descriptions etc. even without a particular marking in this works is in no way to be construed to mean that such names may be regarded as unrestricted in respect of trademark and brand protection legislation and could thus be used by anyone.

Publisher: Südwestdeutscher Verlag für Hochschulschriften Aktiengesellschaft & Co. KG
Dudweiler Landstr. 99, 66123 Saarbrücken, Germany
Phone +49 681 37 20 271-1, Fax +49 681 37 20 271-0
Email: info@svh-verlag.de

Printed in the U.S.A.
Printed in the U.K. by (see last page)
ISBN: 978-3-8381-1875-8

Copyright © 2010 by the author and Südwestdeutscher Verlag für Hochschulschriften Aktiengesellschaft & Co. KG and licensors
All rights reserved. Saarbrücken 2010

Acknowledgements

I would like to thank my advisor Prof. Dietmar Dietrich for giving me the opportunity to write this thesis in his ARS-Team, for his continuous support and guidance regarding this work as well as my academic and personal development. I would also like to thank my second advisor Prof. Harold Boley for the expeditious support across several time zones.

Further thanks go out to the 'old' ARS-Team that introduced me to the research area and its methodologies and paved the way to symbolization and neuro-psychoanalysis. To the technical members of the 'almost new' ARS-Team, who brought the project into its current state (sacrificing many nights of sleep on the way), as well as the psychoanalytical members of the 'almost new' ARS-Team, who gave me tremendous support in order to look beyond the boundaries of my own technical knowledge (sometimes subliminally to an apple in combination with a stomach).

Tobias, for his great support as a colleague and a friend. Brigitte for having an eye on the progress of my thesis during all the support-breakfasts. To all my friends that encouraged me and backed me up during the last eight years of preparing for and finally writing this work.

My parents receive my deepest gratitude for standing beside me and believing in me. Even in the deepest, most troubled water, they offer me support which I can always rely on.

Love and thanks to Isabella for her support and all her love and patience between landing and take-off and between take-off and landing.

Additional Proofreaders

Dr. Dietmar Bruckner
Mag. Isabella Vormittag

and

Dipl.-Ing. Tobias Deutsch
Dr. Klaus Doblhammer
Dipl.-Ing. Clemens Muchitsch
MMag Brit Müller
Dr. Brigitte Palensky
Stephan Stockinger
Dr. Rosemarie Velik
Mag. Sabine Waldhuber
Dipl.-Ing. Heimo Zeilinger

Abstract

One of the most challenging tasks for modern computer systems is to recognize situations and perform actions in the real world – a task that is handled easily by humans. Modern concepts for *Artificial Intelligence* still have serious problems when operating in such scenarios. In bionic approaches, models of human perception and cognitive processes are investigated in order to improve the performance of computational agents. A technically feasible and unitary model of these processes does not exist, however. This thesis introduces the computational framework ARSi09/Lang for the decision-making unit of an autonomous agent, which transfers the theory of psychoanalytical metapsychology into a technically feasible specification. Metapsychological concepts are not adapted but described technically with respect to a possible implementation. By applying a top-down design approach, the functional components of human decision processes according to metapsychology are identified and specified. Mirroring the functional structure of the cognitive processes according to the metapsychological models, interrelationships between the functional modules are defined in the form of interfaces and implemented within the decision unit of an autonomous agent. The application of the developed ARSi09-framework in an autonomous agent probes its performance and results in a modular decision-making framework with an integrated, comprehensive rewarding system that considers external and internal performance measures. In a virtual simulation of an embodied, situated agent that uses the introduced model in combination with methods of *Artificial Intelligence*, the performance of the framework is investigated, revealing considerable potential regarding the interpretation and evaluation of data owing to said performance measures.

Kurzfassung

Eine der größten Herausforderungen für moderne Computersysteme stellen Anwendungen dar, die in der realen Welt stattfinden. Aktuelle Methoden der *Künstlichen Intelligenz* zeigen immer noch bedeutende Mängel beim Einsatz in solchen Szenarien. Einem bionischen Ansatz folgend, werden Modelle der menschlichen Wahrnehmung und Entscheidungsfindung untersucht um aus den Erkenntnissen technische Systeme zu verbessern. Ein technisch umsetzbares, einheitliches Modell gibt es derzeit jedoch nicht. Die vorliegende Arbeit beschreibt das technische Framework ARSi09/Lang zur maschinellen Entscheidungsfindung für einen autonomen Agenten, als eine technisch realisierbare Spezifikation der Theorie der psychoanalytischen Metapsychologie. Dabei wird diese Theorie in der Arbeit nicht adaptiert oder weiterentwickelt, sondern von technischer Seite auf ihre Verwendbarkeit, Implementierbarkeit und Realisierbarkeit im Rahmen einer Entscheidungseinheit für autonome Agenten untersucht und verifiziert. Die funktionalen Komponenten der menschlichen Entscheidungsfindung werden in einer Top-Down-Analyse herausgearbeitet und spezifiziert. Das Zusammenspiel der einzelnen Funktionen wird dabei durch die Verwendung von Schnittstellendefinitionen beschrieben und in der Entscheidungsfindungseinheit eines autonomen Agenten implementiert. Dabei werden das entwickelte ARSi09-Framework und die darin umgesetzte psychoanalytische Theorie in einem autonomen Agenten auf die Probe gestellt. Das Ergebnis ist ein modulares Framework mit einem integrierten Bewertungssystem, das sowohl externe als auch interne Bewertungskriterien berücksichtigt. Zur Realisierung werden Methoden der klassischen *Künstlichen Intelligenz* verwendet, die jedoch von dem übergeordneten, psychoanalytisch inspirierten Framework gesteuert werden und die auferlegten Einschränkungen einhalten müssen. Die Anwendung des Agenten in einer simulierten Umgebung zeigt die Stärken des Systems besonders in der Dateninterpretation und Bewertung unter Verwendung interner und externer Leistungsindikatoren.

Table of Contents

1 Introduction   **1**
    1.1 A Brief History and the Motivation 1
    1.2 The Focus of this Work and its Basic Assumptions 4
    1.3 Possible Realizations 10

2 State of the Art   **12**
    2.1 Towards Modern AI and Demands in Applications 12
    2.2 Building Models in Cognitive Science 16
        2.2.1 Neuroscientific Approach - The Blue Brain Project 17
        2.2.2 Affective Computing - Modeling the Mind in AI 19
        2.2.3 The Ψ-Theory - Cognitive and Emotional Affects Simulation 24
        2.2.4 Emotional Machines 28
        2.2.5 Psychoanalytical Models in Artificial Intelligence 34
        2.2.6 Discussion of Cognitive Architectures 38
    2.3 Simulating Embodiment and the Environment 42
    2.4 Artificial Decision-Making Frameworks 49
    2.5 Evaluating Multi-Agent Simulations 58
    2.6 Artificial Recognition System - Psychoanalysis 62

3 Concept and Model of the Decision Unit   **67**
    3.1 Neuro-Psychoanalytical Prerequisites 68
        3.1.1 From Neurological Foundations to Metapsychology 68
        3.1.2 The Second Topographical Model of Psychoanalysis – Layer 1 . . . 74
        3.1.3 Psychoanalytical Structures Mandatory for Decision-Making 78
    3.2 The General Architecture of the Model 89

	3.2.1	The Embedded Mind – Top Level Considerations and Detailed Functional Combination	89
	3.2.2	Functional Structuring Applying the Top-Down Design Approach .	94
	3.2.3	Functional Description of the Lowest Layers	97
3.3	The Structure of Psychic Processing – A New Approach in Computational Planning		105
	3.3.1	Minimum Requirement Analysis for Structural Planning	106
	3.3.2	The Sequential Coherence of Psychoanalytical Functionalities . . .	108
	3.3.3	Interface Specification of the Functional Modules	113
	3.3.4	Discussion of Expected Advantages and Possible Limitations	118

4 Implementation in Embodied Agents   120

4.1	The Embodied Agent as Implementation Platform		121
4.2	Transforming Metapsychology to Implementation		127
	4.2.1	Utilized Data Structures	128
	4.2.2	The Association Framework Linking Information	130
	4.2.3	Implementing Rules, Searching, and Filtering Mechanisms	132
	4.2.4	Employed Concepts and Implementation of Causal Planning	134
	4.2.5	Global Class Framework, Synchronization Aspects and Sequencing .	136
4.3	Realization of the Primary Process Functionality		138
	4.3.1	Drive and Perception Handling	138
	4.3.2	Primary Decision and Repressed Contents	141
4.4	Realization of the Secondary Process Functionality		144
	4.4.1	Perceptual Preprocessing	144
	4.4.2	Deliberation - Generating the Desire to Plan	146
	4.4.3	Uniting Demands of the Model and Implementation	151

5 Simulation of the Situated Agent   154

5.1	Simulation Environment		154
	5.1.1	Global Demands, Complexity, and Selection Criteria	155
	5.1.2	Customizing the MASON Environment as a Basic Platform	157
	5.1.3	Implemented Entities and their Class Framework	160
	5.1.4	Situatedness and the Agent-Environment Interaction	163
	5.1.5	Available Sensors and Actuators for Complex Agents	167
5.2	Setup and Initialization		169
	5.2.1	Setup of the Environment	169
	5.2.2	Setup of the Decision Unit	171

6	Results			**176**
	6.1	Utilized Evaluation Toolkit		176
	6.2	Simulation Results		179
		6.2.1	Configuration and Impacts	180
		6.2.2	Input Data Generation	187
		6.2.3	Search Parameters and Filtering Mechanisms	191
		6.2.4	Impacts on Decision Making and Information Flow	193
	6.3	Comparison to Classic AI Architectures and Conclusions Therefrom		195

7	Conclusion and Outlook		**201**
	7.1	Key Issues Regarding the Developed Agent Controller	201
	7.2	Hot Spots for Future Research	208
	7.3	Future Requirements to Decision Making Units	212

Bibliography	**215**

A	Abbreviations and Formalisms	**233**
	A.1 Abbreviations	233
	A.2 Usage of Mathematical Formalisms	233
	A.3 Utilized Unified Modeling Language (UML) Version 2.2 Notations	235

1 Introduction

In the late nineties, Prof. Dr. Dietmar Dietrich and his research team at the Institute of Computer Technology at the Vienna University of Technology began to introduce bionic[1] concepts into building automation by applying biologically inspired concepts to field bus networks. This new approach was designed to cope with the rising demands of modern building automation, especially in the area of data processing, condensation, and interpretation, and was first published in 2000 at a conference for factory communication systems [Die00]. Within the same research group almost 10 years later, this thesis introduces an approach for building the decision unit of an embodied, autonomous agent using concepts from the theory of psychoanalytical metapsychology[2]. Although these concepts seem to be scarcely related, the motivation remains the same: Building computer systems capable of perceiving and interpreting real world processes and reacting accordingly to support humans in their everyday business.

1.1 A Brief History and the Motivation

In the beginning of the project, the main problem was the tremendously increasing amount of sensory data within building automation. A centralized computer system was no longer able to handle and interpret the rising number of computer nodes within a building, which increased from several thousand to more than fifty-thousand nodes in the last ten years

---

[1]According to [Nac98, p. 3], bionics systematically transforms structures, processes, and development principles of biological systems into technically realizable applications.

[2]Sigmund Freud, the founder of psychoanalysis, developed a functional, topographical model of the human psyche. This theory is today known as metapsychology. Currently, leading neurologists and psychoanalysts are confirming assumptions of the models of metapsychology using modern neurological methods. Mark Solms is one of these leading scientists and chairman of the International Neuropsychoanalytical Society (npsa).

Introduction

([Die00] and [DFZ⁺09]). To decentralize the necessary computer power, the research team began to compare conventional field buses with *"... the nervous system of higher animals or humans..."* [Die00] and realized first concepts within the project "SmartKitchen (SmaKi)" [Rus03]. The SmaKi was the institute's kitchen, equipped with different types of sensors and actuators and was the host for new conceptual implementations, following the idea of *Perceptive Awareness* and also the implementation platform for the newly developed bionical models, described in [DFR02]. With this platform, it became possible to prove the feasibility of the concepts and to test their functionality in respect to an application in building automation systems for the first time. According to the term *Perceptive Awareness*, control systems have to be able to perceive and recognize situations and react in order to increase comfort, security, safety, and economy ([SRF00] and [FDDR01]). In [Rus03] and [Fue03], an approach using case based reasoning was developed to reach a higher semantic level for categorizing situations. With tactile floor sensors, motion detectors and light barriers, the final stage of extension of the SmaKi was able to detect different ongoing scenarios and assign these scenarios to the individuals in the room. On a visualization screen, visitors were able to see their representation symbols on a two-dimensional plan of the kitchen including the assumed scenario and the predicted action associated by the system [MBV09]. Such scenario patterns could be either predefined in the form of sequences of states [Bur07], or learned during a learning phase by applying statistical methods [BSL07]. A closer description of applying the Hidden Markov Model in building automation is given in [LBVD09] and [Bru07]. With these concepts, the system was able to identify a visitor who was trying to get a cup of coffee and distinguish him from a child that came too close to a hot stove top. Within the proposals SENSE (Smart Embedded Network of Sensing Entities) and SEAL (Smart Environment for Assisted Living) first realizations of the concepts were implemented that showed the advantages of a self-learning scenario recognition system. Within the project BASE (Building Automation System for Safety and Energy efficiency), a system was developed to prolong independent living for elderly people in their own flat or nursing home [Bru07, p. 39]. Within this application environment, the critical topic of observation of persons became relevant. The project showed that simple, wireless sensors such as tactile floor sensors or motion detectors instead of camera systems could cope with the given goals. The system was able to deduce relevant information from e.g. tactile sensors installed within the beds of elderly people. With the knowledge gained during the learning phase, it was able to detect an unusual situation: When the person remains in bed too long, the system detects a salient deviation. Especially the last scenarios show a very important requirement to these systems: the possibility to take a corresponding, appropriate action.

The work of *Perceptive Awareness* built the foundation for the project ARS - Artificial Recognition System - that tries to focus on two main tasks a perceptive awareness system has to deal with: recognizing situations and acting within real world applications [DKM+04]. Inspired by concepts of neuroscientific findings in [KSS00], a new model of symbolization was introduced in [PP05] and [PPDB05] that uses three layers of symbolization: micro symbols, snapshot symbols, and representation symbols. Whereas a micro symbol corresponds to simple incoming sensory data, representation symbols deal with semantically higher information representing current world information [Pra06]. In [Bur07], further neuro-psychological findings on perceptual processes were realized and in [Vel08] a new model of a multi-modal neuro-symbolic awareness were introduced. With this newly achieved level of symbolization, even the highest layer of neuroscientific concepts could be represented. The next layer necessarily had to leave the area of neurological findings regarding brain structures in order to deal with semantically higher concepts and structures of the human psyche. Therefore, additionally to perception, ARS investigated concepts of the human psyche that are responsible for evaluating sensory information and for final decision making. These cognitive processes can be seen on top of the concept of symbolization as introduced in [Pra06]. In [DLP+06] the symbol-generating bottom-up approach inspired by neuroscience was combined with a reasoning unit whose modules are partly inspired by the neuro-psychoanalytical theory in [ST02], following a top-down design approach. The model was intended to be used in building automation. The tight coupling between bodily needs and the psychoanalytical concepts made an intermediate step necessary during the development to be able to apply the concepts, namely shifting the target platform from a building to a more human-like entity: an embodied, autonomous agent or robot. The importance of embodiment with respect to emerging intelligent systems has been stressed by various scientists within the last thirty years with the central conclusion being that all human thoughts are grounded in physical patterns and therefore generated in our own sensory and motor systems while interacting with the world [BS93]. In respect to bionics this requirement has to be considered when developing an embodied, autonomous agent and in [PB07, p. 101 ff.], several design principles for autonomous agents are discussed. Compared to a static system as is the case with the surveillance systems discussed above, an autonomous, self-sufficient, embodied, situated agent is limited to the sensors available to itself. The advantage of being able to adapt its position and therefore apply its actuators from every possible location increases the utility of each single actuator. But one of the most important advantages of such an agent must be stressed again, as it was previously claimed as a disadvantage: The awareness of a situated agent is limited solely to the data provided by its own sensors that are limited to their sensor ranges. The feature

Introduction

of embodiment and situatedness shall be considered the first filtering mechanism for perceptual data that has to be processed. The current situation and the association with the internal values of the agent form a new type of evaluation system. This interrelationship between environment and bodily needs is also crucial for humans. Different models of the human's cognitive processes consider these influences. Neuro-psychoanalysis and especially psychoanalysis were therefore of vital importance for the modeling efforts in ARS. With the goal of realizing a neuro-psychoanalytically inspired decision unit within a robot-like agent, [Roe07] and [Pal07] introduced the first model within the research group. It was compatible with the neuro-scientifically inspired symbolization model [Pra06] and used the data thus produced as an input. Additionally, it formulated a framework for a decision-making unit that was able to react according to psychoanalytical concepts. A first virtual, embodied agent was developed that made decisions in a simulated environment. It had to satisfy its own demands and desires (an implementation of the psychoanalytical concept of the Id), but was also designed to meet predefined social rules (an implementation of the psychoanalytical concept of the Super-Ego) [DZL07]. The model will be discussed in more detail in Section 2.6.

1.2 The Focus of this Work and its Basic Assumptions

Based upon the concepts and findings described above, this thesis concentrates on the development of a decision unit of an autonomous agent and uses concepts from psychoanalytical metapsychology to realize a computational framework for awareness and decision making. Although the target platform is an embodied, autonomous, situated agent (a virtual robot), the presented concepts are still applicable to building automation with some restrictions related to the different body as shown in [LBVD09].

Aim of this Work
    The main task is to transform concepts of psychoanalytical metapsychology into a technically feasible model by applying a strict top-down design approach for the functional description and to evaluate it within an autonomous, embodied, situated agent.

The pronounced aim of this work contains three critical points. First, an autonomous agent shall be run by providing a corresponding controlling unit. Second, this controlling unit of the agent shall be modeled using concepts of a specific theory of the human mind:

the psychoanalytical metapsychology. Third, the model shall be functionally defined by applying a top-down design approach. The concepts of metapsychology cannot be directly applied to a a technical system. They first have to be transformed into a technically feasible model that satisfy the demands of metapsychology on the one hand and the demands of a possible implementation on the other hand. Furthermore, they must not simply be applied to existing implementations because a projection of psychoanalytical concepts onto technical realizations would not convert a technical concept into a psychoanalytical one. The following paragraphs give an overview of the methodologies applied within this work in order to accomplish with the three aforementioned goals for the decision unit of an autonomous, embodied agent.

Cognitive science and Artificial Intelligence already provide decision units for agents. They are realized by using symbolical, statistical, or hybrid implementation concepts. Some of the implementations follow a bionic approach and are inspired by concepts from neurology, psychology, and other areas that investigate the human decision-making process. These architectures therefore represent cognitive models, often inspired by the human or mammalian brain. However, there is a key difference between currently available concepts of Artificial Intelligence and the project *Artificial Recognition System (ARS)*. The majority of existing cognitive architectures in the field of Artificial Intelligence attempt to apply concepts that describe the human cognitive process, but they are merely project cognitive models onto technical realizations. Section 2.2 gives several examples and discusses them. ARS is the first that is able to realize psychoanalytical theory within a technical system. In [DZ08] and [DBZ+09], the basis of a corresponding methodology for this work is defined. The design process must begin with data acquisition from psychoanalytical theory in order to produce a technically feasible, functional specification that can be used for a technical implementation. Compared to other cognitive architectures, ARS therefore does not project different concepts from psychoanalysis onto an implementation. The unified, psychoanalytical theory and defined concepts can be seen on the highest layer, followed by detailed functional descriptions on the layers below. These functional descriptions represent specifications and therefore the top layer of the implementation layers.

Building a model of the human cognitive processes requires a unitary model and cannot consider only parts. Cognitive architectures in Artificial Intelligence during the past decades often combined concepts from different scientific areas and showed theoretically promising results. In practice currently available robots are still unable to autonomously cope with everyday situations as humans do. One main reason for the poor practically results in Artificial Intelligence is the lack of a unitary model of the human cognitive process.

Introduction

When realizing two different, bionically inspired models in a technical system, for example combining the concepts of bodily urges with the concept of a basic emotional system, and connecting them, an interface definition becomes mandatory. It is a necessary part of the unitary model because it describes the interrelationship between the functional modules. Every combination of bionically inspired models would no longer follow the bionic approach anymore until the interfaces are defined from the point of view of technical realization. This thesis therefore relies on a unitary model which has been developed in cooperation with psychoanalytical advisors.

When Prof. Dietrich discussed with Mark Solms, the chairman of the International Neuropsychoanalysis Society (npsa) for the first time, Solms described the project ARS and its goal to join neuro-psychoanalysis and computer technology as adventurous. He was nonetheless interested, however, not only in the outcome in terms of technological results but also with respect to the project scientists' implied assessment of the psychoanalytical model regarding consistency and completeness. With permanent support from psychoanalytical advisors and in interdisciplinary cooperation with technical engineers, a first version of the unitary model of psychoanalysis was developed and discussed within the *1st International Engineering & Neuro-Psychoanalysis Forum* (ENF[3] for short). During this conference, the developed models and specifications were discussed before an international audience of experts in the three disciplines: neurology, psychoanalysis and computer engineering. The outcome of these discussions was summarized in [DFZ+09].

The core development team of ARS consists of a group of psychoanalysts and computer engineers that are defining a technically feasible, functional model under the supervision of Prof. Dietrich. New concepts, functionality, or insights are periodically discussed within a group of leading international psychoanalysts to avoid conceptual flaws. These discussions together with the ongoing work within ARS formed the unitary model, introduced in Chapter 3, and are the basis of a first implementation within this thesis. This background leads to the first two statements that are crucial for the following work:

Statement 1
> Psychoanalytical metapsychology provides a unitary functional description of the human's decision-making process.

Statement 2
> A top-down design approach will be applied to the functional concepts of metapsy-

---

[3]The conference homepage is available at http://www.indin2007.org/enf/ , the resulting discussion forum on http://www.simulatingthemind.info/ (both sources accessed in Nov. 2009)

chology in order to verify the model with respect to the necessary integrity of implementations.

The model of psychoanalytical metapsychology bases upon defined concepts first developed by Sigmund Freud (summarized in [Fre40]) and describes functional interrelations within the human cognitive process. The theory itself will neither be adapted nor further developed within this work. It has been chosen because of its comprehensive and functional description of the processes necessary for human decision making, starting at the perceptual interpretation of internal and external sensory data and leading to the motor-action that performs already deliberated intentions. In a first attempt, the concepts are verified with respect to their technical applicability, implementation, and realization in order to give a technical specification of the functions identified in metapsychology. The psychoanalytical models will be probed within a technical system: a virtual, situated, embodied agent. The derived technical model provides a top level description of the functional relations of awareness and decision making as shown in [ZMD08]. Starting from this level and by using the second topographical model[4] of psychoanalysis, the functional modules are described in a higher granularity using a top-down design approach.

The application of the top-down design to the second topographical model has several advantages. First, each functional module, independent of the depth within the top-down design, is assigned to exactly one of the three instances (Id, Ego, Super-Ego) at the top layer. This methodology ensures that sub-functionalities will follow the principles defined in their base-functionalities. The importance of this approach becomes more clear in Section 3.1.3, when common data structures and types of data processing are assigned to the three instances. Second, every defined sub-functionality can be assumed as necessary for the function of the three instances. It is not possible to unwittingly define functions that will not be used or would not serve only one base-functionality. The latter would falsify the theory of the second topographical model and its claim of covering the complete cognitive process of the psyche.

---

[4]Freud tried to categorize the human psyche within two different models he had developed. The first topographical model distinguishes between unconscious, preconscious, and conscious processes. In the second topographical model he identified the three main instances of the human psyche: Id, Ego, Super-Ego.

Aim of the Implementation
> The overall aim of the implementation described in this treaties is to realize the developed and specified model within an autonomous agent able to perceive and recognize situations, to deduce the need for action according to the situation, to generate plans to adapt the environment according to its needs, and finally to select and execute the best of the possible plans.

The main goal of this work is not only to define a psychoanalytically inspired model for cognitive processing, based on the findings introduced in [DBZ$^+$09], but also to realize it within a technical system. The selected target platform will be an embodied, autonomous agent – a robot. In the following, the implied requirements that have to be met by an architecture developed for the decision unit of an autonomous agent in general will be discussed. They will be the basis for an objective evaluation of the developed system. The above statement regarding the realization of the agent that uses the developed model contains five critical points. *First*, awareness is a critical requirement to the system. Since the perceptual part of the agent does not lie within the focus of this work, the interface to the perceptual system and the actuator system has to be defined. *Second*, the system has to be *situation aware* and able to distinguish between different situations. This requirement is a border case between neurological and psychoanalytical concepts. Certain information regarding a current situation can be formed within the neurological layer, as described above within the *Perceptive Awareness Model*. However, a complete assessment of any given situation often depends on the context and can only be achieved using higher deliberative processes. *Third*, the agent has to be able to deduce the necessity of changing the current situation. Agent-internal performance measurements such as needs have to be matched with the currently perceived environment to distinguish whether the situation is acceptable or not. *Fourth*, a plan has to be generated or at least selected from a predefined knowledge-base that is able to adapt the environment according to satisfy arising needs. And finally *fifth*, the agent has to be equipped with the capability of executing the selected plan. The corresponding actuators of the agent must be accessible in order to adapt the environment. Again, a defined interface is necessary to ensure proper information flow from the developed and implemented, psychoanalytically inspired cognitive model.

The technically relevant theories for such an implementation were defined in the course of a knowledge acquisition in cooperation with psychoanalytical advisors in the form of interdisciplinary discussions as described above. With the technical, functional specification of the necessary submodules, a possible implementation of the implied requirements will be the focus of this work, summarized within the next two statements:

Statement 3
> A framework of an artificial decision-making unit will be developed by transferring psychoanalytical function-descriptions into technical specifications.

Statement 4
> A modular implementation of the developed model will be realized within a embodied, autonomous agent. The implementation of the model does not exclude available implementation concepts of Artificial Intelligence, but provides a detailed specification for their functionality where they are used.

To realize the above statements different methodologies are applied. The first one concerns the selection of the bionic model. Instead of gathering information from different research areas, only one – namely psychoanalytical metapsychology – is used. The functionality of a cognitive framework as described within this work also bases solely upon the theory of psychoanalysis. Future work may see the necessity for additional theories to be able to implement corresponding functional modules because the theory of psychoanalysis does not give a functional description. Therefore, modules that can only be described sufficiently with other concepts have to be integrated into the psychoanalytical model in order to fulfill higher-level specifications. The second methodology implied is the bionic approach that is used when transferring concepts of metapsychology to computer science. The psychoanalytical model of the human mind is transferred into a technical implementation of a decision unit. This is done by applying two concepts: A top-down design approach and a modular description of the functionality. With the former, the highest functional layer of metapsychology – the three instances of the second topographical model Id, Ego, and Super-Ego – is analyzed and each of the three modules are sub-divided in their specific functionalities. Repeating this procedure results in a detailed description of functional modules that constitute the requirement profile for the implementation. This modular framework is necessary since it achieves not only a clear functional structure but also a detailed specification of the communication processes between the functional modules. Thereby it becomes possible to evaluate different realizations of modules in order to identify implementation methods that comply with the proposed model.

With respect to the realization and implementation of a decision unit for an autonomous agent, the metapsychological properties of satisfying needs and the corresponding plans that are a content of the metapsychological term 'wish' are a particular aspect in this work. The functional sequence of forming a wish out of internally and externally perceived circumstances is used to describe, define, and implement a call hierarchy within the functional modules. Structures that lead to a wish are identified and technically implemented. Methods of common Artificial Intelligence are used for implementation. However, these implementations have to work within the specifications of the metapsychologically inspired framework and provide precisely the required functionality.

To provide a framework that is able to fulfill the discussed requirements, the developed model will not only apply a top-down design to the functionalities but additionally to the data structures used therein. As described in Section 3.3.2, two tiers will be identified within the model that describe the employed data structures and their processing methods. One tier refers to the psychoanalytical concept of the primary process. Functional modules that deal with this concept only have the goal to satisfy needs as fast as possible. The second tier is the secondary process and covers deliberative data processing which also includes considerations concerning the environmental reality. The two main data structures that have been identified for these processes are – according to psychoanalysis – the *thing presentation* (for the primary process) and the *word presentation* (for the secondary process). Identification, realization, and implied possibilities of these two data types will be considered the main interfaces between the psychoanalytically inspired implementation framework and the possible use of common Artificial Intelligence to realize specific functional sub-modules. The concepts for thing and word presentations can be seen as abstract information containers and interpreted by implementations of symbolic Artificial Intelligence as (non-psychoanalytical) symbols. This work shows a first approach in applying the developed, psychoanalytical model to a technical realization that uses the various described implementation methods.

1.3 Possible Realizations

As stated in Section 1.2, the aim of this work is to develop a technically feasible model for human-like decision making that can be applied to an autonomous, embodied agent. Psychoanalytical theory is used as an archetype for the human's cognitive process. An assumed precondition for the decision making is the ability of perception and action in order to interact within an environment.

By defining a first, technically feasible model of psychoanalysis two main aspects will be covered. First, technical decision units can rely on identified process structures of the human mind according to the theory of psychology when using the introduced architecture.

The model focuses on the definition of functionality and interrelationship between these functions. It provides a continuous framework that is necessary for the cognitive process of decision making. A simulation will evaluate the accuracy of the model and the project team's psychoanalytical advisors will be able to verify the investigated second topographical model and its associated functional concepts.

By realizing the first implementation 'ARSi09/Lang' of the introduced model, an example is given on how to apply psychoanalytical theory to a concrete technical system. The implemented concepts of psychoanalysis endow an autonomous agent with the following features in particular. The agent architecture requires a minimum system of bodily related performance measurements but provides a detailed functional description on how these measurements influence the decision process. The agent becomes situation aware, and since the current situation is always associated with the current bodily state and already experienced influences within the situation, the architecture provides a framework for evaluating ongoing situations. These evaluations are used within the framework for defined data filtering mechanisms as well as the final decision making. Most important, the architecture provides a concept of data reduction by using the described evaluations and will be able to narrow down the search space for further implementation of data processing. With these filtering mechanism the architecture provides a dynamic, context-sensitive generator of wishes and a detailed specification for further planning in an agent. This would especially improve common implementations of artificial architectures such as BDI-Systems (Belief, Desire, and Intention) [GPP$^+$99], where desires are reduced to a set of predefined and weighted rules. Furthermore the psychoanalytical model provides a concept for handling social restrictions while interacting with the environment and copes with the demands of ethical reasoning [AA07].

Future work on the introduced model can now be embedded in the created implementation in order to investigate impacts caused by newly added changes. With the provided simulation and data visualization framework, impacts of changes can be efficiently comprised and evaluated.

2 State of the Art

The demand on technical applications to process steadily increasing amounts of data makes it necessary to find new approaches in modern computer technology. The field of Artificial Intelligence (AI) has been working on this issue since its beginning. The core of the emerging intelligent agent therefore needs a model for perception and decision making. In the following, different approaches in modeling such cognitive processes will be discussed and categorized, focusing on their advantages and disadvantages with respect to their applicability. The discussion of the described models is the basis for the decision unit established within this thesis. With respect to a possible implementation of the developed model, currently available implementations of reasoning frameworks as well as existing simulation environments for autonomous, embodied agents will be discussed, and the possibilities of evaluating the quality of an embodied, intelligent agent in regard to these frameworks outlined. This leads to the last topic of this chapter, the formerly developed cognitive architecture within the project ARS: Artificial Recognition System. It is the basis for the present work.

2.1 Towards Modern AI and Demands in Applications

Since the early 1960ies, the number of transistors on an integrated circuit and therefore the processing power of CPU's has been continuously increasing in exponential fashion - according to Moore's law as explained in [Moo65]. In conjunction with this phenomenon, the demands on computer systems have also increased dramatically. In modern building automation, as already discussed in Section 1.1, the amount of computer nodes within a large building increased from several thousand nodes in the year 2000 [Die00] to more than 50.000 nodes in the year 2009 [DFZ+09, p. 2]. These nodes, generating and processing data, cannot be handled by a centralized computer system. [Rus03] therefore underlines the necessity of using decentralized systems, making it further possible to use different physical media types for data transfer.

Today, computer systems have to fulfill tasks in real world environments. To cope with these tasks, bionic approaches were applied in order to model and implement computational perception ([FDDR01]) and decision making ([DLP+06]). The biological object of interest in this case is the human body containing all senses and capabilities to act, the human brain with its faculty for condensing sensory data to corresponding symbols ([Pra06], [Vel08]), and the human psyche with its ability to perceive, deliberate, and initiate actions ([LZD+08]). Although human perception would not be possible without the former two (the body and the brain), one main task of the human psyche is to perceive, to filter, and to evaluate the current situation an individual is placed in. Additionally to the perception of the environment, the human psyche is responsible for detecting certain needs and determining possibilities to satisfy these needs in time.

Nowadays, the area of Artificial Intelligence provides a wide variety of symbolic or statistical implementations, but still computer systems are not able to cope with everyday situations. A corresponding model is missing that is able to realize human deliberation processes within technical systems. The following section gives a short historical overview with respect to agent based modeling.

Inspired and influenced by Wiener et al.'s book *Cybernetics* [Wie65] released in 1948, and Turing's articulation of machine learning, the field of Artificial Intelligence was established at the Dartmouth workshop in 1955. McCarthy, Minsky, Newell and other researchers launched the research area and defined the demands AI was expected to meet. With the advent of powerful chess computers, symbolic AI reached one pinnacle of its success by beating a human chess master in a chess game. A different example for a system that appears very complex when investigating the behavior but in fact consists of a simple functionality is the computer program ELIZA[1], developed 1960 by J. Weizenbaum. It demonstrated why programs that behave in a humans-like way are not necessarily intelligent. The implementation in this case was based on elementary pattern-matching algorithms, re-arranging

---

[1]ELIZA (1966), PARRY (1972), RACTOR (ca. 1983), and MegaHAL (1998) are so called *"chatterbots"*, and are trying to simulate a conversation with a human narrator. The conversation in ELIZA and PARRY was based upon rather simple, partly grammatical rules and in some cases the program effectively suggested to be a human dialog partner. Both ran on a Z80 computer using less than 64KiB of RAM

incoming sentences into questions that are plausible simulating human behavior as described in [Wei66]. The output was an elusively human-like conversation, at least for the first few minutes. However, modern service robots show that the usage of rule based reasoning as it is applied in the game of chess or ELIZA, is not enough to handle real world problems and situations. These problems in applying classical methods of symbolic AI are still prevalent, since a real environment can neither be described entirely, nor is such an environment static. With the emergence of statistical AI, one of the most urgent disadvantages of symbolic AI was addressed: Handling states that were exceptional and not predefined. In symbolic reasoning, the occurrence of an undefined input could not be handled, a problem that is often referred to as the frame problem [PS99, p. 65] or as Varela summarizes in [VTR93, p. 15ff] that it is not easily possible to describe every possible state of an everyday environment although it is necessary for common (monotonic-logic) AI algorithms. With statistical methods, the probability of similarity to existing patterns could be used to assign unknown and new input values to the most likely pattern. A system might react to such a stimulus with the wrong output, but at least it continues working and does not ignore new input data. The implementations of such statistical systems (commonly, these systems deal with the task of statistical pattern recognition) either used statistical approaches (like Bayesian Networks, Markov Models, etc.) or dynamic systems theory (differential equation systems and artificial neural networks as a special kind of dynamic system as argued in [Pal07, p. 10]). Such artificial neural networks, or generally spoken connectionistic systems, need an initial phase of training with a relevant training set of input data. The information of the system's knowledge is distributed across the whole system structure. It gives a proper result according to the information learnt and stored, but the learnt knowledge itself is not accessible in a symbolic form. Shaffer therefore argues that *"[...] Bayesian, or evidential, decision-theoretic characterizations of decision situations fail to adequately account for knowledge [...]"* [Sha09].

However, the findings in AI described above are highly useful for implementations. Although there is a need for other solutions in the area of complex service robots and rational agents, symbolic and statistical AI is still the basis of implementation for further abstraction layers, as discussed in Chapter 1. One necessary abstraction was defined by Brooks in [Bro91], who suggested focusing on the interaction between an agent and the environment and further argued that embodiment is mandatory for an agent. *"Any interactive agent must have a perceptual or input system that provides a primitive representation of the agent's environment or situation."* [JW06, p. 62]. Today, it is considered *"[...] one of the greatest mistakes of traditional AI ...]"* [DS03, p. 119] to treat problems of sense, action, and environment as irrelevant or negligible. Embodiment and situatedness can be considered the core prerequisites for applying cognitive models of the human psyche to autonomous agents and must be the first step to shift from purely logical or computational models to biological models, following a bionic approach.

When talking about an agent (which stems from the Latin *agere*, "to do"), this paper specifically refers to a rational [RN03], autonomous, proactive, reactive and social [Woo00] agent. A rational agent acts with intent to achieve the best outcome or the best expected outcome, according to its defined goals. Wooldridge and Jennings additionally define the latter four properties listed above in [Woo00]. The ability to operate independently makes the agent autonomous and implicitly requires a decision unit with beliefs, desires, and intentions, which will be described in closer detail in Section 2.4. The agent must have the ability to act in its environment, to execute its intentions and to achieve certain goals. This makes the agent proactive and requires a motivation system which forces the agent to act rather than being totally passive. Furthermore, the agent has to be able to react to different stimuli, especially from the environment, to meet the requirements of a reactive agent. This demand makes a sensor interface to the environment mandatory. Lastly, the social aspect requires an ability to interact and cooperate with other agents to achieve given goals and necessitates communication with other agents or an assessment of other agents to cope with agents having different interests by negotiation or cooperation. In [DS03, p. 192], six demands on self-aware agents are described, which extends the previously given list by two further requirements. First, the environment has to be sufficiently complex and challenging to allow complex responses. And second, the agent must contain an inner representation of the world and itself in order to react deliberately instead of reflexive.

Brooks did not limit the requirements of necessary embodiment to service robots interacting in a real world, but extended it to any kind of agent, like virtual agents, or software agents (described in [Bro92], [LBG97], [BBI+98], and [BAE+04]). By calling his newly defined field of research *embodied intelligence*, Brooks stated the necessity of understanding the sensory-motor basis of 'natural agents' like animals or humans first before it would become possible to understand intelligence. It is clear that Brooks suggests a bottom-up design approach with his statement. There is no doubt that human level intelligence necessarily needs a body. Sensors and actuators are a part of our body, and are the basis for all considerations in the cognitive process as Pfeifer argues in [PB07]. However, starting *only* at the lowest layer of sensory-motor interaction will not provide a model of cognitive processes on the highest layer. These different layers must not be confused, since they deal with different types of problems. As described in Section 2.2.1, cognitive models on the highest layer cannot be expected to simply 'emerge' as soon as the lowest layers are sufficiently defined. Only a certain behavior can 'emerge' out of the combination of several functionalities, as it is the case in the *subsumption architecture*, a robust layered control system for mobile agents described in [Bro86].

Based upon the statements on embodiment, the field of embodied intelligence became an area of various new models and concepts. *On the one hand*, Brooks and others showed the power of emerging intelligence within agents. He introduced the *subsumption architecture*, a purely reactive architecture, where functional layers with simple tasks are combined in order to produce a complex behavior. This concept follows a clear bottom-up design. *On the other hand*, cognitive architectures (some of them purely deliberative) provided by researchers in the field of *embodied cognitive science* have been developed and implemented within embodied agents to make them flexible and autonomous. The design of these models follows a top-down design approach, where principle cognitive models are characterized and their functionality described with respect to a corresponding implementation. The cognitive frameworks ACT-R/PM (an attempt to combine the deliberative architecture ACT-R with a perceptual motor system as described in [Byr01]) and Robo-Soar (described in Section 2.4 and in more detail in [LYHT91]) are two exemplary implementations. However, the available models are limited to certain parts of the human cognitive process. ACT-R and Soar, for example, focus on the cognitive processes of information storage and do not consider emotional or motivational aspects. Inspired mostly by the work of the neuroscientist Damasio in [Dam94] and [Dam03], scientists in the field of AI like Minsky in [Min06], Sloman in [SCS05], Picard in [Pic00], or Breazeal in [Bre02], claim that emotions influences not only the decision-making process, but perception as well. A comprehensive model of the human's complex cognitive processes seems to be missing. This circumstance and the recently established areas of Artificial Intelligence as introduced above will be the basis for the following considerations.

In the following Sections 2.2 and 2.4 the modeling methodologies of various cognitive architectures and their implementations will be discussed. As mentioned above, a cognitive architecture does not necessarily exclude the use of symbolic or statistical AI. Cognitive architectures are arranged on top of an implementation that need not contradict this architecture.

2.2 Building Models in Cognitive Science

Building models for intelligent decision units is one of the main tasks in the field of cognitive science. Theories of different sciences, such as psychology, psychoanalysis, neuroscience, sociology, or computer science, to name a few, are cooperating in their research efforts. Typically, each science has its own, historically grown point of view and also its own procedures to build models of the mind and the behavior of a human being. The following sections will investigate five different approaches of building an architecture for the cognitive process. The approaches are applying different methodologies in building the model and are following different approaches in their implementations and applications. The applied methodologies are discussed in detail and their design flaws are highlighted. The discussion leads to the applied methodologies used in Chapter 3, where a new, psychoanalytically inspired decision unit for an autonomous agent will be developed.

2.2.1 Neuroscientific Approach - The Blue Brain Project

The *Blue Brain Project* as described in [Mar06] was launched 2005 by the Brain Mind Institute (BMI, at the Ecole Politechnique Fédérale de Lausanne) in cooperation with the company IBM.

In the past, IBM's mainframe computers were used, to apply vast numbers of simple, logical rules to strictly defined, logically problems to derive solutions. One of the most famous examples is the chess game between Garry Kasparov and Deep Blue [Hsu02], a mainframe computer applying conventional methods from computer science. Markram calls this application of Artificial Intelligence in [Mar06] 'linear intelligence', according to the linear increase of pretended intelligence by increasing the number of *if-then-rules* stored in the computer systems memory.

The *Blue Brain Project* attends to go far beyond this approach. The following section gives a short summary according to [Mar06]. IBM's latest supercomputer called *Blue Gene* is used to simulate a model of the brain from a neurological point of view. In a bottom-up design approach, a specific cellular region of the mammalian brain, the so called neocortical (sensory) columns located in the visual cortex, is modeled. Based on different, currently available and widely accepted neurological concepts (the Hodgkin-Huxley model, which is describing the mechanism of action potentials in neuron cells, is for example one of the used models), neocortical columns are built. Starting from modeling atoms, molecules are modeled that again can be formed together to model DNA (Deoxyribonucleic acid) molecules. Using these genes, proteins are modeled to form particular cells, the neuron. This is an example for applying the bottom-up design approach: The simplest unit in the overall model is defined, modeled, and can be used to form the next higher layer. In this case, the smallest part that builds the lowest layer is represented by the atom that acts as the basic component to model molecules. The project aims for developing a complete model of a particular brain region – and in longer terms the whole brain – to test the used models and to verify new models. If it is possible to embody information processes by emulating the human brain structure is a central question of the project.

The model of the *Blue Brain Project* deals, on its highest level with a huge amount of connections between neurons. One simulated neocortical column, for example, is consisting of 10.000 neocortical neurons [Mar06, p. 156]. A minimal simulation of such a micro circuit structure consisting of neuron that again are receiving inputs from thousands of other neurons therefore requires massive computational power [Mar06, p. 156]. However, this lower bound alone requires a massive increase of computational power to simulate neocortical columns. Since the *Blue Brain Project* is using a 4-rack system of IBM's Blue Gene/L architecture, 22.4 TFLOPS (equals $22,4 \cdot 10^{12}$ floating point operations per second) are processed according to [Mar06, p. 154]. However, the figures of maximal possible processing power, advertised by IBM in this article, must not be confused with the actual goal of the project to simulate a human brain structure. In fact, the simulation of the highly parallel processes within the human brain structure can also be realized on a single core processor, as soon as a corresponding model for the interrelationship of neurons is existing.

Databases with the results and the statistics of past experiments on the real neocortical columns, as described in [DBG+07] are used to bring the model into a simulation environment and to – virtually – place the neurons into the right place and define the interconnections between them as described in [DBG+07]. Since the Blue Gene/L architecture is providing about 130.000 Dual Core CPUs (up to 64 racks with 1.024 computer nodes each - one node consists of a Dual Core CPU, the Blue Gene chip), one neuron is mapped onto each processor whereas the axons, interacting the neurons are physically represented by the MPI[2] based cables. Using optimized algorithms, the simulations could be run nearly as fast as the human brain [DBG+07].

These facts of the *Blue Brain Project* are impressive, but one of the major problems in the developing process of the model is that there are lots of ways to engineer and to implement the functionality of the defined layers of the model. Using statistically interpreted findings of the human brain is one applied methodology in the *Blue Brain Project*. The simulation based upon a bottom-up designed model is exemplary to evaluate existing models and change them and their implementations on the different layers in order to verify the impacts

---

[2]The message-passing interface (MPI) described in detail in [GLS99] is a standarized programming interface for parallel processing in distributed computer systems.

to the whole simulation. As soon as a possible 'emergent intelligence' is claimed, it is unlikely that the bottom-up design is able to lead to human-level intelligence because of the missing functional top layer, defining cognitive processes that are leading to human-level intelligence. A system with emergent intelligent behavior that can be interpreted as human-like behavior must not be confused with a system that models and realizes cognitive processes of the human psyche.

Limitations to digital computing biological processes are the spatial resolution on the one hand and the constraints made by modeling the biological processes with algorithms. Even it is, in principle, possible to simulate the human brain with current technologies like specialized ASICs (application-specific integrated circuits), it is wrong to imply that whole-brain simulation including mental processes is possible without the knowledge and a model for the higher levels of the cognitive process - namely the psychic apparatus. Although the dedicated goal of the *Blue Brain Project* is to simulate and evaluate current theories in neuroscience, the wish to track the emergence of intelligence back to the level of neurons still remains. This unrealistic aspect in particular will be discussed in section 2.2.6. However, the findings of non-invasive investigation of human brain structures together with the already developed models that can be verified in simulations like the *Blue Brain Project* are essential for the generation of symbolic data in modern computer systems. In [Vel08], a new approach of multi-modal perception is introduced that is following the concepts of neurology. These symbol generation methodology will be used in Section 3.1.1 and are forming the symbolic input of the model, introduced in Chapter 3.

2.2.2 Affective Computing - Modeling the Mind in AI

Behaviorisms, present since the early 20th century as historically described in [OK98, p. 6], uses objective methods to describe behavior totally by identifying the stimulus and the response. This method considers the analyzed object as a black box. A methodology that is commonly used for example in a passive, electrical two-port network [GHLM01, p. 172 ff.] that is only considered as a black box the integration into the whole circuit. This consideration becomes applicable, because the necessary, internal functionality of the object – in this case a passive electrical circuit – is of no concern as long as the circuit works within the given specifications. In cognitive science, behavioristic models are also used to describe the functionality of the mind. [Pal07] shows that most of the low level approaches to model emotional computing in AI are based on behavioristic, ethological, and neuro-biological theories that are not considering personality-oriented, psychological theories of emotions.

State of the Art

The model of the mind presented by Aaron Sloman and his team is conceptually described in [SCS05] are considered as such a behavioristic approach. Although Sloman never declares the model as behavioristic approach, the following section will discuss the reasons for this assumption.

In 1991, the Cognition and Affect (CogAff) Project has been started by Aaron Sloman and Glyn Humphreys. The two main topics consciousness and affects were investigated by defining a general framework for a cognitive architecture that is capable to cope with those keywords. Like most of the comparable architectures, in the model shown in Figure 2.1 the horizontal axis consists of three areas: Perception, central processing, and action. The novelty is, compared to other models, the differentiation on the vertical axis. There, cognitive processes are distinguished between their evolutionary development, which is directly indicating their level of semantic meaning.

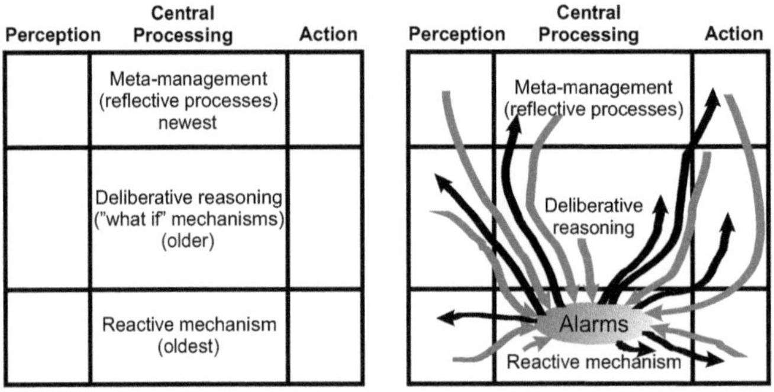

Figure 2.1: CogAff Scheme - the Nine Areas of the Cognitive Architecture [SCS05]

From bottom up, the so called *'Reactive mechanisms'* are forming the lowest level of the hierarchical model and are depicted as the oldest system. This level covers immediate internal or external action without any necessary reasoning. No multi-steps are taken between perception and action and no alternatives are calculated.

The next layer in this model is called the *'Deliberative reasoning'* layer where predictions and explanations are given to compare and select preferred options in possible reactions. This layer already requires a short term storage to construct necessary temporal structures for planning.

On the third and highest layer, the *Meta-management* is placed. Internal processes are monitored that can be categorized using a specialized ontology of possible occurring values.

Also self-categorization in comparison to other agents is done within this layer. The internal processes can therefore be evaluated, controlled, and modulated within this layer.

In the model, each of the three layers has its own implementation of perception, central processing, and action. This categorization makes it possible, to develop different models of cognitive architectures by leaving some of the nine blocks out if they are not needed. As an example, it is possible to use only one perception unit delivering the input for all three following central processing units and the same can be done with the action side. Moreover, it is not necessary to use the meta-management layer when developing a simple rule-based decision unit for a robot. The architecture is a very rough framework for classification and as it has been shown, no reasonable constraints have been made in terms of the model or the implementation until this point.

The model gets more precise, when the way of embedding the theory of emotions is highlighted. Here, a clear assignment of an already existing neuroscientific model defined in [Dam94, p. 134] to the three layers is made:

- *Primary emotions* are embedded in the reactive layer and are independent from higher reasoning. There, emotional values like primitive fear are implemented.
- *Secondary emotions* include hypothetical reasoning abilities about the world and possible future events, such as worries about possible accidents. To do so, the deliberative layer is needed.
- *Tertiary emotions* are representing emotions that are connected to the Self of the observed individual such as self-blame and can be found in the meta-management layer that monitors and observes processes of other layers and systems.

Such determinations are most important in defining cognitive models. Although Sloman's definition describes where the particular emotion is located and gives also an example to distinguish between e.g. the primary emotion 'simple fear' and the secondary emotion 'worry' (fear about the future), the model fails to define the underlying processes and structures of the different emotion types. Emotions are used only as evaluation values in different layers within the architecture. According to A. Damasio in [Dam94] – and as described in detail in Chapter 3 for psychoanalytical affects – also the type of information processing with emotions is, at least in theory, known and described. It shows one of the main problem in transferring a theory from one scientific field to another. Without being an expert in both fields, it has to be carefully outlined why parts of a model have been used and other parts taken out.

State of the Art

In the CogAff framework, affects are triggering probably conflicting actions. As a simple behavior it is suggested to just select one, a complex behavior would have to satisfy both although incompatible states of affects. Affects are further used to reward positive or negative consequences of processed actions to learn and develop a better behavior in the future.

Another mechanism used in the CogAff framework is also following a bionic concept: The alarm mechanism is inspired by the limbic system and can be compared to the hormone system in our blood circulation. Its purpose is to support a rapid interlayer-communication between any dedicated module in any direction. This assumption allows the model to be used almost everywhere without any restrictions. The previous sectioning of the layers is therefore technically obsolete and – considering the architecture – it only distinguishes between the semantic complexity of the information, the layers are dealing with. There is no doubt that most of the functional units within the human brain are interacting and interfering. The challenge of building a model is to defined those interferences.

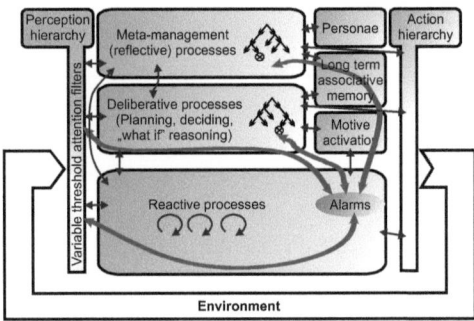

Figure 2.2: The H-CogAff Scheme (Human Cognitive Affective) [SCS05]

The HCogAff framework, shown in Figure 2.2, is the attempt of Sloman's team, to apply the *CogAff Scheme* to the human adult brain (the H stands for human). Since there is no remarkable modification, except of adding several memory modules, representing several sorts of knowledge (e.g. motive activation module and long term associative memory), it is not necessary to discuss the model, described in [SCS05] in detail. However, it is a good example of violating the defined layers by applying additional communication channels that enables interlayer communication.

Sloman's intention was to present a model consisting of nine modules, whereas each can be used on demand to describe the mind of humans, other animals, and human-like machines. He calls this model the CogAff framework and claims: *"The [...] framework should, in principle, be applicable beyond life on earth, to accommodate many alien forms of intelligence, if there are any"* [SCS05, p. 225].

This statement indicates the core problem of the model. According to this approach, the behavior of any creature can be categorized in three main blocks: perception, central processing, and action. By observing the behavior within a specific environment it is assumed that the functionality of the modules can be defined. However, categorization alone is not enough for describing the functionality of the human cognitive process. Cognitive processes of the mind cannot be explained by categorizing behavior into the nine behavioral black boxes as suggested by the *CogAff Scheme*.

By describing this general model, Sloman suggests that *"[...] many engineering goals can be achieved using shallow concepts and shallow theories[...]"* [SCS05, p. 225] that are defined by comparing the behavior of the implementation with the real behavior and shallow theories that are linking conditions to an observable behavior. This may be a good approach in developing simple but effective agents for computer entertainment. Diverse project – for example the robot *Kismet* developed at the MIT Media Laboratory and described in Section 2.2.4 – can be based upon this approach, but they have nothing in common with modeling a mind. The fact that a robot behaves like a human in one certain situation does not mean that the robot 'thinks' like a human. It can never be sufficient to implement rules that are connecting environmental circumstances with proper actions for modeling a mind, not even if a variable is called 'emotion' within the implementation. R. Pfeifer states in [PB07, p. 345] that with projects like *Kismet* progress can be made in building human-machine interfaces. But it cannot be answered, why humans control these particular facial expressions.

To summarize this subsection, Sloman's model can be seen as a good template to allocate parts of existing theory to the described nine sections. They are influenced by emotional theories as explained in [Dam94, p. 132ff] and theories about different levels of cognition, as described in [Lur73, p. 128ff]. On basis of that, existing models can be organized and more easily compared to each other. It is further a basis for discussion of the minimal requirements concerning a human-like decision framework. The term emotion in the *CogAff Scheme* is, albeit introduced as a concept from the human cognitive process, only a value system. The model of the emotional systems behind stays undefined. A developer for decision units in Artificial Intelligence would not be able to build a technical system out of these descriptions, because the main information about the functional system behind it is missing. Comparatively the same is the case for the integration of the alarm system. It is no problem to implement a technical system that is a sink for any type of information

State of the Art

from each point of a system. One example would be a TCP/IP port, where any part of the system listens to this port. It would allow inter-process communication, but it would violate the abstraction layers of the model. By using such an implementation, the defined layers of the *CogAff Scheme* are reduced to the same abstraction layer. In the development process of the model introduced in Chapter 3, the communication therefore strictly follows the layered architecture and its defined interfaces.

2.2.3 The Ψ-Theory - Cognitive and Emotional Affects Simulation

The Ψ-*Theory* is, according to [Dör08, p. 96], an integrative cognitive theory based upon three main columns: cognitive, motivational, and emotional processes. These three components are together forming the main structures for the Ψ-*Theory* of the psychological processes. To describe both, processes and structures of these subsets and to show that a mathematical formalism can be used, a simplified form of an artificial neuronal network is used. The theory is based upon sub-symbolic information processing only and does not use symbols that are including semantical information of certain objects. The usage of hybrid approaches, using sub-symbolic as well as symbolic approaches, is suggested to be avoided because of a possible, multiple description of one problem on the two different layers. Further, the model reduces the human psyche to a few main parameters that are defining the basic behavior of an individual. Changing some of these main parameters, a happy and extroverted daredevil can be changed into a ruminant, shy philosopher, as it is stated in [Dör02, p. 15].

In [Dör02, p. 21], Doerner claims that it is possible to build models and in a further step simulations that are an exact copy of the reality. It is stated that this becomes possible by reverse engineering the reality molecule by molecule. Further, it is believed that the construction of an artificial psyche is possible by adding a sufficient number of processes consisting of states and neuronal networks. This belief has to be discarded here from a scientific point of view. It is not possible today, to even measure the state of the human brain within one distinct point in time because of the duration of the scan when using e.g. functional magnetic resonance imaging. Influences that cannot be foreseen although they might (or might not) be totally insignificant for the model at a certain point in time, as it is the gravitation of Jupiter in a simulation of a pendulum on earth, will always remain. Therefore, models and simulations within the main chapters of this thesis are not claiming to be an exact copy of the reality – neither in case of a simple pendulum nor in case of a model of the human psyche.

The Ψ-*Theory* is implemented [Dör02, p. 249] and behavioral tested [Dör02, p. 263] in a computer simulation. An agent has the ability to move across an island that contains a finite number of places that are connected with specific paths and are forming the directed graph of movement. Energy and water are the main parts of the agent's homeostasis, because it is driven by water steam. Energy is gained by the collection of different nuts using a robots tentacle. The nuts are converted to oil that is combusted to heat the water. Water can be grabbed by a water nozzle. The agent can detect damage of its body and a variable for pain is adopted if it is hurt. Additionally to water and nuts that are needed for survival, so called nucleotides are available within the world, have to be collected. A good agent collects as much nucleotides as possible and survives as long as possible.

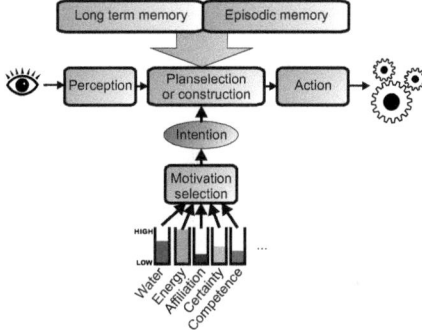

Figure 2.3: Data and Data Processing in Psi [Dör02, p. 27]

Figure 2.3 shows the main modules of the architecture. The perception of the external environment is represented by an image of the situation according to the knowledge and the expected horizon. Additionally, for each agent a set of urges is defined that are represented by a certain quality (energy, water, etc.) and the corresponding quantity, which is the level of the quality as depicted at the bottom of in Figure 2.3. In [DGMM06] these value systems are called *tanks*. The deviation to the optimal level generates the quantity of the need and is representing the motivation to satisfy this need. This motivation is also influenced by the already learned knowledge about the goals. The motivational, multi-stable system consists of the following six needs: hunger, thirst, pain, affiliation, certainty, and competence. A global homeostasis is the basic goal that has to be guaranteed. To select a certain need for further processing, the *expectancy-value theory*[3] is introduced, where the need with the highest product of expectancy of success and value of need satisfaction is selected. After the selection of the most important motive, a competing motive has to have a level that is higher than the active motive plus a certain threshold. This method avoids behavioral oscillation. The selected motive results in the intention to reach the motive. Together with data from the perception, this information is influencing the plan selection or construction functionality. This module accesses already stored plans and perceived episodes to generate the plan that is able to follow the selected motive, according to the current situation. When a plan is generated, the actions of the plan are executed. Dörner states in [Dör02, p. 96] that logical reasoning, as suggested in classic symbolic Artificial Intelligence is not enough to build a comprehensive model of the human's cognitive process. With motivation and emotions, different cognitive processes, like thinking, remembering, or even perceiving are influenced. And these emotions again can be changing during the former listed processes. Emotions are not defined as explicit states but emerge from modulation of the information processing and action selection.

To verify the quality of the defined framework and its implementation a comparison to the behavior of real persons in the same situation has been made. Because the simulation platform was implemented in form of a visualized computer program, it became possible to watch the agents that are equipped with the Ψ-*Theory* as well as to give the control of an agent to a human operator. The test did not include the possibility for an agent to have an own personality, to modify its own behavior, and to reflect about its own actions, although it is stated to be realizable within the framework of the Ψ-*Theory*. The results of the human operated agents were categorized and seven different main-strategies among the human test persons could be found, e.g. the survival strategy, location oriented strategy, action strategy. Together with the amount of deaths, the collected nucleotides, the visited places, and the own estimation of competence during a defined time period the behavior of the agents could be compared to the behavior of the test persons. The main advantage of this comparison is that different weak points within the model became obvious, as described in the following:

- *Weak backward memorization* - A taken action that turned out to be wrong did hardly influence further actions in a similar situation.
- *Bored by action* - Once an object is processed by an actuator, this type of object becomes uninteresting.

---

[3]In [DGMM06, p. 3] the author denotes the theory as 'expectancy-value principle'.

- *Uncoordinated exploration* - The exploration of the agent is in a very random way and not planned in detail.
- *Underestimation of energy shortness* - When the agent is low of energy, the search for energy sources is not increased. Collecting nucleotides has therefore the highest priority although the agent runs out of energy. The agent therefore does not fear death or pain as much as real test persons do.
- *Exploring the new* - The agents are always exploring new objects and the priority is very high compared to the internal homeostasis.
- *Overeating* - Agents never take more energy than necessary, test persons do have a longer reserve.
- *Exploring objects* - Agents are testing systematically all actions – albeit any plausibility – on new objects.
- *Locked strategy* - When an agent is following a certain strategy, it hardly changes its behavior.

The enumerated problems that have been detected when analyzing the behavior show the advantages of the virtual simulation. First, the behavior that was generated by the implemented Ψ-*Theory* can be analyzed in order to verify corresponding parts of model. In the simulation described in Section 5.1 a similar approach is followed. However, the adaption of the model within the Ψ-*Theory* is, due to the missing abstraction layers hardly to realize. Especially when considering a Ψ-*Theory* model that – according to [Dör02, p. 21] – is a perfect model of the human brain, including the same number of neurons.

Summarizing, the Ψ-*Theory* describes the cognitive processes on one single layer: the artificial neuronal network (ANN). A possible implementation of the different functional processes, such as perception, motivation, intention, action planning, memory, and action, is described by using only the components of an ANN. With neural connections between the different functional systems, they are influencing each other. There is no abstraction layers used, where higher layers can use and rely on the functionality of their lower layers. The approach of this theory therefore does not differ in principle from Brooks' *subsumption architecture*: Simple functionalities are implemented and connected together with the result of emerging intelligence. The main difference is that Brooks refers to a robot's emergent intelligence, whereas the Ψ-*Theory* claims the emergence of human level intelligence.

2.2.4 Emotional Machines

One part of the research in Artificial Intelligence is the simulation of emotions. The main goal of this research area is to improve human computer interaction that is more intuitive to a human operator. One example for such research is the project called *Kismet*, an artificial, toy-like robot head that is capable to control its artificial facial muscles to create different facial expressions as well as voices, and changing its posture, described in more detail in [Bre02]. The robot has been developed by the MIT Media Lab - Personal Robots Group with C. Breazeal as project leader.

In [Bre02, p. XII], it is assumed that *"[...] social robots [...] will have to be socially intelligent in a human way."* The aim of the project is therefore not only to provide a testbed for concepts of human social intelligence, but also to understand, define, and engineer human social intelligence to gain an optimal human-machine-interface.

According to the given definition, a social robot is able to interact with, understand, and even relate to humans, in a personal way. It should be able to understand humans and itself in social terms. Additionally, a human should be able to understand it in the same social terms. The social robot has to adapt and learn during its lifetime to be able to cope with new situations. An understanding of itself, others, and the relations between is mandatory for the interaction.

Breazeal states in [Bre02, p. 36] that when people are interacting, playing, and teaching the built robot as if it is infant or very young child, the project can be seen as a success. The measurement of the output is in this case a pure subjective one and does not necessarily need human social intelligence as long as the system behaves socially intelligent. Based upon the given demands, the target platform has to fulfill the following requirements:

- The system has to be embodied – a robot has to be built.
- A face-to-face interaction is needed – the robot gets a human-like face.
- It has to behave believable – interaction has to be in a life-like-quality.
- The system has to be human aware – a perception of other persons and a detection for facial expressions is needed.
- It should be able to communicate – the generation of facial expressions used to be understood by interacting humans.
- Socially learning has to be implemented – giving the possibility to estimate the actual situation in a social way.

Due to complexity, the latter one is not discussed in details within the project. To emulate social intelligence, Breazeal first examines the behavior and especially the abilities of infants when interacting with a caregiver. Based upon these examinations, the requirements to *Kismet* were defined, especially focusing on face-to-face communication and the ability to learn the meaning of facial expressions, as described in [TB06]. According to them, the facial expressions are mainly representing emotions.

The internal apparatus that generates the behavior of the robot is called the "Synthetic Nervous System" and several key components are serving as the basis for the technical assumptions. The implemented variety of infant-level social competencies are developed by adapting models and theories from the fields of psychology, cognitive development, and ethology as stated in [Bre02, p. 5]. Especially psychology provides models for the attention system, facial expressions, the emotion system, and various perceptual abilities.

Analyzing the various forms of social exchange between an infant and its caregiver, the model is focusing on the several aspects [Bre02, p. 33], discussed in the following paragraphs. To get and give an affective feedback, the attention is directed to the interacting person, in this case the caregiver. Avoiding boring or overwhelming events, a regulation of arousal has to be done by interaction.

Therefore, the need for a balancing agenda arises that defines what can be done to keep the arousal in limits. One possible response would be to answer with the same type of recognized behavior, but partly converted to the positive if the current internal state is also positively engaged. Repeated behavior is better accepted, because the behavior becomes predictable, repetition and variation of actions is introduced. To provide a better detection of causal connections, timing and contingency is necessary. To improve the current communication and language-learning, several sorts of games are established that improve the learned contents. This particular aspect of learning is technically picked up and described in [BGTB06], using a virtually simulated robot with arms that can play with bricks available in its close environment.

State of the Art

So called 'subjective internal states' are necessary that are representing intents, beliefs, desire, and feelings. The following responses have to be generated from the "Synthetic Nervous System":

- Affective response - facial expression are reflecting the current condition
- Exploratory response - new, unknown objects or scenarios are triggering exploratory behavior
- Proactive response - a damaging stimuli will be avoided by turning away
- Regulatory response - actions are set to keep the environment neither under- nor overstimulating

Figure 2.4 shows the main framework for the Synthetic Nervous System. Getting sensory information about the world and the interacting person – as it is the caregiver to the infant – the *Low Level Extraction (System)* extracts sensor based features from the world. These features are encapsulated to percepts in the *High Level Perceptual System* that influences directly the robot's behavior, motivation, and motor processes. The *Attention System* determines the most salient and therefore relevant stimuli. In the *Motivation System*, the actual urges are generated and processed. It is distinguished between the *Homeostatic Regulation*, processing pure bodily needs, and the *Emotion System*, generating and handling emotions according to the external and homeostatic circumstances. The *Behavior System* implements and arbitrates between competing behavior and selects the task with the highest priority to define the current goal. This goal is carried out by the *Motor System*.

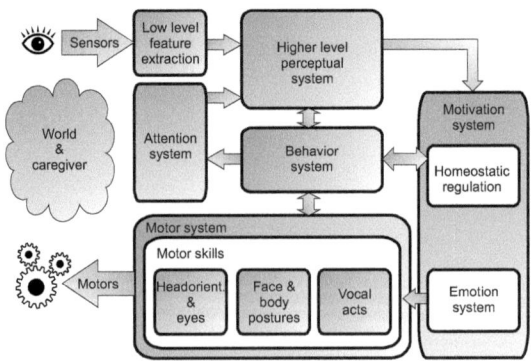

Figure 2.4: Overall Cognitive Model of *Kismet* [Bre02, p. 44]

This basic framework and its parts can be categorized to fit into the CogAff-Framework discussed in Section 2.2.2. Based upon categorized behavior, main function blocks are defined that can be implemented by following theories of human decision processes. In the following, the implementation of the *Motivation System* and the *Behavior System* are now discussed in detail.

The motivational system has to process more complex stimulus patterns in the environment in order to be able to select an adequate behavior out of a highly flexible behavior repertoire. It has to cope with the simultaneous existence of a multitude of motivational tendencies and provides corresponding actions as the basis of social organization. Using the module *Homeostatic Regulation* described in [Bre02, p. 105], critical parameters are monitored to stay within a bounded range. This can be values for the temperature, energy level, amount of fluids, etc. Each value of the homeostasis is mapped to a specific need value. This generates the desire to get in contact with the needed stimulus in the appropriate time. Each drive is modeled as an idealized homeostatic process that maintains a set of critical parameters within a bounded range. The direct mapping between drives[4] (a lack of homeostatic equilibrium) and emotions can be seen in Table 2.1.

Emotions are centrally involved in determining the behavioral reaction to the social environment in the *Emotion System*. The used concepts of emotional systems are described in [Roe07, p. 25] in further detail. The emotions, used in the system are idealized models of basic emotions. Each emotion serves as a particular function (often social). Each emotion also arises in a particular context and therefore motivates *Kismet* to respond in an adaptive manner. The *Emotion System*, described in more detail in [Bre03] directly influences the robot's facial expressions that are again inspired by emotions of humans.

The *Emotion System*, shown in Figure 2.5 is the mediating logic between environmental (the high level perceptual system) and internal (drives and behavioral system) stimulations and generates either social or self-maintaining action-tendencies ([Bre01, p. 110]).

---

[4]The term *drive* is used in the model of *Kismet* in a different context and does not rely on psychoanalytical theories. In this work, a psychoanalytical definition is given in Chapter 3.

Antecedent conditions	Emotion	Behavior	Function
Delay, difficulty in achieving goal of adaptive behavior	Anger, frustration	Compliant	Show displeasure to caregiver to modify his/her behavior
Presence of an undesired stimulus	Disgust	Withdraw	Signal rejection of presented stimulus to caregiver
Presence of a threatening, overwhelming stimulus	Fear, distress	Escape	Move away from a potentially dangerous stimuli
Prolonged presence of a desired stimulus	Calm	Engage	Continued interaction with a desired stimulus
Success in achieving goal of active behavior, or praise	Joy	Display pleasure	Reallocate resources to the next relevant behavior (eventually to reinforce behavior)
Prolonged absence of a desired stimulus, or prohibition	Sorrow	Display sorrow	Evoke sympathy and attention from caregiver (eventually to discourage behavior)
A sudden, close stimulus	Surprise	Startle response	Alert
Appearance of a desired stimulus	Interest	Orient	Attend to new, salient object
Need of an absent and desired stimulus	Boredom	Seek	Explore environment for desired stimulus

Table 2.1: Mapping for homeostasis - drives - from emotion to behavior via executing a function. ([Bre01, p. 584] and [Bre02, p. 111])

The emotive reaction cycle of *Kismet*, described in [Bre02, p. 112], can be divided into three states:

Affective Assessment: Perceiving the triggering event either from the external perception or the internal urges represented as drives.

Emotional Elicitor: The evaluation of this event according to the intensity, relevance, intrinsic pleasantness, and goal oriented influences the value of the emotion.

Emotional Arbitration: Generates a characteristic, emotional expression via an action throughout the face, voice, or posture directly and sets the action tendencies that motivate a behavioral response in the behavior system.

Intrinsic pleasantness is implemented as a hardwired positive effect on emotions. For example has praising speech a positive influence on the emotions, scolding speech a bad influence. The affective appraisal is also goal directed and therefore depends on the active goal of the robot. Since *Kismet* is neither conscious nor self-conscious, a subjective state of feelings is not included. Also it does not have the possibility to sense physiological states or activity in its body.

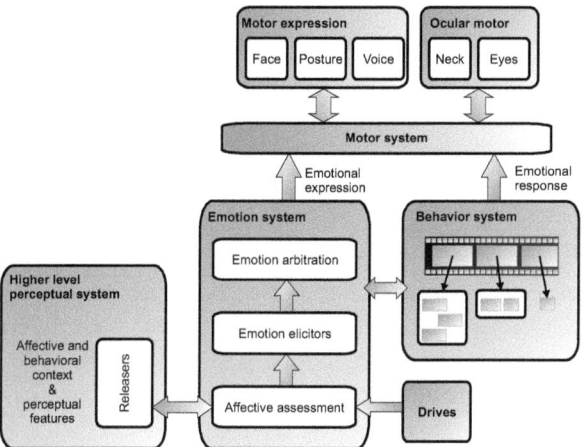

Figure 2.5: Emotion System of *Kismet* [Bre02, p. 113]

The *Behavior System* includes a set of action patterns in dependence on human infants actions. A reduced set, allowing the infant to communicate with the caregiver is introduced by [TAA79]. There, based upon an ethological behavioral protocol, five phases are identified that characterizes social exchanges between three-month-old infants and their caregiver: Initiation, Mutual-orientation, Greeting, Play-dialog, Disengagement.

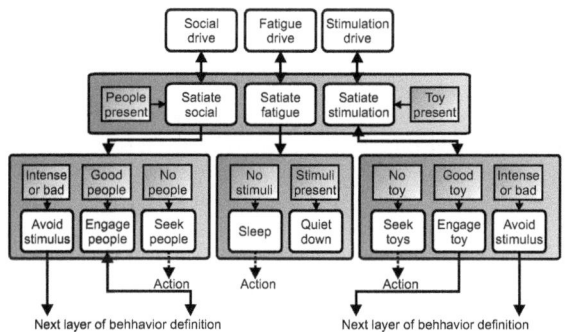

Figure 2.6: Behavior Generator of *Kismet* [Bre02, p. 133]

State of the Art

Figure 2.6 shows the mapping between the perception and the action in form of a tree that categorizes the perceived situation. The three predefined drives of the robot are satiated by different actions (sleep in the case of fatigue) or objects (person or toy) in this model. When an object is missing, the environment has to be changed so that the object is appearing. When the object is present, it is evaluated whether it is satisfying or not. Interaction is engaged in the positive case, otherwise the taken actions are avoiding further interaction.

In this example, emotions are not used as a central system that influences the decision process of the robot. In fact it is a direct mapping of the intensity of a value that is supposed to represent a specific emotion to the settings of the servomotors that alter the mimic of the robot. The work, as well as the results of this project are remarkable, however the social intelligence of the system is represented by a couple of if-the-rules connecting certain perception patterns to behavioral actions that are evoking facial expressions in the robot's face. Simulating facial emotion expressions due to simple control for the expressions can advance the building of good human-machine interfaces [PB07, p. 136]. The system behind describing how humans control the facial expressions is not covered by this research. The values that are influencing the facial expressions of the robot have to be 'grounded' [PB07, p. 136, 345] with a corresponding emotional model to their origins. A robot's emotion will not be the same like human's emotions, because of the different components that are available for grounding. Emotions can only emerge by the particular dynamics (functions and functionality) of the robot itself.

Nevertheless, the development of human-machine-interfaces takes advantage in making the machine more human-like in a behavioral and lookalike way. Therefore, a lot of projects exist that are developing human-like behavior as it is done in the case of the *Kismet*-project. Brooks uses the development to emphasize the importance of embodiment for autonomous agents in [BBI+98]. Although the current architecture of *Kismet* cannot be considered as a cognitive architecture, these projects will provide a serious implementation platform to test future cognitive architectures. They have to be used instead of the direct mapping of perception with emotional reaction in order to design an intelligent computer system. However, the test application used in this work will rely on a virtual agent as introduced in Chapter 5.

2.2.5 Psychoanalytical Models in Artificial Intelligence

When Artificial Intelligence discovered the need for more distinct models of the human mind and how it works, also psychoanalytical models have been investigated. It has been tried to extract the essences out of the psychoanalytical theory and to transform it to a technical model. Psychoanalysts were also interested, because they wanted to have their theory verified under the aspect of scientific, engineering methods. Two of the earliest research teams will be introduced that have been trying to bring psychoanalysis and Artificial Intelligence and especially embodied cognitive science together. Afterwards, one example for using psychoanalytical theory in a technical framework will be discussed.

M. Leuzinger-Bohleber and R. Pfeifer are publishing since the early 80s together, emphasizing on the importance of embodiment and the benefits, using psychoanalysis as a key model. Mental processes are – with the current technology – not directly observable, natural science therefore cannot describe these processes objectively. Therefore, *"Only subjects can describe mental processes–the mind!"* [LBP06, p. 66] and psychoanalysis is delivering a model of these mental processes [LBP06]. It is underlined that human's interaction with the surrounding is based upon the continuously changing sensory stimulation. It is the main reason why cognitive science is using autonomous robots that are interacting with a real world environment. Leuzinger-Bohleber and Pfeifer were applying new concepts from embodied cognitive science to central issues of modern psychoanalysis and discovered similarities in dealing with unconscious mechanisms and adaptive functioning. *"We think that psychoanalysis has much in common with cognitive science: it also deals with (unconscious) mechanisms underlying adaptive or maladaptive functions of the mind and tries to integrate complex (clinical-empirical) findings in theoretical models."*, Leuzinger-Bohleber stated in [LBP06, p. 68] Most recent results are regarding the description of memory and a psychoanalytical description of how memory systems are composed. In [LBSP92] and [LBP06] the memory system is interpreted in a psychoanalytically way. Memory should rather be seen as a theoretical construct, than a functional block that is explaining the current behavior by events that happened in the past. The described functionality of this construct is clearly separated from the underlying brain mechanisms, meaning that mind and brain are two different abstraction layers. Further, memory must not be seen as a data storage but as a complex, dynamic, re-categorizing, and interactive process that is always connected to sensory- and motor experiences. The direct coupling between the sensory and motor processes is essential for the function of the memory. The memory content itself is divided into the subjective side that includes past experience and an objective side that represents neural patterns generated by sensory-motor interaction with the environment. This classification will be further discussed in 3.1.3.

The team of S. Turkle on the Massachusetts Institute of Technology also tries to consolidate findings in Artificial Intelligence with the theories provided by psychoanalysis. As Turkle writes: *"Artificial Intelligence and Psychoanalysis - The new Alliance"* [Tur89, p. 241]. According to [Tur89], the classical Freudian theory has many overlapping concepts that can be used to describe internal objects. Those concepts would be *memory traces, mental representations, introjections, identifications,* and the *idea of inner structures* such as the *Super-Ego*. Unlike this, the object relation theory is more specific about what the psyche is containing. A society of inner agents or "micro-minds" is used as a description for the mind's contents. These contents are formed by the interaction with other people and build the fundamental blocks of our mental life. Turkle emphasizes on this difference between the classical Freudian theory, using single internalized objects (namely the *Super-Ego*) and the object relation theory, where each object can be seen as an autonomous agent. Further it is postulated that people are not fundamentally pleasure-seeking, but object seeking. In the classical theory, the main actors on memories, thoughts, and wishes are just a few main entities. Object relations theory describes a more dynamic system with multiple processors and processed content, an approach that is comparable to emergent Artificial Intelligence. Turkle therefore notices the possibility of an implementation in Artificial Intelligence by using a multi-agent architecture.

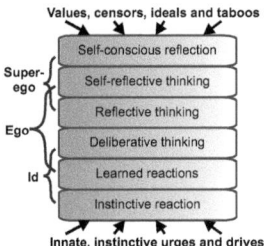

Figure 2.7: Minsky's Model of the Mind and the Mapping to Psychoanalysis [Min06, p. 148]

According to [Tur89], the difference between *drive theory* and *object relation theory* can be compared with common information processing and emergent AI: Intelligence arises out of the interaction between multiple agents. Minsky's idea of a so called *Society of Mind* ([Min06]) uses this theory and defines a censor so that the whole system can ignore contradictory agent voices. According to Minsky, intelligence, artificial or otherwise, cannot be exist without repression [Tur89, p. 259]. He defines in [Min06, p. 115] six layers to categorize the mind and assigns them to the second topographical model that is describing the human psyche by the usage of three parts, namely the *Id, Ego,* and *Super-Ego,* as it is shown in Figure 2.7. The assignment does not make sense, because the processes of reacting, thinking and reflecting that are compared to the three psychic instances (described in detail in Chapter 3) are simply not capable of the assigned functionalities. The Super-Ego indeed influences self-conscious reflections and self-reflective thinking. However, the functionality of the Super-Ego is not thinking or reflection.

Turkle identifies in [Tur04, p. 23 f] the inner censors as barriers against forbidden thoughts and shows that psychoanalysis and Artificial Intelligence have the following in general:

- The idea of the autonomous *Ego* (meaning an independent instance that makes decisions)
- The existence of *intentional actors* that can influence the mental states
- The need for self reference in theory building
- The need for objects such as censors to deal with inner conflicts

While *object relation theory* explains the mind by postulating many minds in it, which is the main idea of connectionism in AI, Turkle also introduces the idea of the "Ego psychologists" to be used in AI. There, the Ego as an agent is described that is capable to integrate the psyche with the help of defense mechanisms that are coping with the contradictory inputs. In her most recent research, Turkle is investigating the impacts computers can cause on humans and the role of human-machine-relationship e.g. to systems like *Kismet* described in Section 2.2.4 as described in [Tur06], [Tur04] and [Tur07] and so left the area of modeling cognitive processes.

In the closer past, A. Buller described in [Bul02] how to equip robots – both, simulated and real world – with a sub-domain of psychoanalysis: psycho-dynamics. He postulated in [Bul05] that psycho-dynamics deals with the fundamental role of unconscious processes and the existence of conflicting mental forces and defense mechanisms. Psychoanalytical theory also concerns these mechanisms, but considers also a sexual and aggressive drive in the development of personality. The term *psycho-dynamics* refers to the dynamic transfer between pleasure and displeasure of the observed individual. Achieving pleasure is the initial force that drives the agent to take several actions instead of resting in the same state. Tension and defense are the main antagonists in Buller's theory [Bul09], the basic dynamic complex in his introduced machine psycho-dynamics. While one of the agent's tension-systems is trying to suppress all other tension systems and is forcing the individual to take some corresponding action to satisfy the tension, the defense mechanisms are regulating the whole system and are a necessary component in the decision process of action selection. Lowering tension means achieving pleasure [Bul08], which is stored in a working memory system called MemeStorm, described in [BS02], to support reinforcement learning. The

State of the Art

structure of MemeStorm, shown in Figure 2.8, is one possible implementation example for the object relations theory that was also applied by Turkle.

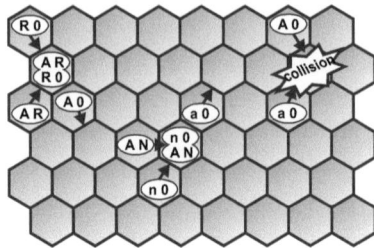

Figure 2.8: MemeStorm – A Tile-Based Working Memory [BS02]

Each *"meme"* is representing an arbitrary type of information and is able to interact with other *memes* by a predefined genetic methodology. In the case of Figure 2.8, two *memes* are meeting in the upper left corner, where one is representing a fact and one is representing a rule. Combining those two together, a confirmed fact appears. In the upper right corner, two contradicting facts are generating an exception and are refused in the memory system. The two-dimensional field formed by hexagons constitute the underlying memory. Combining the two parts of his theory – the tension-system and the memory system – Buller implements his theory on virtual agents that are exploring new habitats by negotiating an unsafe area [Bul08]. Liu picks up the idea of Bullers machine psychodynamics in [LA08] and creates a virtual avatar agent called qViki that is able to generate facial expressions on the bases of perceptual information, like the project described in Section 2.2.4 by Breazeal.

Both works are using the mapping to the psychoanalytical structure for description purpose only. In their model, the characteristically behavior of the three Freudian entities were only projected into the occurring functionality. The technical models are not based on the theory of psychoanalytical metapsychology.

2.2.6 Discussion of Cognitive Architectures

The five varying efforts to define cognitive architectures presented above are only a few of the large number of concepts applied in the area of Artificial Intelligence. However, each of the selected models represent one typical way of modeling cognitive architectures. In this section, these models will be compared and their advantages and disadvantages are discussed.

The *Blue Brain project* is a good example for the application of a bottom up design. Starting with models from the sub-molecular layer, entire brain regions like the visual cortex of the human brain are constructed within the simulation. The methodology in this case is to define a satisfying physical model for the interrelations in the lowest layer. Based upon the defined layer, the next layer is assigned which relies on the previous layer but defines additional physical models. From the point of view of a bottom-up design approach, each component defined on the highest layer consists of components defined on the lowest layer. In the case of the *Blue Brain Project*, a neo-cortical column, for example, consists of the molecules defined in one of the lower layers. It has to be emphasized that different *physical models* are described within this approach. In [Mar06] it is stated that an extension of the model to a simulation of the entire brain can lead to emerging intelligence. In this case,simulation of the entire brain means to expand the physico-chemical simulation to every other brain structure in addition to the neo-cortical region as is the case in the current status of the simulation. The problem within this argumentation is the expectation that simulated physico-chemical base structures would automatically lead to a functional model of the human psyche that emerges from these basic physico-chemical structures. There are two main arguments that can disprove this assumption. First, within the development process of the simulated neo-cortical brain region it was not expected that higher layers would emerge from the combination of elements defined in the lower layers. The simulation model for sub-molecular interrelations did not form the next higher layer. It provided only the basic components for the next higher layer. Within the model of the *Blue Brain Project*, each layer needed a definition of its own components and a model that defined the interrelationship between these components. Up to the neo-cortical brain region, it was not expected that the next layer would emerge automatically. Therefore, it is not likely to assume that the highest layer – the psychic layer – should emerge from the lower layers of the physico-chemical brain simulation. Second, the bottom-up design approach lacks in the knowledge of the top-layer demands in the beginning of the design and modeling phase. In this case, the methodology can be compared to an attempt to develop a computer program like the simulation introduced in Chapter 5 by starting with an estimation of the number of necessary transistors within the CPU that will run the program. In summary, the expectation of self-forming higher layers conflicts with the abstraction into layers itself because the functionality of a higher layer would depend on the definitions of the underlying layer. The clear interface definition between layers in a layered model would be dispersed. The model that will be introduced and developed in Chapter 3 is based upon the psychoanalytical theory of the human psyche. This theory will be considered the top-layer definition and the model developed by applying a top-down design approach to avoid unnecessary definitions on lower layers such as unused implementation details or the specification of a sub-molecular layer.

While the *Blue Brain Project* is a typical example of a bottom-up design approach, it was not primarily designed to become a cognitive architecture but rather a simulation platform for testing physico-chemical interaction. The projects discussed in the following are designed to control the behavior of an agent. Therefore, the abstraction layer will be considered on a higher level than was done with the *Blue Brain Project*.

The *CogAff Scheme* provides a general design that identifies nine possible main functional parts of a cognitive process. Whether these parts are implemented in a specific organism or robot depends on the individual. As argued in Section 2.2.2, the defined layers are based upon the observation of living organisms and their capabilities of cognition. They can be applied to any further organism or robot architecture [SCS05]. These nine functional modules are not mandatory for each organism or robot but the identified modules reflect and describe the behavior of the individual. Sloman introduces the CogAff Schema as a platform which can contain different theories of emotionally influenced cognition and is not limited to certain models and theories. In further works ([Slo04a], [Slo04b], [SC05], [SCS05], [DFZ+09], [Slo09]), Sloman also integrates various theories for emotionally influenced cognition into his scheme and combines them. The *H-CogAff Scheme* is one example of this approach. Two main criteria have to be discussed in detail. First, the design of the model follows a behavioristic methodology in identifying the main components of the model rather than identifying the functions that are responsible for this behavior. This approach neither gives any specifications on the functionality nor about the way a system can be realized. Second, the functionality is integrated by using assorted concepts from psychology, neurology, etc. that are assigned to the behavioral definitions of the architecture. The behavior is considered the controlling layer of certain functional realizations. However, behavior only results out of functionality and must not be the main component of a functional model. By describing the behavior from a distant point of view, it will never be possible to reproduce the exact functionality of the observed object. A further problem of the different integrated theories used for a possible implementation (e.g. the *H-CogAff Scheme* in [SCS05, p. 227]) is that each of the concepts may be considered complete (such as the emotional system theory) but the interface definitions only follow project internal definitions instead of definitions given by the theories used. The model developed in Chapter 3 therefore only uses a functional approach and does not consider behavioristic findings on any of the layers. Moreover, only the theory of psychoanalysis including the defined functionality and its interfaces between identified functional modules will be used.

The Ψ-*Theory* described in Section 2.2.3 reduces the cognition process to a combination of finite state machines and structures that are comparable to artificial neural networks. The complete functionality of the model is not only realized by using these basic components, it is also modeled with these components. The various functional processes identified in the model are described with finite state machines and a combination of neural networks that process perceptual and stored thresholds. The main problem within this approach is the missing abstraction layer architecture. Each of the functional modules is described within the same layer. The different functionalities merely describe containers for the underlying state functions charts. In the following Chapter 3 higher brain functions are considered too complex to describe them on a single abstraction layer. Furthermore, functionality and implementation have to be considered separately. Using components of the implementation in the functional top layer description has to be avoided. Abstraction within layers is a powerful tool for describing complex systems like the cognitive process, as shown in [DKM+04] for *situation modeling*, and will play a central role in this work.

The robotic architecture of *Kismet* described in Section 2.2.4 has the goal of simulating emotions. Actually, the focus of the project is not simulating emotional models but invoking the projection of emotions onto the system by a human observer. Used the term 'emotions' in this case is misleading because the system is not capable of 'feeling emotions' but rather invokes an emotional association within an observer. The observer projects emotions onto the system because of the system's behavior. In the case of *Kismet*, the simulated facial expressions are interpreted by a human observer as if the machine were human. The project group of *Kismet* built a system exhibiting similar behavior to that which is normally induced by emotions within humans. However, the implementation behind this is reduced to a basic set of rules. For the work that will be introduced in Chapter 3 the criticism against the emotional behavior of *Kismet* will lead to a functional approach instead of a behavioral one. It must also be stated that it is not sufficient to evaluate a system architecture only by its behavior. Behavior can be one performance measure of a cognitive architecture but additional measures concerning internal functionality need to be defined.

The psychoanalytically influenced discussions on cognitive processes, as introduced in Section 2.2.5, represent the currently existing approaches of applying psychoanalysis to technology. However, these models give a description of selected parts of psychoanalytical theory and try to project them onto existing technical implementations. They do not establish a psychoanalytical model and realize it within a corresponding technical implementation. In [Tur89], Turkle projects the psychoanalytical *object relations theory* onto Minsky's artificial network referred to as the 'society of the mind'. Minsky himself attempts to project the second topographical model onto the developed layers of his architecture [Min06, p. 148]. He does not specify how a technical system can be realized using psychoanalytical theory. Only Buller tries to realize selected concepts from psychoanalysis by using an electrical circuit like illustration to describe the dynamics of the system. However, he focuses on several selected topics and does not provide a global model realizing psychoanalytical concepts.

To improve the described research situation, the project ARS (Artificial Recognition System) attempts to develop a functional model of the human psyche using psychoanalytical models. Its purpose is to give a feasible specification for a concrete realization of psychoanalytical theory. It will be the host platform for psychoanalytically described functional concepts of drives, affects, and other defined primary and secondary processes. The following work, developed within the project ARS, introduces a functional model of the psychoanalytically defined cognitive process in Section 2.2.5. Starting from the second topographical model as the highest functional layer, underlying layers are defined in a top down manner. Additionally, one possible implementation is elaborated that follows the concepts defined within the corresponding functional model.

2.3 Simulating Embodiment and the Environment

Embodiment and the possibility to interact with an environment are mandatory tasks for intelligent agents in the area of Artificial Intelligence as described in Section 2.1. To test a developed cognitive model, it is therefore necessary to provide a simulation environment where an embodied agent can be placed in. Since there are already simulation platforms for computer simulations available, this section first discusses four selected simulation platforms. In the second part, already implemented cognitive architectures – that can be placed into the decision unit of the simulated embodied agent – are discussed, regarding their underlying cognitive modeling approach as discussed in Section 2.2, their used implementation models, and their performance in solving different tasks. Based on these frameworks, efficient methods in evaluating the results of cognitive architectures are defined, developed, and discussed and will be further used to evaluate the proposed concept of this work in Chapter 6.

Simulation environments for continues as well as discrete computer simulations have become a powerful tool for verifying new developed models in almost every field of application. Therefore, to simulate embodied autonomous agents, a variety of possible simulation platforms are available. In a first categorization, it can be distinguished between simulation environments that are providing a visual graphical user interface and pure simulation libraries that can be arranged within a specific programming language to run the simulation as a simple executable[5]. One typical examples for the former ones is *Matlab* with its extension *Simulink*, a graphical simulation environment from *The Mathworks*, the corresponding software manufacturer. Matlab offers the possibility, to define the function flow of the developed model either visually by using functional models that can be connected with each other or by using the integrated, high level programming language for describing the necessary functionality. However, *Matlab* is designed to run simulation of dynamic systems and does not support multi-agent simulations. In contrast to graphical simulation environments like Matlab, simulation libraries are developed for one specific programming language like Java, C++, etc. The main advantage of the libraries is that the defined functionality can be compiled to an executable that can be run on the target platform with high performance. In the following *AnyLogic*, a product of *XJ Technnologies*, will be introduced as one example of a simulation environment, which is not specialized to multi agent simulations only. The advantages of usability and disadvantages of performance of such comprehensive simulation frameworks will lead to the subsequently three discussed simulation environments that were specifically designed for multi agent simulation.

AnyLogic

Any logic is a simulation environment and supports several different types of simulation. In Figure 2.9 four different categories of simulations are identified that are supported by *AnyLogic*: *System Dynamics (SD)* is describing a system of modules, representing certain transfer functions defined by differential equations, which are interacting with each other and building feedback loops. The topic has its root in modeling organizational flowcharts for e.g. controlling company internal processes. To describe global physical systems (and System Dynamics is a sub-area of it), *Dynamic Systems (DS)* is used. Physical state variables and the corresponding algebraic differential equations are used as definition components for the simulation. The former two are mainly dealing with continuous processes. The connections between them are working with aggregates and do not distinguish between the items that are sent to the next module. Whereas *Discrete Event Based (DE)* and *Agent Based (AB)* simulations are mainly handled with time discrete simulations. The former is used to simulate passive entities, analyzing flowcharts, transport networks, and resources during the simulation time. The latter describes active entities – so called agents – with their individual decision unit and direct interaction with the environment the agents are placed in. A global system behavior is not defined in agent based simulations. It is

---

[5]The executable file is able to initiate a new process that runs the simulation without the necessity of installing the complete simulation framework.

State of the Art

emerging out of the interaction between the different agents.

Compared to *Matlab, Labview, SWARM, FlexSim,* or *ModelMaker* that are focusing on one of the previously described modeling approaches only, *AnyLogic* claims, as shown in Figure 2.9 to be a multi-paradigm simulation tool. Simulations of electrical circuits or physical interrelationships using corresponding differential equations or discrete characterizations can be simulated as well as emergent behavior of multi-agents, such as pedestrian simulations. In the following, the possibility of agent based simulations in *AnyLogic* will be discussed in further detail, with respect to a realization of a multi-agent simulation in Chapter 4.

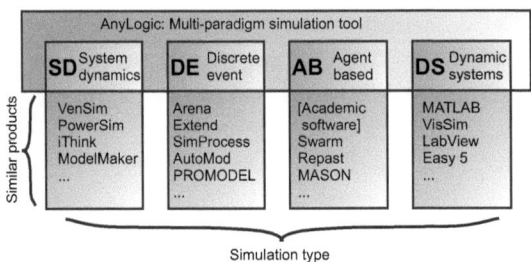

Figure 2.9: Anylogic's Multi Paradigm Approach [BF04, p. 16]

For a rapid development of agent based models, libraries for defining agent behavior, communications, and environmental models are provided as well as packages for the graphical visualization as it is extensively used in [BBF+99]. Therefore, a framework can be used that deals with the requirements of discrete, event-based processing and agent based simulation. The necessary prerequisites of timing, scheduling, threading are already supported. Besides the possibility of a graphically definition tool for flowcharts, the programming language is Java and also the output of a completely defined model are Java binaries. This makes it possible to include self implemented external Java-classes or existing libraries from third party providers. A first approach in simulating an agents decision unit that will be described in Section 2.6 was already implemented in *AnyLogic* in previous works [DZLZ08]. Although *AnyLogic* provides a good platform for rapid prototyping to simulate the agent's decision units (including a simplified simulated environment), the solution lack in stability, performance, and the ability to distribute agents to e.g. processes, processors or computers. The latter has been solved, using external classes that were supporting this functionality but the other criteria remain. Event triggered processes – such as sensing, acting, moving, or collision handling – could be defined by so called *time charts* using customized Java-functions as transition conditions. However, the simulation environment produces auto-generated Java-code of all graphically defined flow-charts that can hardly be read and are therefore non-transparent to debugging. Furthermore, *AnyLogic* does not provides a built in physics engine. In the simulation of robot-like agents the integration of a physics model become necessary, especially when the interaction between a robot and its environment has to be considered.

For a rapid prototyping in agent based simulations, the framework for scheduling, positioning and visualization provided by AnyLogic is sufficient. In multi-agent based simulation, performance is a critical factor that requires a slim scheduling algorithm for the amount of agents. Also the integration of a physics engine can improve the performance of the simulation. With these demands, simulations can take advantage of the more customized Frameworks that are currently existing. In the following paragraphs, three different frameworks especially designed for agent based simulation will be introduced.

Swarm
First developed in *Objective C*, Swarm is a set of libraries that enables the implementation of agent-based models. A wrapper framework exists that enables the usage of the library also in a Java native framework. It is developed for studying biological systems in the field of Artificial Life to identify unifying dynamical properties of the life-form called Swarm-agents [Dan99].

State of the Art

Providing the developer with the basic framework for timing and scheduling, agents are grouped in a temporal container, the so-called swarms. A swarm can also consist of several sub-swarms and each swarm contains a scheduler that handles the included sub-swarms and agents. Also an agent contains a schedule, which can be interpreted as the agent's task list consisting of the actions that have to be processed by the agent.

The development process is a classic bottom-up approach. First the agent's behavior is implemented one by one with respect to the frameworks specific methods that are automatically called during the simulation. Then the behavior of the next higher group-container is implemented and finally the highest swarm – a container that includes every group – is defined. This hierarchy, described in closer detail in [MBLA96], has the advantage that different types of agents can be inspected in their behavior, population, etc.

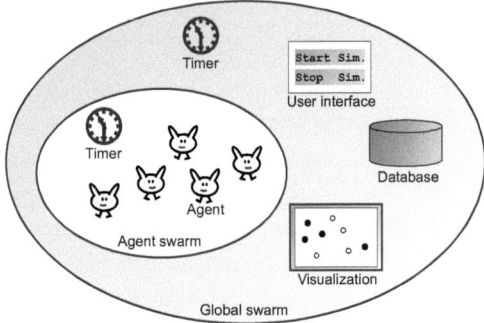

Figure 2.10: A Swarm of Observer Agents Measuring a Model of Agents [MBLA96]

A further performance-ensuring design decision is the conceptual framework that strictly differs between the model and the visualization. Therefore visualization libraries are provided as well as special data structures that are supporting a rapid development of inspectors where the agents and swarms can be monitored [RLJ06]. Figure 2.10 shows a Swarm of observer agents for visualization that are observing a Swarm of agents. Also the objects used for the visualization, user interface and data storage are considered as swarm objects within the global swarm object and are therefore also scheduled by the defined timers. Swarm has been developed first for biological research – for example for simulating cell behaviors – but is now applied to many research areas, also in computer technology. However, for agent based simulation of robot-like agents in a simulated environment, Swarm does not provide specific treatment for these 'real-world-simulation-logic' such as a physics engine. Although the interaction between agents and environment can be implemented, using third party solutions, the basic framework is not addressing this specific issue. Being one of the first implementations of agent based simulation only, Swarm influenced more recent developed simulation frameworks. Two of them will be introduced in the following.

Repast - Recursive Porous Agent Simulation Toolkit
Like Swarm, *Repast* is a Java library to simulate agents within a virtual environment. One main attempt was to implement a Swarm-Simulation in native Java. However, some decisions regarding the design principals: The hierarchy of a swarm-construct was not transferred, although it would be possible to implement such a hierarchy in the *Repast* framework. The main focus of this simulation framework is the area of social science, where social behavior has to be simulated. Most of the tools that are available are addressing this specific research domain.

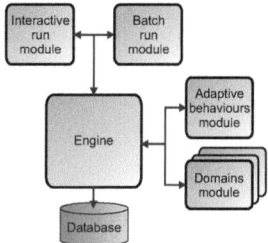

Figure 2.11: The Main Components of Repast [NCV06]

Figure 2.11 shows the basic architecture of Repast [NCV06]. Whereas the engine-, logging-, interactive-run-, and batch-run-modules are the representing the core of the framework, the other modules are optional. Like the former simulation environments, the engine is responsible for the type of scheduling, the distribution of the action-commands, and the animation of the simulated agents. It also supports, in cooperation with the interactive- and batch-run-module, the control of starting, stopping, and stepping functionality of the simulation. The logging module supports the possibility to record data and the interactive-run module is the interface between visualization and data modules. The adaptive behavior module is holding the self implemented algorithms creating the behavior of an agent. Neural network and genetic algorithm solutions are partly included in the framework. Repast provides also several packages for analyzing and visualizing data in 2D and 3D environments (an example can be found in [TNH+06] for a predator-prey scenario) and with the add-on software integration for Eclipse, called Repast Simphony [NTCJ07], the development process is very similar to the graphical simulation environment of AnyLogic.

To summarize, Swarm and Repast support the agent developer with the basic framework for scheduling and interaction with the environment but more detailed environmental or agents

State of the Art

functionality has to be embedded manually. This either increases the time for development of robot-like agents in a simulated environment or slows down the core framework due to the integration of external libraries. This would be necessary in using a physics engine and therefore, one further simulation framework will be introduced.

MASON - Multi-Agent Simulator Of Neighborhoods

MASON is a Java-based discrete-event simulation core library and visualization toolkit and can be used for agent based simulation [LCRPS04]. During the development process of MASON, performance for millions of agents in "swarm" simulation and therefore the ability to distribute the agents logic domain-independent back-end systems were defining the main requirements and influenced the design process. MASON should be (and is) a fast, orthogonal, minimal model library for multi-agent-simulation that grants the possibility of developing and embedding additional features.

From the point of view of the development of a robot-like-agent simulation in a simulated environment, this brings two main advantages. First, the integration of a robot-like agent library including environmental objects can be integrated without unsolvable or conflicting problems. Second, the framework can be easily extended and customized by adding third-party libraries. One of the existing libraries is an integrated two-dimensional physics engine.

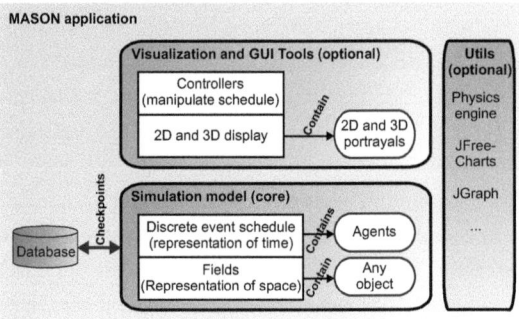

Figure 2.12: The MASON Layer Architecture [LBP+03]

The basic ideas of handling multi-agent-simulations are similar to Swarm and Repast, but the implementation is done more pragmatic with respect to performance. The modeling layer is strictly separated from the visualization layer [LBP+03], as it is depicted in Figure 2.12. The possibility of either running the simulation with or without a visualization is reached by having a main class that holds the simulation-state (`SimState`) and a main class that holds the visualization state (`GuiState`). Electively the application can be run for presenting the data visually or generating the calculated data and write it do disk.

Scheduling is done by the discrete event schedule, included in the MASON's core library. Each agent is called by the framework in each step or in other, predefined and agent-specific multiples of a simulation step. Additionally, high performance container classes for the position of any object in the simulation are provided. Each logical unit that has a visual representative has to implement a corresponding portrayal class that is registered to the scheduler of the visualization and defines the appearance in the simulation. So called *Inspectors* can be used to visualize and alter the values of the agent's model classes. For a visualization of agent specific values a charts library is included. Since the simulation is an open source Java project, any Java library can be included into the project.

A typical example of a multi-agent based simulation realized in MASON is given in [PL04], describing the implementation of an ant-forging simulation. Chapter 4 and 5 will discuss the application of the MASON framework in multi-agent-based simulation in more detail. It has been selected due to its advantages of performance in scheduling and physics simulation and its flexibility of adding new components to the framework.

The presented simulation platforms are necessary to realize a simulation environment for an embodied agent. The following sections will focus on existing implementations of frameworks for the decision making of an autonomous agent. In a typical agent-based simulation, each agent contains an instance of its own decision unit in order to react on changes in the environment.

2.4 Artificial Decision-Making Frameworks

Embodied, autonomous agents have the possibility to perceive information about their environment and are able to change it by executing certain actions. The process that is necessary to come from a certain perception to a corresponding action is taking place in the decision unit of the autonomous agent. The following section discusses existing architectures for this decision making process.

The classic approach of data processing in intelligent autonomous agents within one processing step is depicted in Figure 2.13. According to [Bro86], the sensors of the agent are first accessed and the sensor data has to be written into defined registers and transferred into a type of data that can be processed by the further modules. Then, a model of the currently perceived situation has to be created, to be able to make a plan to meet the actual requirements. This model includes knowledge about the environment and the agent's current state. The created plan results in an action or a sequence of actions that has to be executed by the actuators of the agent.

Figure 2.13: A Traditional, Functional Decomposition of a Mobile Robot Control System According to [Bro86]

Using specified interfaces, the two modules Modeling and Planning that will be called *Deliberative System*, can be implemented as an independent part. Therefore, the deliberative work is located only within these two modules. Today's implementations of symbolic Artificial Intelligence are requiring symbols as an input from the sensing module. The *Deliberative System* uses these symbols as the central information structure that is processed and stored, and generates new symbols that are representing the system's actions.

In the following chapter, four different models for *Deliberative Systems* will be introduced and compared to each other. Additionally, existing implementation of the models will be investigated. The conclusion and selected basic concept of the models will be used as a basis for the development of the implementation, described in detail in Chapter 4. The chapter will show a possible implementation of the psychoanalytically inspired model and will use several implementation details discussed in the following paragraphs.

Software systems for decision making generally include cognitive architectures as well as agent architectures. A main task in developing such systems is to hold knowledge and to process perceptual data according to this knowledge. It will be shown that knowledge representation is a central issue in all introduced agent architectures and therefore also the central bases of these architecture. The following architectures can be used for *knowledge-intensive agents*, which have, according to [JW06], to achieve a human-level Artificial Intelligence. The frameworks differ in their nomenclature and methodology, so that is necessary to give a definition of the main parts that are relevant in agent architectures.

Jones distinguishes between the following seven functional processing steps in the agent's *decision unit*: Perceptions, Beliefs, Desires, Active Goals, Plans, Actions, Outputs [JW06]. Simple perceptual elements are forming the agent's beliefs, representing the current situation and additional logical knowledge. It can be distinguished between justified beliefs and mere assumptions. The former one is investigated in particular within belief revision [GÖ8, p. 148 ff]. The desires are formed by a list of goals the agent already decided to reach but that are not eligible in the current situation. However, desires can be communicated to other agents or to anticipatory planning while achieving the active currently active goal.

After the selection of an active goal, the agent has to calculate a plan to reach this goal. Plan switching is an optional task that supports flexible considerations of investigating current desires but requires interruptible plans consisting of atomic actions. Such a plan consists of several actions that are necessary to complete the plan. In general different action types are used to execute an output command, to update the current beliefs, and to select a new goal or desire.

The output can be seen as the activity in the environment. During all of these seven steps of the described information processing chain, data is handled and processed in different forms and with respect on different consequences. The knowledge-base has to be kept consistent, beliefs, assumptions, desires, goals, and plans have to be maintained according to the changing environment.

BDI – Belief, Desire, Intention

The BDI architecture introduced by Bratmans theory of human perception [Bra87], is technically transferred and applied to real world applications by Georgeff in [GI89]. It was developed for reasoning systems, coping with the demands on continuously changing environments. The architecture was, for example, applied to handling malfunctions on the space shuttle or controlling autonomous agents and robots. Wooldrige also introduces an implementation concept called LORA (Logic of Rational Agents) in more detail in [Woo00] applying the BDI framework.

The basic idea of the BDI-Framework is to functionally subdivide the implementation of a deliberative process into three main modules: Belief, Desire, and Intention. A typical application can be seen in [KKSD08], where an agent has to operate in a discrete world called the 'tileworld', having a belief of the environment, several desires to achieve, and an actual intention to do something that is necessary to satisfy the currently selected desire.

Whereas BDI does not make any restrictions on actions, perception, and human-like deliberation processes, as critically discussed in [GPP+99], it clearly defines the three main modules including their functionality and information types. However, it is not distinguished between justified beliefs and assumptions, but a general mechanism for maintaining justified beliefs is provided. Belief revision, described by Gärdenfors in [GÖ8] is one possible framework and implementation of the mechanism. The clear distinction between beliefs and desires allows a BDI-System to monitor goals that are currently not chosen to be claimed. Processes using logical inference are selecting a desire to an active goal. This active goal is called *intention*. In several implementations, there is no difference between the intention (or active goal) and the corresponding selected plan. Without specifying a plan language, it is assumed that there exists a plan library or the plans are generated outside of the basic agent framework.

Different processing paths can cause different actions at the same time that have to be prioritized. One possible strategy is a direct mapping from the active goal to the plan using a simple lookup list. After each atomic action was successfully processed, the current plan can be re-evaluated. Is the selected plan still leading to the goal, the next actions are sequentially executed. Otherwise, a new plan has to be selected. The output type related to the action of the system is not further specified by the framework. The main advantage in this functional modeling approach is the clear distinction between a world model and a desired plan library and execution. The novelty of this approach can be seen in the creation of an additional model that holds and handles desires that influence the agent-specific planning. A more detailed description of the Lora-architecture is given by Wooldridge in [GW99, p. 54-61]. A comparison between the functional modules of the BDI architecture and the ARS model (Artificial Recognition System) also described in this thesis is given in [LZD+08].

Soar

Soar is a cognitive architecture for *knowledge-intensive agents* with roots in the theory of cognitive psychology and computer science [LNR87]. The goal of this architecture was to find a minimum set of mechanisms that are necessary to produce intelligent behavior as explained in [JW06]. The main focus lies on functionalities of knowledge and belief representation, mechanisms for learning and intention selection, and the integration of different reasoning methods.

Long-term knowledge is represented in the *problem space*, whereas the *physical symbol system hypotheses* claims that any physically realized, intelligent entity can be treated as a formal symbol processing system.

It is not distinguished between knowledge and specific beliefs about the environment (the agent's world model repository) in terms of the data structure of the symbol. The same symbol-structure is also used for the representation of primitive perceptual elements, which is the interface to the environment. An automatic reason maintenance system fosters justified beliefs out of the perceptual primitives and removes old ones. A deliberative process leads to a so called assumption, which is the agent's estimation of the current

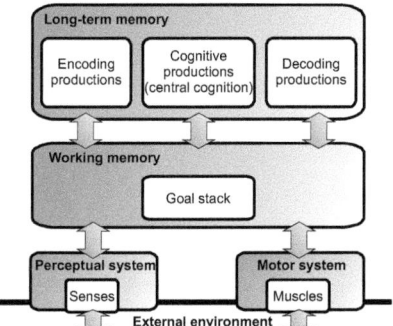

Figure 2.14: Architecture of SOAR

situation. Based upon these assumptions, the next action is selected from a current plan that represents directly the achievement of an active goal. In Soar, it is not necessary that an agent has an explicit representation of a plan as long as an action is connected to the active goal.

The deliberate goal commitment is done in an explicit process. External planning libraries can be used, as long as the results are transferred into Soar's belief representation language. The framework does not give any further specifications or restrictions. The deliberating process is based on a working memory, holding all different types of information, a decision procedure that detects representatives that are requiring an action, a working memory manager that deletes irrelevant information, a production memory that can add new entries in the working memory, and a chunking mechanism [New94, p. 185] that is the basis of the learning mechanism for that rules. Because there are only actions and no plan that has to be processed, reconsideration can be done after each action. The output is a motor command that is represented in the belief language of the system. This allows a deliberation of the output, using the agents complete knowledge without restrictions.

Although the Soar architecture can be used to realize a decision unit of an autonomous agent, a functional specification regarding the process that lead to an action are hardly defined. The framework focuses on knowledge representation, the functionalities perception, planning, and action have to be considered within the specific realization. However, especially these functionalities are considered as crucial for an autonomous agent.

ICARUS

After the memory-oriented architecture of Soar, an implementation of an agent-based model will be discussed that does not consider the memory as the central component:

ICARUS is a cognitive architecture that makes strong commitments to memories, representations, and cognitive processes and uses concepts of human problem solving, reasoning, and skill acquisition, as specified in [Lan06]. In contrast to Soar, it is an architecture, designed directly for embodied agents placed in an external environment. This is clearly an impact to the design of the architecture.

State of the Art

The general principles can be divided into five main conceptual parts:

- The cognitive symbols for perception and action are grounded.
- Available concepts and skills are represented as distinct cognitive structures.
- Memory entries of the long-term memory are hierarchically organized.
- Concepts of higher semantic skills or routines are based upon existing lower ones.
- Short-term memories are always connected to their corresponding long-term memories.

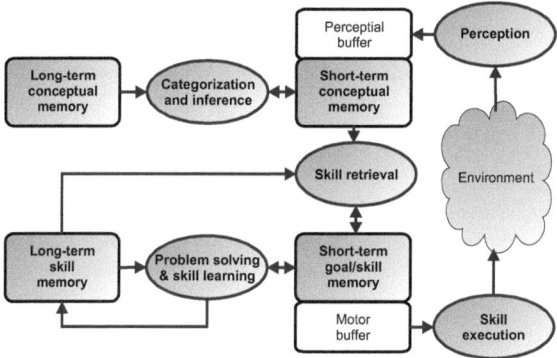

Figure 2.15: Functional Processes of the ICARUS Architecture and Their Connections to Memories [Lan06]

The analysis of these principles shows a tight connection to a possible implementation. Clear restrictions are made and therefore the possibility of defining clear interfaces is granted. As in the previous described architectures, the starting point of this architecture also lies in the data representation and the corresponding memory system. As depicted in Figure 2.15, it is distinguished between long-term memories, containing knowledge and procedures and short-term memories, containing beliefs and goals. Starting from the perception of the environment in the perceptual buffer, the currently perceived situation is matched against the specific concept of perception, represented in the bottom-up designed conceptual memory. Each set of perception can be mapped to one or more specific concepts. When a concept matches, a new instance of this conceptual memory entry is created in the perceptual buffer. This shows the main advantage of ICARUS: A perceptual symbol is automatically grounded to the sensory data, and can use this information in the further processing cycle. The concept followed in the conceptual memory, where every symbol in the perceptual buffer has a corresponding parent symbol, is also applied to every other symbolic instance within the short-term memory. A short-term memory entry only consists with a mandatory, corresponding parent symbol in the long-term memory.

As in the BDI framework, the belief memory holds the information about the current environmental situation according to the perceived symbols. Each of these entries in the belief memory are related to the corresponding concept. On the lower part of Figure 2.15, the goal and intention memory holds an ordered list of goals. Each goal has a link to the corresponding skill-template that defines and describes the abilities the agent has. The goals are hierarchically assembled by subgoals that are further divided into the necessary skills and actions. Thus, the knowledge-representation tree of the goals is – unlike the perceptual concept memory – organized in a top-down hierarchy. Through the motor buffer, the agent's actuators are driven.

According to [Lan06] psychology distinguishes between performance processes and the learning processes. In the ICARUS framework, performance processes are handling contents of the short-term memory. These can be functions responsible for memory retrieval, pattern matching, skill selection, inference, and problem solving. Learning processes are only processing and changing data in the long-term memory, where the existing knowledge is refined or replaced by a new one, for example as described in [LC06]. For such higher cognitive functionalities, ICARUS incorporates a means-ends problem solver (described in detail in [Vel94, p. 39] and [GW99, p. 56]) and a learning module for the generation of new skills in the skill memory.

Compared to the former described cognitive architectures, the programming language is more complex, due to the higher abstraction level. This higher-level constructs allow a much simpler programming and more rapid construction of intelligent agents [Lan06].

Amongst other existing cognitive frameworks[6] the former described three cognitive architectures and their considerations are the basis for the technical implementation described in Chapter 4. The BDI framework gives a fast possibility of allocating data and functionality to the three main blocks of BDI, namely beliefs, desires, and intention. The Soar framework shows how processes can be identified, specified, and further implemented and the ICARUS framework is chosen because of the strong mapping between knowledge and sensor-generated data.

---

[6]In the literature of Artificial intelligence a wide variety of frameworks exist. They mainly differ in their field of application. In the following, a view selected frameworks are listed: ACT-R ([ABB+04] and [WL07] in which a comparison to Soar is given), EPIC ([KM97]), or Clarion ([SMP01]) and further models for agent based decision units e.g. subsumption architecture ([Bro90]), Prodigy ([Vel94]), or GRL ([Hor00]).

For most of the mentioned architectures, specific implementations exist, using the restrictions defined in the framework as necessary requirements to the implementation. The BDI framework is used by many implementations as an archetype, e.g. BDIM [BR98b], [BR98a], JACK [BRHL99], and the open source version Jadex [PBL03] (for a comparison of those former two see [Che03]) and CoJACK [ERBB08] as a further development of JACK [Hub99b], JAM [Hub99a], and Jason [BHW07]. The BDI framework is used to differ between the three data types – data holding information about the beliefs, the desires, and the intentions – and the corresponding processing functions that are altering the data bases. A central part of the implementations are the agent programming language in which rules and knowledge can be defined. It can be distinguished between agent oriented programming languages, using mentalistic notions [GW99, p. 67], and logical-formulas based language [Woo00]. A detailed descriptions of the different agent languages is given in [MDA05]. The BDI implementation Jadex, as mentioned above, will be considered for implementation in Chapter 4. With a LISP-like logical programming language it allows the declaration of rule-based beliefs, desires and intentions. The usage of this formal, abstract language makes the development of the agents logical reasoning unit more convenient than implementing each detail in e.g. Java-code directly. The designer of the basic knowledge can focus on the definition framework rather than on programming skills.

As shown on the example of the BDI framework, a huge set of available, specialized frameworks and implementations exists. Comparisons can hardly be made between the different, implemented sub-frameworks and are even more difficult between the different frameworks. Projects like the APOC Framework [SA04], a general universal agent architecture framework standing for Activating-Processing-Observing-Components, are trying to compare different agent architectures by providing a standardized set of components, necessary to describe a cognitive architecture. This intermediate step of restructuring the model using only the provided elements makes a direct comparison of the main structures and their implementations possible. ADE, an Architecture Development Environment for Virtual and Robotic Agents [AS05] is the corresponding, available development tool for building such intermediate steps.

The discussed frameworks for decision units are the basis for the considerations in the Chapter 4 regarding implementation. For evaluating the developed decision-making unit, a simulation platform is introduced in Chapter 5. With this framework, it further becomes possible to compare the decision unit with other, already existing implementations by using standardized interfaces. The following section will highlight the possibilities of evaluating the performance of decision units.

State of the Art

2.5 Evaluating Multi-Agent Simulations

To evaluate the outcomes of an rational agent, distinct criteria have to be defined. The combination of sensing, deliberating, and acting results in a large number of factors that can be evaluated. This combination grants the possibilities of *autonomy, pro-activeness, reactivity, and social ability* to a rational agent. The following section compares existing evaluation techniques for autonomous agents and acquires a set of factors that will become the basis for evaluation in Chapter 6. In [RN03, p. 38], the PEAS description (Performance, Environment, Actuators, and Sensors) is defined to describe the task environment of a rational agent. According to [RN03, p. 35], *"[...] it is better to design performance measure according to what one actually wants in the environment, rather than according to how one thinks the agent should behave."*

For the following considerations, a simplified agent is assumed that is embedded in an artificial environment. The agent is able to influence this environment and has, as a motivation to do so, a certain and measurable goal. For example collecting objects would be a very simple task in such a simulated environment. Further, the agent itself has a homeostasis, keeping certain values between defined thresholds, and certain directives to change the environment.

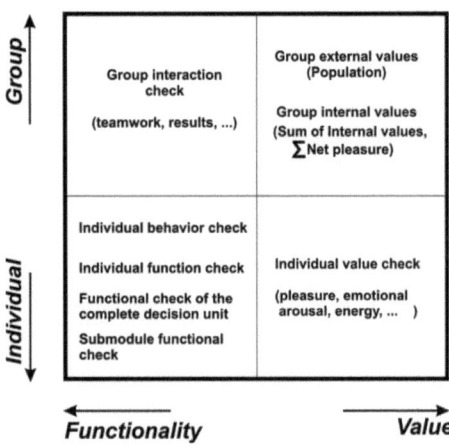

Figure 2.16: Four Categories of Evaluating an Agent's Performance

Figure 2.16 shows one possibility to divide measurement categories of autonomous agents. The performance measure can be applied either to the functionality or the qualitative and quantitative values of the agents. The former can be seen as the deviation between the given functionality according to the specifications and the observed functionality. The latter uses predefined and measurable values that are changing during the simulation time. The second dimension of Figure 2.16 distinguishes between one single agent and a group of agents. When examing a single agent, only values regarding to this agent are of interest. Group values are either measure variables that reflect the competence (e.g. as an average of the single agents) of a group of agents in terms of quantity or quality.

The individual's functionality can be measured in several layers of the simulated agent. A submodule functional test does not have to take place necessarily during the simulation runtime but can also be processed in the context of a test routine. When a functional module of an implemented decision framework has to be tested, a test function would have to call this function block with all possible combinations of input values and evaluate the outputs according to the specification. This approach can be identified as *software unit testing*. In this form of testing, each functional unit has to pass a specific test procedure that detects faulty terminations. This procedure makes the quality of the implemented function capable of measurement as depicted in [IEE87].

The same procedure can be applied to the implementation of the entire decision unit of the agent. This test can be compared to an impulse response in signal processing. By embedding the decision unit into a software unit tester, specific simulated input variables can be applied and the output of the system evaluated. Running times and delays are not primarily important in discrete simulations of autonomous agents because the time between one atomic simulation step to the next can be seen as constant. The function call hierarchy and therefore the functionality between an input and the corresponding output is most important and can be analyzed within such a simulation, even within one simulation step.

When a rational agent is supposed to achieve given goals and is able to show certain behavior to achieve them, the individuals functionality of meeting the requirements can be measured. Evaluating if a goal has been achieved is one simple possibility to measure the performance of an agent. But also values like time, distance, or quantity of achieving a goal can be measured in a second step to get more insight into the process of achieving the goal. Further, the applied actions for achieving a goal have to be compared with other possibilities for reaching the goal by using for example different sub-plans. For the evaluation of complex decision making, it has to be considered that short term goals – as they are common for episodic environments, where future actions are completely independent from past actions – may have a worse impact than long term goals – as they are common in sequential environments, where the current decision could affect all future ones.

Taking a more detailed look at the agent's individual values, this part of measuring system strongly depends on the models that are used within the agent. Most agent simulations are using the energy level of the agent as a simplified and more technical homeostatic system that has to be, at least, greater than zero. Without energy, the agent is unable to function and its lifetime is typically expired. Supposing the agents goal is to keep alive as long as possible, the only performance measure for this goal can be the lifetime (assuming an infinite lifespan is impossible). Measuring the lifespan within agent simulations – either for single agents or for groups of agents – is often used in literature. In [HDN03] and [HDNB04] the lifetime of agents using the developed agent architectures is measured and compared to get results of the functionality. Especially in multi-agent and swarm simulations, the lifetime is of importance to predict the steady state of the artificial ecosystem.

Besides of the bodily-related values (energy, processor load, network traffic, ...), an agent can also have internal values that are not directly influenced by bodily circumstances. Especially affective agents as described in [Pic00] are using virtual constructs of emotional value systems that are basically identified as being both, physically and cognitive. These systems can be seen as a summary of past impressions of the agent and are significantly influencing an emotional agents behavior. An agent that avoids negative emotional arousal can be evaluated and identified as a better agent than one that is significantly influenced by its overwhelming emotional system, as shown in [HC08] or [PKKK08]. In such systems, *pleasure* often serves as a common currency to support reinforcement learning algorithms and strongly depends on its definition. A system that experiences more pleasure during a given time or its lifetime can be evaluated as the better system, as long as this pleasure seeking can be inhibited in order to meet long term goals. In terms of humans, this concept seems obvious, but also in terms of technical systems it is applicable. It is possible to define a decrease of a robot's pleasure value, as soon as the current drawn by an electrical load (e.g. a motor) exceeds a certain threshold[7]. This value of displeasure certainly becomes a significance to the systems lifetime.

Functionality and internal values can be closely connected to each other. In [MM07], Marcarelli et al. are discussing the insight learning implementation of their agent. Using a

---

[7]A motor, for example, draws about ten times more current during start-up or in terms of a blocking motor than it does during the normal run. This characteristics is used to detect the mechanical end stop of motor actuators without using an ultimate limit switch as it is explained in [Lan01] and can also be utilized in robots.

Bayesian Network, they are investigating the utility of the simulation and are also evaluating the information contained by the network. They argue that more trained agents that are mentally simulating the impact of their actions are taking the better solution. Especially when virtual constructed keywords in simulated agents like "consciousness" or "self-awareness" and their corresponding values have to be measured, as it is done in [McC07] and [SLH07], the measure values are highly depending on the definition of the value that has to be measured.

The upper left quarter of Figure 2.16 measures a group's performance in terms of functionality. It does not only measure if teamwork is better than egoistic behavior but also the number of team actions during a given time or lifetime. Additionally the outcomes can be measured. In [Dör02], the agents have to collect as much units of an available resource as possible as described in Section 2.2.3. Building teams of different types of agents, the amount of collected resources within a team can be used as a measure of performance.

The upper right quadrant describes the groups values. Again, especially in multi-agent swarm simulation, the population of agents is a typically used measure. It can be seen as an external value to measure the group's performance by calculating the average population. These values are labeled as *group internal values*. Measuring the total amount of gained pleasure of a team of emotional based agents would be one possibility to evaluate the performance of such a group. In Section 4.4.2, the 'Gross agent pleasure' will be defined, based on this idea. One further realization regarding group internal values is the *Total net pleasure*, introduced by Anderson and Anderson in [AA07]. Although this value is used as a decision criterion for further actions of so called ethical agents, it can also be used as a performance measure for a dedicated group of agents. The *Total net pleasure* is defined as the sum of pleasure for each affected individual, where the pleasure is weighted with the product of intensity, duration, and probability as shown in Equation 2.1.

$$Total\ net\ pleasure = \sum(intensity \cdot duration \cdot probability)\ for\ each\ affected\ agent \quad (2.1)$$

In Anderson's ethical agents, the net pleasure is calculated before a certain action is taken. When the intended action results in an increase of the net pleasure, the action is taken, otherwise it is discarded. It is a simple implementation of hedonistic act utilitarianism, which can be seen as the opposite of the deontological approach, where each action can be assigned to be good or bad, regardless to its consequences.

The values of performance measurement do not depend on the type of environment and the type of agent only, but also on the situation, the agent is. In the Chapters 4 and 6, each of the discussed measuring values will be applied to the agent. The suggested four areas of evaluating the performance must not be investigated only separately. Otherwise it is possible that conflicts of interests between the individual agent and their corresponding group and the origins are not detected. However, the *total net pleasure* shows the main challenge in performance measuring: Evaluating the taken action of an agent requires a complete knowledge of the environment. Even with this knowledge, the measured value evaluates only the behavior in a certain situation but does not necessarily give a proof for the behavior in other situations, especially in new and therefore unknown situations.

The above described topics gave an overview on already existing cognitive frameworks and their implementations. Simulation environments were introduced in order to show the possibilities to test the implementations of developed cognitive frameworks within the decision unit of autonomous agents. Various decision-making frameworks were discussed that are implementing planning algorithms in order to react on certain changes in the environment. Finally, a framework for evaluations for decision units was described that summarizes the methods to measure the performance of the simulated agents. Before introducing the computational framework that will be described in Chapter 3, the previously work within the project ARS will be summarized and discussed and will be the basis for this work.

2.6 Artificial Recognition System - Psychoanalysis

In the year 2006, when I joined the Institute of Computer Technology at the Vienna University of Technology, Prof. Dr. Dietmar Dietrich and his team were developing the project *Artificial Recognition System (ARS)*. Their research focused on the development of an architecture for data processing and decision making and followed a bionic approach as already described in [Die00]. In 2006, two separate teams existed with different research foci. The group *ARS-PC (Perception)* was investigating neurological theories for data processing and symbolization in order to develop a technically feasible model that could be used in modern computer systems. With the work of G. Zucker (né Pratl) [Pra06], a first hierarchical model for data symbolization was developed that has been implemented and improved, especially by the further works of W. Burgstaller [Bur07] and R. Velik [Vel08]. The developed models can be described as passive models. Environmental information was perceived and processed via corresponding sensors and translated into higher level semantic symbols.

State of the Art

In parallel to the efforts of ARS-PC, the group ARS-PA (Psychoanalysis) around B. Palensky [Pal07] and C.Rösener [Roe07] had developed *"[...] a new cognitive architecture for automation systems and autonomous agents [...]"* [Pal07, p. 69]. The research findings regarding this architecture will be introduced and discussed in the following paragraphs because they lead to the fundamentals of the model introduced in Chapter 3. The designed, cognitive architecture is shown in Figure 2.17 according to the introduction in [Pal07, p. 69 ff.].

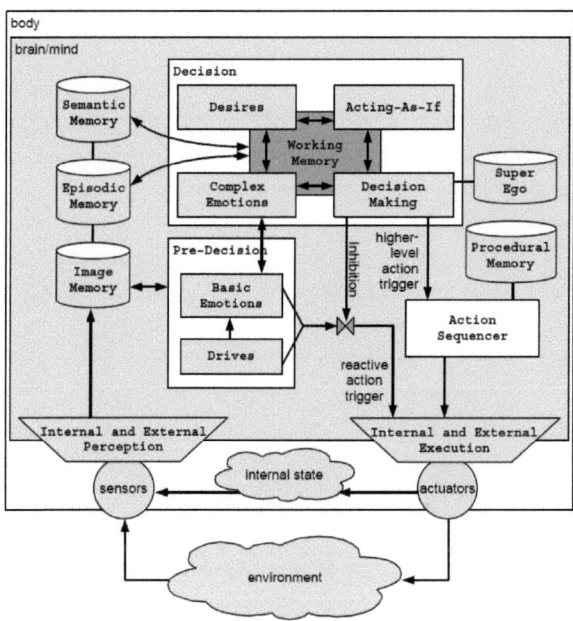

Figure 2.17: The Architecture of the *Artificial Recognition System - Psychoanalysis (ARS-PA)* Introduced by B. Palensky in [Pal07, p. 73]

The model is based on selected, neuro-psychoanalytical concepts that were defined by the International Neuropsychoanalytical Society (npsa) as described in detail by M. Solms in [ST02]. The model distinguishes between three principle regions: the environment, the body, and the brain/mind. The environment of the agent that implements the architecture can be perceived through the sensors of the agent. They are part of the agent's body. Essential internal states of the agent – such as the current energy level or temperature – can also be perceived through the agent's sensors. According to the symbolization methods described in [Pra06], the module *Internal and External Perception* transforms the sensor values into higher semantical symbols. This component can be compared to the neurological functionality of the human brain. The area named *brain/mind* of the agent therefore only deals with symbols that represent the perception of the internal state of its body or the environment. This stream of perceptual symbols are then matched against a set of so-called images, which define specific sub-sets of the perception. The images, stored in the module *Image Memory* typically contain perceptual symbols that normally appear together. An image represents a specific kind of situation the agent is currently in. If an image matches the currently perceived stream of symbols, the image is recognized and is forwarded to the module *Pre-Decision*.

Within the *Pre-Decision* module, two concepts of neuro-psychoanalysis are applied. First, *Drives* are generated out of images that have their origins within the internal states. They are seen as a boundary phenomenon, signaling the needs of the body to the mind. In [Roe07, p. 81], the following drives are defined: *hunger, temperature imbalance, stress, lust*. Second, the module *Basic Emotions* is evaluating the currently perceived information, containing drives and environmental images, by generating so called basic emotions. In [Pal07, p. 83], the following basic emotions are defined, following the description in neuro-psychoanalysis in [Pan98] and [ST02]: SEEKING, FEAR, RAGE, PANIC/LOSS, PLAY, and LUST [8]. For the development of the model introduced in Chapter 3, the significance of these concepts must be discussed. In the case of the drive, the model uses the term from psychoanalytical theory but does not consider the psychoanalytical functionality of drives, including data structures such as *thing presentations* or *affects* and functionalities such as *pairs of opposites*, the *Fusion of drives* and *defense mechanisms* (all these terms will be described in detail in Chapter 3). Instead, the values of the internal states are directly mapped onto the predefined drive-systems. These drives are described to influence one of the basic emotional systems, namely the SEEKING system. However, Panksepp bases his concept of basic emotions in [Pan98] on findings regarding the neurological structure of the brain. The interconnection between the defined drives of the model and the basic emotion representing the SEEKING system is a mixture of different layers within modeling. Although the efforts of the International Neuropsychoanalytical Society are describing new connections between neurological and psychoanalytical principles, there remains a gap between these two research areas. The model in Chapter 3 therefore relies on psychoanalytical theories only.

Back to the ARS-PA model of 2006: The perceived images with the influenced basic emotions can lead to a reactive action and trigger the actuators of the agent, or are for-

---

[8]Panksepp uses the upper case notation in [Pan98] to indicate the existence of an emotional system behind.

warded to the module *Decisions*. Based upon previously gained semantic, episodic, and socially influenced knowledge, a *Working Memory* provides all necessary information for the decision-making process. This process considers four modules that influence the decision process. Complex emotions leave space for higher cognitive emotions [BLPV07]. The following list is defined in [Roe07, p. 116]: *hope, joy, disappointment, gratitude, reproach, pride, shame*. They are influenced by basic emotions but *"[...] give an evaluation of past events"* [Roe07, p. 117]. The module *Desires* holds a list of wishes *"[...] to re-experience a once pleasurable (satisfying) situation"* [Pal07, p. 85]. They are influenced by the current activation levels of complex emotions ([RLD+07], [LBP+07]) and are also connected with certain courses of action that already lead to a satisfaction in the past. Based upon the most urgent plans, the module *Acting-As-If* evaluates the impacts of executing the suggested plans in the current situation. The *decision making* selects the plan that satisfies the current drives best, has the least negative impact during execution and fits the demands on the social rule set, defined in the module *Super-Ego*. Several psychoanalytical concepts can be found within this structure. However, the Ego has several functionalities that are not considered within this model or can be found outside of the module *Decision Making*. Nevertheless, a first top-down design approach has been applied, by identifying the module *Decision* with the the psychoanalytical *Ego* and the module *Pre-Decisoin* with the psychoanalytical *Id*. The third psychic instance according to psychoanalytical theory is present with the module *Super-Ego*. To complete the description of the architecture shown in Figure 2.17, the module *Decision Making* is capable of executing a selected plan via an *Action Sequencer* as well as inhibiting and suppressing reactive actions. The *Action sequencer* uses routine sequences from the *Procedural Memory* and forwards the action symbols to the *Internal and External Execution* module, where symbols are converted into specific motor actions. The actuators are part of the body of the agent and are able to influence the internal state as well as the environment. This closes the circle and agent-environment interaction becomes possible.

In summary, the model of ARS-PA introduced in [Roe07] and [Pal07] in 2007 defines a cognitive architecture for an autonomous agent. It contains reactive as well as deliberative routines for an agent and uses concepts from neuro-psychoanalysis. Despite applying a first top-down design approach, by using the psychoanalytical structure of *Id, Ego, and Super-Ego* as the highest layer, the functionality was not further defined from a psychoanalytical point of view. The underlying functionalities were developed solely by engineers and therefore excluded the psychoanalytical expertise in the design process. Furthermore, concepts from neurology like the basic emotional system are represented on the same layer as concepts from psychoanalysis which are actually considered to be above the neurological layers. This result is the basis for development of an improved model, which will use only concepts of psychoanalysis, in Chapter 3. To ensure consistency and completeness, a top-down design approach is applied to the second topographical model of psychoanalysis.

3 Concept and Model of the Decision Unit

Based upon the considerations and research results of the cognitive architecture presented in Section 2.6, this chapter presents a new approach in developing a cognitive architecture for the decision unit of an autonomous agent. Introducing a technical model for awareness and decision making based on the theory of psychoanalysis, this chapter focuses on the topic of emotional planning in embedded autonomous agents and uses the structure of the psychoanalytically defined wish and its underlying information-processing structures as an archetype. A top-down design approach will be applied to the functional modules defined in metapsychology to determine, if the descriptions and definitions in metapsychology are sufficient to be implemented in a computational system. In the case of insufficient specifications, the main obstacles impeding a proper definition are located. A call-sequence for the technically described functional modules is assembled, defining the interconnection between the modules to form the final, artificial decision unit. The main modules, responsible for a final decision are discussed in detail with respect to their technical implementation. The necessary constraints identified from other frameworks, which are defined and discussed in Section 2.2.6, will be the basis for the development process. Furthermore, content related constraints will be developed in a technical determination of necessary data types and structures of metapsychology mainly in Section 3.1 and 3.1.3. The aim of this chapter is to design and specify a technically feasible model for a psychoanalytically inspired decision unit rather than provide a specific algorithm for handling perceptual data. The combination of several data evaluation and filtering mechanisms reduce the design space for an applied, technical implementation. One possible implementation will be presented in Chapter 4 to show the resulting performance of the developed model.

3.1 Neuro-Psychoanalytical Prerequisites

Before designing the functional modules for the psychoanalytically inspired decision unit, a few prerequisites have to be defined to describe the gathered technical and psychoanalytical information. Chapter 3.1.1 gives a brief overview on the structural conditions, the decision unit is embedded in. The necessary preconditions for the interfaces handling input and output data will be defined. They represent the ability to perceive and act within a simulated physical environment. Since the core of the introduced model is based on the structural model of psychoanalysis, Section 3.1.2 gives an overview of this model and discusses its further use. Finally, Section 3.1.3 identifies already defined data structures in the theory of psychoanalytical metapsychology, describes the areas for the mandatory application of these data structures, and gives a first description of a possible implementation. Based upon the supplied definitions, Section 3.2 introduces the developed model.

3.1.1 From Neurological Foundations to Metapsychology

To develop a cognitive architecture for an autonomous, embodied agent, as defined in Section 2.1, the two main components *perception*[1] and *decision making* can be identified. Perception can be viewed as the necessary interface between an agent and its environment. Without knowledge about the environment the agent is embedded in, no further reasoning is possible. The decision making creates the connection between the perceptual interface and the action interface, a mandatory component for the efficiency of a proactive agent. Comparing the two described concepts of perception and decision making to the human cognitive process, the following parallels can be observed. Besides sensor modalities, the human brain structure also plays an important role in the process of perception. It consists of neural connections and converts data from the human sensory organs into more object related information. In [Pra06], [Vel08], and [Dam94], it is argued that this object related information can be referred to as *perceptual symbols*[2]. A symbol can therefore represent

---

[1]With the term perception, only the transformation process from the physical values measured by sensors to a representing symbol is meant. Often, the term awareness is used instead in order to avoid conflicts with the conscious perception. Within this work, perception only refers to information from the environment or body of the agent on different abstraction layers, without the demand of consciousness perception.

[2]The word *symbol* has different meanings in psychoanalysis, artificial intelligence and computer science according to its context. Therefore, the phrase '*perceptual*' is added in terms of describing object related information constructed from sensor data. The psychoanalytical meaning of a symbol differs drastically from this definition, therefore a *psychoanalytical symbol* will always be announced as such symbols that are used in Artificial Intelligence to apply logical operations are referred to as *logic symbols*.

the abstract ideas of objects, characters, images, voices, colors, etc. Velik states in [Vel08] that: *"According to the theory of symbolic systems, the mind is a symbol system and cognition is symbol manipulation."* In literature, a *perceptual symbol* is also called an *image* [Dam94], to visualize the tight connection to the sensory organs, in this case to the eyes. Lurija shows in [Lur73] the different locations of brain areas that process sensor data from the different sensory organs. He further divides each brain area that is responsible for a certain modality into the three areas of data processing, the primary, secondary, and tertiary cortex. Whereas essentially only sensor data of like modality is combined in the first layer, the tertiary cortex connects information from all the senses together into one single construct, the *perceptual image*. Following a neuro-biological concept, technical implementations are typically achieved by using a bottom-up design approach. An artificial neural network would be an example for a corresponding implementation.

In the opposite direction, the *decision-making unit* needs information about the environment[3] to achieve the goals of a certain agent. The theoretical models of the psyche in psychoanalysis, more precisely named *psychoanalytical metapsychology*, constitute one description amongst others of the process of human decision making. In psychoanalytical metapsychology, two particular topographical models were defined by Freud. The first topographical model distinguished between the three agencies unconscious, preconscious, and conscious and served as a top level description of the mental process. In 1923, Freud conceived the second topography of the mental processes that distinguishes between the three agencies Id (primary drives of the individual), Super-Ego (concerning social rules) and Ego (as a mediator between the former two and the final instance before the execution of an activity).

Metapsychology must not be confused with psychoanalytical therapy, where patients and their innermost desires are analyzed to reveal and solve hidden problems. However, therapy was the necessary input for building the psychoanalytical metapsychology. In the last decades, medical technology and especially medical imaging procedures made it possible to narrow the gap between neurology and psychoanalysis. With modern functional magnetic resonance imaging (fMRI) the resolution of the non-invasive imaging increased and it became possible to explain and prove parts of various psychologically and psychoanalytically described phenomena. According to Leuzinger-Bohleber in [LBP06, p. 63], PET, fMRI, and the studies by *"[...] Kaplan-Solms and Solms [2], have initiated a boom and intensified dialog between psychoanalysis and the neurosciences during the last 20 years or so."*

---
[3]The environment of a decision unit (the human mind can be seen as a specific natural instance of it) includes the body as well as the external environment of the agent.

Concept and Model of the Decision Unit

M. Solms and J. Panksepp founded the new research platform of the *International Neuropsychoanalytical Society (npsa)* with the goal to bring the two areas together and describe selected topics in neuroscience as well as in psychoanalysis. Figure 3.1 shows the two main areas. Neurology is identified as a bottom-up design approach that explains mental processes from the neuronal point of view, whereas psychoanalysis is identified as a top-down design approach, explaining the mental process from the point of view of the main functional structures of the human psyche. The interface between them is still hardly understood but as mentioned above, the *perceptual symbol* appears in both areas. The output of the brain structures as it is described in neurology is a *perceptual image*, which corresponds to the input of the psyche according to psychoanalytical theory.

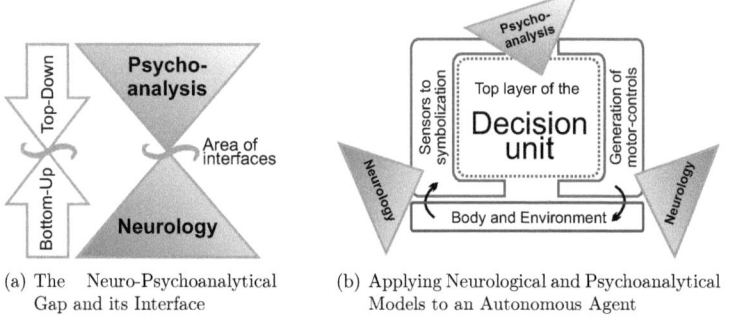

(a) The Neuro-Psychoanalytical Gap and its Interface

(b) Applying Neurological and Psychoanalytical Models to an Autonomous Agent

Figure 3.1: Concepts from Neurology and Psychoanalysis Forming the Decision Unit

The focus of this work is the technical realization of a decision unit for an autonomous agent and therefore the formulation of a corresponding model deduced from psychoanalytical theory. The previous works of [Pra06], [Bru07], [Bur07], and [Vel08] are assumed as necessary technical preconditions for sensor data processing and generation of *perceptual symbols* as described in their works. This is the foundation for realizing a psychoanalytically inspired decision unit. Figure 3.1 shows the used design principles and the alignment of neurological and psychoanalytical theory.

Figure 3.1(a) visualizes the bottom-up design approach used for the realization of symbolization in ARS. For the description of the decision unit, a top-down design approach is applied and will be described in this chapter. Figure 3.1(b) shows the decision unit, based on psychoanalytical theory, provided with sensory data from the body and environment of the agent in the form symbols. Environmental sensations are transformed into *perceptual symbols* by the *symbolization unit* on the left hand side and then passed to the decision unit. On the right hand side, *action symbols* which represent complex action commands to the body are passed from the decision unit to the *motor-control unit*. Complex action symbols are translated into the corresponding motor-controls that control the actuators, which in turn influence the environment or the body of the agent. For the decision unit of an autonomous agent, it is mandatory to be able to distinguish between data from the external environment and the bodily values. One possible solution for this requirement to the implementation is to strictly divide the symbolization unit into three parts using the same implementation attached to different sensors. One part deals with exteroceptive sensory information from the environment only (visual, acoustic, tactile, ...), the second part receives data from proprioceptive sensorsmeasuring the relative position of body parts (e.g. degrees of bending the knee), and the third part is connected to interoceptive sensors that measures bodily values (heart pressure, temperature, hormones, status of organs, ...). The necessary boundaries of the agent's mind can therefore be formed by the four communication channels (introduced in [DS03]), placed in the 'area of interfaces': the exteroceptive, proprioceptive, interoceptive, and executing channel.

Based upon these neurologically inspired technical prerequisites, the decision unit is supplied with the necessary information and possibilities for executing actions that are mandatory for an autonomous agent as defined in Section 2.1. As introduced and discussed in Section 2.2, various, partly psychologically inspired cognitive architectures for decision units of autonomous agents already exist. In this thesis the efficiency of a decision unit for an autonomous agent based upon the theoretical models of psychoanalysis will be examined from the technical side. From this technical point of view the psychoanalytic concept of the cognitive process offers two main advantages. First, the theory completely describes the decision process between the previously described interfaces, namely perception and action. As will be highlighted in more detail in Section 3.3, this does not generally imply the existence of a detailed specification of each functionality. What is crucial is the existence of a global description including the interaction between the functional units with a more detailed and more granular functional description of each functional unit. Psychoanalysis, having its origin in the 1890's when it was founded and developed by the psychiatrist S. Freud, describes the mental apparatus in this way, starting from a top layer of description and characterizing the identified functional units in more detail. Second, the theory provides a model in which different functional units are identified and their workings and interactions with other functional units described. In psychology, a behavioristic description of a function is often sufficient. Observing the actions of a group of individuals within a defined scenario makes it possible to predict the behavior of a person by e.g. the use of statistical methods. Although statistical methods applied to groups of test persons are one possibility of analyzing human behavior, knowledge about the function that initiates this behavior is limited to a set of observed values and a statistical method of data interpretation. The functionality itself remains unknown without further interpretation and deduction. Psychoanalytical theory, on the other hand, tries to model the functionality in order to be able to explain the behavior [DFZ+09, p. 34].

Freud's metapsychology is based on two different topographical models, developed sequentially in time. Both can be seen as the top layer of a top down design approach. Although both are accepted *topographical models*, they are not attempts of anatomically localizing certain functionalities within the human brain structure. Due to the unavailability of non-invasive methods of investigating the brain structure, Freud decided to work on a theoretical topography only, regardless to the corresponding brain region. Leuzinger-Bohleber describes in [LBP06, p. 63] that *"[...] it is well known that Freud never gave up his hope that some day developments in the neurosciences might contribute to a "scientific foundation" of psychoanalysis in terms of the natural sciences. One reason why Freud himself did not continue his own attempts [at] such a neuroscientific foundation of psychoanalysis, his 'Outline of psychoanalysis' [1], was his confrontation with the obvious limitations of the methodologies of the neurosciences of his time [2]. He then consistently defined psychoanalysis as a pure psychology of the unconscious. ..."*

The *first topographical model* identifies three main parts of the human psyche: The unconscious, the preconscious, and the conscious part. This represents a rather uncommon and daring opinion at Freud's time, namely that human decisions are not entirely conscious. For the development of a decision unit for an autonomous agent, the *first topographical model* will not be considered. Essential definitions of processes and their functional structure from this model will be used but the definition of consciousness and further machine-consciousness is beyond the scope of this work. Further, a coherent consolidation of the two topographical models could not be found in literature and would require detailed expertise in psychoanalysis. Freud himself abandoned his original organizing principle and redrew his map of the mind [ST02, p. 99]. In the *second topographical model*, he rearranges the structure of the human psyche and identifies three main functional units: The *Id*, the *Ego* and the *Super-Ego*. The left part of Figure 3.2 shows a replica of the original, conceptual drawing of Freud's second topographical model (Id, Ego, Super-Ego) [Fre33, p. 78]. It is visually integrated into the decision unit of an autonomous agent depicted on the right hand side.

Supplied with perceptual information, the three units are the functional instances of the psychic processes. Dealing with contradictory inputs, the Ego has to make final decisions

Concept and Model of the Decision Unit

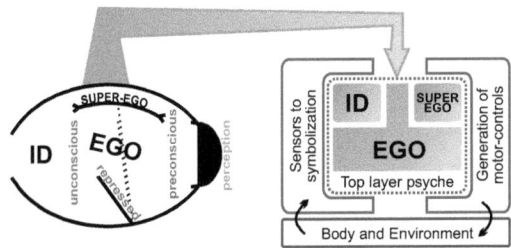

Figure 3.2: The Second Topographical Model of Psychoanalysis - Id, Ego, and Super-Ego (left) and the Integration into an Autonomous Agent (right)

that are influenced by the self-related part – the Id – and the socially-related part – the Super-Ego. The picture shows a close relation of the Id to unconscious processing and a close relation of the Ego and Super-Ego to preconscious processing. It also refers to the existence of repressed content, an information that once has been preconscious and became unconscious due to specific mechanisms.

The basic parts of the second topographical model and the necessary psychoanalytical terms will be defined in the next Section (Section 3.1.2). With these prerequisites Section 3.2 shows how the second topographic model can be transferred into a top-down designed, functional model.

3.1.2 The Second Topographical Model of Psychoanalysis – Layer 1

To be able to apply the Freud's second topographical model, which is also called the structural model in psychoanalysis, to the decision unit of an embodied, autonomous agent, the main functionalities and interactions between the three identified modules Id, Ego, and Super-Ego have to be identified. The following passages therefore refer directly to Freud's *Outline of Psycho-Analysis* [Fre40] and summarize the knowledge gained during my cooperation with the psychoanalytical advisors within the project ARS which is also described in [DFZ+09, p. 54]. Figure 3.3 shows the top layer of the decision unit and the basic functionalities of its components that will be discussed in this chapter.

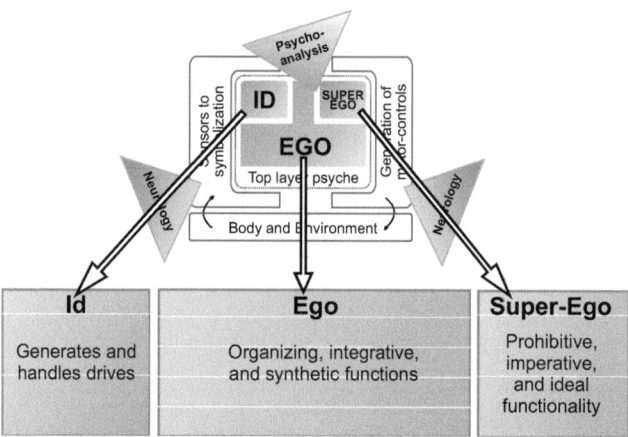

Figure 3.3: The Second Topographical Model - The First Layer in the Top-Down Design Approach

According to Freud in [Fre40], the three agencies introduced previously form the entire human psyche. This division allows a modular consideration of functions related to the individual's body, functions related to the social environment, and functions which mediate between the demands of the body, the physical environment and the social environment.

Representing the most basic and instinctive functionalities, the *Id* represents the source of all arising drives and handles these drives and demands, which in turn originate in the individuals body. Without any knowledge of abstraction, space, time and causality, and without considering the environmental conditions, the *Id* requests the satisfaction of a drive immediately. The *Id* quasi relies on its own psychic reality, which only perceives the bodily demands and exclusively follows the psychoanalytical *pleasure principle*, meaning these processes are primarily concerned with avoiding displeasure and obtaining pleasure [Lap73, p. 181]. A decision unit consisting only of an *Id* representation would lead to a purely reactive agent, exclusively pursuing the satisfaction of its urges by taking unreflected actions. Environmental demands and requests would be completely ignored by such an agent. This unorganized and, with respect to the demands of reality, often contradictory way of information processing is called *primary process* and the data structures used by it are called *thing presentations*. Both terms will be described in detail in Section 3.1.3.

However, the agency of the Id which represents the instinctual functionality of drive-satisfaction has a powerful opponent. The *Super-Ego* is the agency that holds and executes socially prohibitive, imperative, and ideal functionality and provides gratification to the Ego when these rules are observed. It can be seen as a social reward system providing constraints, demands and awards for certain behavior in specific situation. In early childhood, the contents of the Super-Ego are formed by parental interaction. *"The basis of the process is what is called an 'identification' that is to say, the assimilation of one Ego to another one, as a result of which the first Ego behaves like the second in certain respects, imitates it and in a sense takes it up into itself."* [Fre33, p. 63]. In the case of an artificial agent, such a prohibitive social rule-set could be learned by e.g. supervised learning that only affects the agent's social-prohibitive rules. However, the topic of learning is beyond the scope of this work and will not be investigated with regard to psychoanalytical theory. Therefore, Chapter 4 will not describe the aspect of necessary learning algorithms for such systems. Theoretically, an agent obeying only its *Super-Ego* would be following social rules only and would be neither proactive (due to the lack of an internal drive) nor survivable (due to its lack of the missing information about its own bodily needs).

Having two psychic antagonists – the *Id* and the *Super-Ego* – that are capable of generating contradictory, implicit action tendencies, the psyche needs a mediating agency, as it would otherwise be incapable of any action. This conflict-balancing mediator resides in the last of the three agencies, namely the *Ego*. It represents the mediating system between all organizing, integrative and synthetic functions of the mind. Guided by the input of the *Id* and *Super-Ego* as explained in [Str99a] and [Str99b], it has to control instinctual action tendencies and determine whether a drive can or must be satisfied, delayed or entirely suppressed. Though the *Ego* follows bodily demands, it also assumes the duty of self preservation within the environment, the individual is situated in. Therefore, it has to be self-aware but also stimuli-aware, meaning that it must perceive and understand its environment. Additionally, it stores past experiences with certain stimuli from the environment. Excessively strong stimuli are avoided as far as possible, while moderate stimuli are absorbed in order to adapt the environment to the individual's advantage. This functionality, psychoanalytically denoted as unconscious, is executed in a so-called *primary process*, and its similarly unconscious contents are known as *thing presentations* which are connected to corresponding *word presentations*. These terms will be described in Chapter 3.1.3. This work will identify and use the functionality of the primary and secondary process defined in psychoanalysis without considering the concept of unconsciousness or consciousness. Although the *Ego* appears to be surrounded by the two other instances, it is the last instance that is responsible for reacting, e.g. by initiating motor actions, but it is also the first instance that perceives information from the environment. It is capable of changing the incoming stream of perception in specific ways that will be described in Section 3.3. In [SSK97], the following further functions of the *Ego* are identified: reality check, reasoning, memory, consciousness, triggering motor functionality, cognition of senses and wishful satisfaction of certain drives, defense mechanisms, inhibition of drives, etc. One of the main intentions in applying the top-down design approach is to categorize the list of functionalities of the three psychic agencies, in order to construct a model that can be described in a tree-shaped graph, where the root of the tree is the decision unit of the agent, containing the three child node which themselves contain further child-nodes. A technical model using this functional tree structure will be established in Chapter 4. In decomposing functionality in a top-down manner, it will be investigated whether Freud's structural model can be realized within the decision unit of an autonomous agent.

Two major problems could arise while following this approach. First, the structural model itself and/or the available resources describing its functionalities could turn out to be incomplete in terms of a functional description allowing a technical implementation. If this is the case, there are basically two possibilities of implementing the incompletely described functions: Using other theories besides psychoanalytical ones, or simply using a purely technical concept and implementation. In both cases, it is mandatory that the further steps towards implementation must not conflict with the specifications and demands defined in the higher layers. A clear distinction must be made between the psychoanalytical model and the implementations or further theories of different origin[4]. Second, a functional unit could appear that is assigned to two different paths within the tree. In this case, the functionality will be listed several times in the tree-shaped graph structure as it will be depicted in Figure 3.13. In this case, the tree-view would be an unnecessary restriction for this visualization and the usage of a directed acyclic graph would improve the results. However, it will be shown that functionality in different regions of the top-down design approach of the structural model is not identical. The functionalities of the introduced model in Section 3.2 are completely unique within the reached granularity of the top-down design. On the investigated levels of description, no function will be used twice. On lower layers and especially on layers describing of the implementation the same functionality will be used in different modules.

---

[4]This work does not use any theoretical background besides the theoretical models of metapsychology in psychoanalysis. Therefore, the presented implementations of the psychoanalytical models are purely technical and do not rely on psychological, philosophical, or other theories.

3.1.3 Psychoanalytical Structures Mandatory for Decision-Making

To implement a functional model of the human mind with the main task of data processing, it is essential to analyze and specify the core data structures and processing types that are commonly used. The following section gives an overview of the defined data structures that are omnipresent in psychoanalytical metapsychology. The different terms will be described in their structure and functionality with respect to their implementation in the computational model. Since these structures are the main basis for conscious and unconscious deliberation in the human psyche, it is mandatory to use these structures within the implementation[5] as well. In the following, a distinction will be made between *general data containers*, *data structures* including an elementary form of functionality and specifications for *data processing* only. After these three main categories, two basic concepts of memory structures will be introduced which are crucial for the theoretical consideration although they will not be part of the model and implementation itself.

General Data Containers

The following described terms can be seen as general data containers and are able to carry different types of information. These containers will be used by the used specializations later on. Within the framework of psychoanalysis three main categories of data structures can be identified: *memory traces, thing presentations*, and *word presentations*.

Memory traces

Memory traces constitute the most basic data structure. It can be seen as the first psychic element that is confronted with incoming data from the neurological components of the perception. According to [Fre33, p. 75] the *memory traces* are a psycho-physiological concept for the representation of memories in the mind. This means that each datum that can be remembered, whether it originates from external sensory data or from psychic deliberation, becomes manifest in a *memory trace*.

When a generated perceptual symbol or group of symbols, which are the output of the neurologically inspired symbolization model described in [Vel08] and shown in Figure 3.1, is compared with existing memory traces, there are two possible options. If the incoming symbol resembles a memory trace that already exists, a *thing presentation* (discussed below) is generated. In metapsychology, the term *cathexis of memory traces* is used (a definition can be found in [Fre15b, p. 150]) to describe the procedure of activating the corresponding memory traces. When the incoming symbol is not entirely known and therefore does not have a representative memory trace, an adapted new memory trace is created and

---

[5]However, conscious computing is not the topic and goal of this work.

the corresponding *thing presentation* is generated [Fre00, p. 538]. According to Solms in [Sol96], continuous combined innervation of different inner and outer perceptual modalities are the basis for building psychic representations in the form of memory traces. They evolve when remaining traces of such perceptions are organized into mnemonic structures.

This means that every type of data which is stored, and can therefore be recalled in some specific form, is represented by a memory trace. In addition, memory traces are also associated with other memory traces that generally appear in conjunction. When a particular set of sensor data usually activates two memory traces and for some reason only one of those memory traces is activated, the tight association between the two induces the activation of the associated memory trace. The process can be seen as a concept for fault tolerance in the perception and can be compared to the basis of classical conditioning. However, the corresponding reflexive actions are generated on a neurological layer in this case.

To summarize, the memory trace is the system responsible for storing and retrieving previously perceived or processed object information, and associations can be established between related memory traces. The result of an activated memory trace is a thing presentation (in terms of a perceptual stimulus) [Fre15c, p. 201] or word presentation (in terms of a psychic stimulus, former perceptions) [Fre23, p. 20] and an attached affect. These three components originating in the memory trace system represent the data structure that is processed by the psychic apparatus. In reaction to an incoming environmental sensor data during a certain situation, the symbols are activating memory traces that match the perceived symbols[6]. In this work, a memory trace is considered a stored pattern or template and produces a thing presentation when activated. The thing presentation is the psychic representative of a memory trace or at least a part of a memory trace. However, the system of memory traces can also generate affects and word presentations, which will be discussed below. Although Freud abandoned his research on the connection between sensory data and memory traces and especially their connection to the thing presentation due to the lack of brain-imaging methods, the memory traces clearly represent the border between neurological and psychoanalytical findings. They are described in more detail by Solms [7] in [ST02, p. 147].

Thing presentation

---

[6]Metapsychology does not provide a comprehensive explanation on the process that is responsible for selecting the corresponding memory traces, but presumes that it is done accordingly.

[7]M. Solms is neurologist, psychoanalyst and founder of the International Neuropsychoanalytical Society (npsa).

Generated by activated memory traces, the thing presentation[8] is the psychic representative of a stimulated memory trace. Together with affects (described below), thing presentations are the main processing data type in the primary processing part of the psyche. They are psychic representatives of three different types of information that are delivered to the previously discussed memory traces: tension of organs (as a deviation from homeostatic values), information regarding the body, and environmental information. When a thing presentation contains homeostatic information, it describes the quality of a drive tension. Body- and environment-based thing presentations represent the perceived or remembered values, shapes, smells, or objects in general. In contrast to word presentations (described below), thing presentations are independent of linguistic symbolization [DFZ+09, p. 55]. This means that they are not a symbolic-logical construct like the language of thoughts defined by cognitive science ([Den87, p. 227], [Fod75]). They are directly associated with the perceived information produced by the sensed objects through e.g. visual, tactile, or acoustic impressions [Fre91, p. 121ff]. In metapsychology, the functions of the psyche which deal with thing presentations are strictly primary process-bound.

From a technical point of view this means that each generated datum that has its origin either in perceptual sensations or processes that recall past experiences, first appears as an object called a thing presentation. These thing presentations can only be manipulated by primary processes (explained later in detail). They have normally a corresponding assigned affect and can be related to other thing presentations through associations within their corresponding memory traces. There is no limitation for the semantic complexity of a thing presentation. The thing presentation can describe a simple shape, color, smell, etc. as well as a complex situation the individual deals with. However, a thing presentation is not decomposable. It may be associated with other thing presentations that are similar but no knowledge exists on this level that would allow such a decomposing procedure. Also *"[...] cognitive psychologists have found [...] that humans consistently map certain visual and motor representations onto abstract, nonphysical concepts"* [CMW06].

Word presentation
Whereas thing presentations are the main content of the primary process (described in detail below), word presentations are the main content of the secondary process. Every information represented in a thing presentation that has to be processed in the secondary process, needs an attached word presentation. A word presentation is the psychic concept or description for the perceivable object and not a set of sensor-stimuli. It includes the characteristics of e.g. sound, scripts, or motion [Fre91, p. 121] that can be applied to

---

[8]According to [DFZ+09, p. 59], a presentation is the psychic representative of a perceived object information and is defined in [Fre15c, p. 201].

every object that fits into the defined concept. The word presentations are processed and organized in the secondary process of the psyche. They are the basis of thinking and enable inter-subjective communication on non-communicable thing presentations between individuals. They make it possible to reflect on past, present, and future events [DFZ$^+$09, p. 59]. A word presentation is assigned to a specific thing presentation. The exact process is described in Section 3.2.

Information and knowledge can be accessed directly and logical operations and organizations can be applied, as will be explained later for the secondary process. A word presentation has a connection to its corresponding thing presentation and affect. It is a concept of something (e.g. the concept for an object in the environment) and may consist of several sub-concepts, and is therefore decomposable into its component parts. The association to related word presentations in specific situations can be accessed through the association network of the corresponding memory traces, where the templates of word presentations are stored in the same way as for thing presentations. Whereas the thing presentation is the direct link between the sensor data in the form of *perceptual symbols* and the psyche, the word presentation is the interface object between psychic contents and a reasoning process that considers the available information.

Functional Data Structures

The terms memory traces, thing presentations and word presentations, as described above, can be seen as global concepts without any specification regarding the content of the information contained within each of them. A thing presentation can be the representative of a bodily need, an environmental perception or even a recalled memory. The same is valid for word presentations with the additional possibility of processing this form of data. Finally, memory traces are the most general concept, because they represent past experiences and sensations, can generate thing and word presentations, and are necessary for associating these types of objects. In the next part of this section, three data structures will be discussed that possess more content specific constraints, and which will be of direct use to the technical implementation: *drives, affects,* and *wishes*.

Drive

In [Pal07], Palensky defines the drive according to Freud [Fre15a, p. 122] as a pivotal element of the psychoanalytical mediation process between the outside world and the needs of the organism. This statement becomes explicit, when focusing on the origin of the drive that lies within homeostasis and the organs of the human body. A drive is the first psychic representative of the demands of the bodily organs and signals a bodily need, as defined in [Fre15b, p. 111]. According to [DFZ+09], organic processes are transferred into psychic processes and are represented by a structure called drive. The drive representation consists of two components, the thing presentation and the affect. Whereas the thing presentation of a drive contains quality and therefore the information of its content (the origin of the bodily tension is not accessible, but conclusions can be drawn [Fre15a, p. 122]), the affect holds the information of the amplitude of the tension. The higher the tension within a bodily organ, the greater the affect that quantifies the corresponding thing presentation. However, the concept of drives is defined in a more complex fashion in metapsychology. According to [Fre15a, p. 122], a drive additionally consists of (or is at least closely associated with) the following drive-contents:

The *source of the drive* represents the organ that is generating the bodily tension and is no longer accessible in the psyche. The *aim of the drive* is always to reduce the tension of the bodily organ but can be accomplished in different ways. The *object of the drive* is the necessary object that reduces the tension of the organ.

According to the actual situation, the drive object and the aim of the drive can be changed during the psychic processes [Fre72, p. 70]. Freud noted in [Fre15a] that the study of the somatic source (which is the source of the drive) is not part of the research in psychology. Therefore he classifies drives not according their originating organs but according to their *drive contents*. Drive contents can be differentiated regarding constructive and destructive content. To nourish, repress, sleep, breath, relax or reproduce are typical constructive drive contents and are representatives of the so called *life instinct* or *libido*. To bite, excrete, kill, regress, disintegrate, halt and retreat are examples for destructive drive contents and are representatives of the so called *death instinct*. Each of the drive representatives can be associated with its oral, anal, phallic and genital component of the sexual instinct. This definition will only be used as an additional flag within this work and will not be described in further detail. Additionally to this categorization (it is referred to as drive content categories in Section 4.3.2), each drive representative within life instinct has a counterpart within death instinct. Together they constitute a pair of opposites [Fre15a, p. 127].

Based on this definition, the drive can be considered a data structure that holds the information of its drive content directly in the form of a thing presentation for qualification and an affect for quantification. Additionally, it is attached to one or more thing presentations representing appropriate objects or actions that can reduce the tension.

Affect
In [Fre15b, p. 153], the term affect is defined as a quantifiable psychic representative of a drive. It can be said that the quantification is the level of displeasure caused by the corresponding bodily urges. A decrease of displeasure results in an increase of pleasure. Although it is widely accepted that the spectrum of affects is more diverse [Pal07, p. 65], in this concept additional information is always contained within the combination of an affect and a thing presentation or also a word presentation in the case of pre-consciousness or consciousness. In [Roe07, p. 25], an overview of different classifications of affects and emotions in current literature is provided. However, a clear mapping of Freud's terms affect to other authors cannot be found in literature. Damasio, for example, uses the terminology in neuropsychology and distinguishes between primary, secondary and tertiary emotions where each of these three constructs implies a different level of consciousness [Dam00, p. 55]. In connection with a thing presentation, affects can cover all these constructs, therefore within this work the term emotion or feeling will not be used.

Following the neuro-psychoanalytical approach presented in [Sol96], affects have their origin in both, the body in the form of drives as well as the environment in the form of being part of the perception through the body. They are intimately related to bodily, yet unconscious experience of the changes in our environment and represent the most basic evaluation of incoming sensory stimuli. This circumstance makes it necessary to extend the above described concept of the affect. Instead of holding only information regarding the level of displeasure caused by the tension of a bodily organ, the construct also has to deal with the gain in pleasure that is connected to an environmental object that satisfies the respective drive and therefore reduces the tension. Therefore, affects that reflect the tension of a bodily organ represent only the level of displeasure, while affects associated with environmental sensations can contain either a level of pleasure or displeasure.

Artificial intelligence (AI) and cognitive science also realize the importance of emotional evaluation in perceptual systems of reasoning units, in particular regarding autonomous embodied agents. In [SM08], a brief overview of the main concepts in AI is given, including the theories of Minsky, Brooks, Sloman, Picard, Varela, etc., where emotions increase the quality of perception and reasoning.

Wish

When a bodily need is not sufficiently covered, the corresponding psychic representative emerges in the form of a drive as described above, consisting of a thing presentation and an affect. After passing unconscious and filtering mechanisms operating according to the primary process (described in detail in Section 3.3) the drive is attached to a corresponding word presentation and converted into information of the secondary process. This preconscious structure that is capable of becoming conscious and is involved in the conscious process of deliberation is called *wish* within this work (in contrary to Freud's definition of the unconscious wish). Like the affect, the wish does not necessarily have to be evoked by a drive or an actual perception but can also be evoked by recalled memories in combination with a drive. However, these more abstracted wishes which do not primarily aim to immediately satisfy drives (e.g. buying a new car), are also derived from concepts of the drives (e.g. buying a fast car to impress others may satisfy a phallic category of a drive; buying an additional car may satisfy the anal category of a drive) and therefore indirectly satisfy these drives.

A wish motivates an individual to reestablish a previously experienced situation that led to the satisfaction of a need and an increase in pleasure (and corresponding decrease in displeasure) as defined in [Lap73, p. 270]. It is associated with the need that will be satisfied, an object or action that satisfies the wish (this can be the same as the object that satisfies an associated drive), and an internalized experience. Internalized experiences comprise emotional and cognitive aspects and additionally associated patterns in the form of word presentations. One of the most important associations is the planing of actions that lead to the satisfaction of the corresponding wish. Since the wish is the representation of a previously experienced, satisfactory situation, it also has to include at least one plan of actions or perceptions that led to the fulfillment of the wish in the past. The utilized data structures are again accessible by the memory traces and are presumed in the following chapters.

The main work that defines the *wish* and its formation is Freud's "The Interpretation of Dreams" [Fre00]. There he identifies the dream as a direct medium of wish-fulfillment:

> "[A] dream is a (disguised) fulfillment of a (suppressed or repressed) wish." [Fre00, p. 160]

Freud gives an illustrative example for the connection between the dream and the drive, which originates in the somatic sensation caused by thirst. He describes his own dream of drinking water in great gulps:

> "The somatic stimulus was apparently its only source, and the wish derived from the sensation (the thirst that is) was apparently its only motive. The case is similar [to] other simple dreams in which a somatic stimulus seems able by itself to construct a wish." [Fre00, p. 232]

Finally, the following quotation of Freud's interpretation of dreams shows the combination of the functionality of the dream and the satisfaction of a drive and wish:

> "Thus the wish to sleep (which the conscious Ego is concentrated upon, and which, together with the dream-censorship and the 'secondary revision', which I shall mention later [p. 488 ff.], represents the conscious Ego's contribution to dreaming) must in every case be reckoned as one of the motives for the formation of dreams, and every successful dream is a fulfillment of that wish." [Fre00, p. 234]

The discussion of the dream offers good examples of the connection between drives and wishes. In closing, the contents of a wish will be discussed from a technical point of view. A wish can be seen as a combination of a drive (which in itself is a combination of a thing presentation and an affect, specifying the origin and the severity) and a word presentation. This construct makes it possible to further process a drive in the secondary process, such as the process of planning. Therefore, a wish must have a connection to one or several objects and actions capable of satisfying the wish. When referring to an object, this does not necessarily mean a physical object but can also be an action, an environmental change, and so forth.

Data Processing

The definitions given above covered data structures which are integral components of the human deliberating psyche. They are templates that can contain different types of information and can be seen as global concepts that are necessary for a technical implementation. These concepts will be the classes that hold information. What is still missing is a general definition of how this data is processed. In metapsychology, the manner of data processing is manifested in two complementary "principles in mental functioning" [Fre11][9]: the primary process and the secondary process. These processes describe, on the one hand, how drive energy is shifted and discharged, and on the other hand depict a *"certain type of thinking"* [Ari64] in terms of organization of information.

Primary Process

The primary process describes a type of organization and processing of psychic contents in the form of thing presentations and affects. All processes contained therein follow the pleasure-principle. In this mode of information processing, unpleasant excitement is avoided and contents are aligned and organized with respect to the demands of the drives. The current conditions of reality and the possibility of a delay are not considered. It is therefore characterized by a free discharge of quantities of excitation, a so called unbounded "mobility of cathexis": *"[...] exemption from mutual contradiction, primary process (mobility of cathexes), timelessness, and replacement of external by psychical reality [...]"* [Fre15c, p. 187].

The main processing types are thing presentations with their affects that represent scenic ideas, composed of sensory-motor stimulus situations as described in [Sol06a]. They constitute a symbolic data construct for perceived bodily sensations and the processed data is concentrated on concrete experiences of the body in the current situation.

The functional characteristics of this type of process are limited due to its unorganized behavior. However, according to Solms in [ST02, p. 100], it subject of several constraints that must be discussed. These parameters are of utmost importance since a technical realization must not conflict with them: Mutual contradictions of two symbols (each represented by a thing presentation and its affect) in the same process are possible. Therefore, it is possible that two symbols of contradicting meaning are allowed and may even be considered equal in one and the same process. This contradicting meaning becomes especially relevant in

---

[9]In this early work of Freud, the structural model of Id, Ego and Super-Ego did not exist. However, the pleasure-Ego can be identified as the later Id and the reality-Ego as the Ego. By defining the structural model, Freud described the functional processes of the psyche in more detail. However, the general concept of Freud's work does not seem to contradict with the structural model (Freud utilized both) and gives a more generic definition of the concept for the primary and secondary process.

the case of negation. However, the missing concept of negation does not exclude negations in principle. Instead of meaning *'not the negated object'*, the object and its negation can be seen on the same layer. In [Fre25, p. 235], Freud associates this negation with the ability to consider repressed content although this content is forbidden for consideration (*"[...] thinking frees itself from the restrictions of repression [...]"*). The negation does not produce a new concept, but is considered an additional information regarding the object.

Furthermore, Freud describes the primary process thus: *"the governing rules of logic carry no weight in the unconscious"* and therefore *"[logical] contraries are not kept apart from each other but are treated as though they were identical"* [Fre40, p. 48]. The organizational form is completely timeless and constructs of sequence and past time spans are of no relevance. Additionally, external perception can be replaced to fit psychic wishes and ignore external limitations, constraints or obstacles [ST02, p. 103].

With the exclusion of any form of logic, the question arises how the information represented by thing presentations can be organized on the symbolic level of the primary process. According to [Ari64], one of the main criteria is the functionality of comparing two psychic representatives of perceived data with each other. In contrast to the secondary process, two such psychic symbols are identical, when they are similar. Visually speaking, symbols are assumed to be associated as long as they have similar parts in common. By considering these similarities to be identities, similarity *becomes* identity ([Ari64, p. 52]), which would never be possible in Aristotelian logic, where only like subjects are identified.

With this modified possibility of comparison, it becomes possible to discuss the organization of the content in primary process functions. As mentioned above, the content is aligned and organized with respect to the demands of the active drives. According to [Ari64], in primary process organization objects are considered as identical as long as they have at least one attribute in common. In this case, the above defined relational compare-operator becomes true. The formulation of a primary class will be discussed in more detail in Section 3.3.

In summary it can be said that functions which follow the primary process satisfy the pleasure principle without respect for apparent limitations in the environment and without respect to time. The content is aligned to the actual drives of the individual instead of formal logic. Contradictory objects are considered as equal as long as they have at least identical parts in common. In terms of object oriented programming, two instances of the class that represents a thing presentation would be identical as long as they have just one attribute in common.

Secondary Process

In the *secondary process*, word presentations constitute the majority of the processed content. The secondary process follows the reality principle (described in detail in [Sol06a] and [Sol06b]), where constraints from the surroundings in the form of known logical rules can be considered. Furthermore, evaluations are made regarding what is agreeable and what is real (even if it happened to be disagreeable). With these features, the secondary process is able to inhibit the free discharge of drives (or as Freud put's it in [Fre15c, p. 187], the "mobility of cathexis") by hypercathexis. Solms describes this behavior in [ST02, p. 100] as *"[...] the capacity to inhibit drive energies [...]"* and identifies it as the *"[...] basis of all the Ego's rational, reality-constrained, and executive functions."* Described in [Sol06a], this ability of inhibition is reached by transforming floating drive cathexis to bound cathexis that can be expressed in structural-functional terms.

The word-like symbols that designate and signify concepts of certain classes form the structural precondition of secondary process thinking and can be identified as the word presentations described above. Here, the class is a collection of objects to which the concept applies. In technical terms, the concept can be seen as the class-definition itself, whereas the objects that can be assigned to a certain class are specific instances of the class. These objects are identified according to the Aristotelian logic, where *"[...] only like subjects are identified"* [Ari64]. When all relevant members of two instances of a secondary class are the same, the instances are identical.

In terms of employed logical concepts, the secondary process includes all the logical possibilities that cannot be applied in the primary process. The organization of the secondary process includes data processing that allows cross-relations concerning the logic of time, location, and especially learned social rules to become applicable within this type of organization. Due to the possibility of inhibition, actual scenes don't have to be realized immediately in order to discharge arousal and trial actions become possible.

Once again considering a technical specification, the secondary process deals with word presentations that represent concepts and can be applied to different occurrences of perceived objects. Objects are considered identical if and only if the classes and therefore each of their members are the same. Within these data structures, logical considerations can be performed, including a reality check (is the actual perception real or hallucinate) and the generation of trial actions (what if an action is executed).

Tertiary process

To conclude the description of the two different types of psychic processes, the fictive construct of a tertiary process can demonstrate the possibilities of these organizations.

According to [Ari64], the creativity process (which is called tertiary process in the approach that tries to extend Freud's theory) arises by using patterns of the primary process and reorganizing them to fit in the constraints of the secondary process. Creativity searches for new objects by first breaking down the barriers and constraints of the secondary process, forms new concepts in a primary process structure and reestablishes them in a secondary process fashion. In [Ari64] and [Sol06a], the authors underline the tight connection between the primary and secondary processes, especially in the process of creativity. The example of the tertiary process puts the primary and secondary process in an illustrative relation. However, this work will not consider it for realizing an agents decision unit.

3.2 The General Architecture of the Model

From the point of view of software design, it is necessary to start from a global concept that meets the demands of the specifications before implementing specific functionality. Bottom up design as depicted in Section 2.2.1 is not acceptable in complex software design due to the low probability of meeting the specifications in the end. To allow a smooth technical implementation, also the model is described with respect to these considerations. The structural model, describing the functional interrelationship within the human psyche is therefore described in the form of a top-down-design approach. As described in Section 3.1.2 and depicted in Figure 3.3, the main concept bases on the complex of Id, Ego, and Super-Ego. These functional units are described in more detail in the theory of metapsychology. The following sections will apply a top-down design approach to the structural model by using the theory of metapsychology. It is representing a tree of functionalities with the psyche as its root node, the Id, Ego, and Super-Ego on its second layer as subnodes, and results on the lowest layer in a description of a single, atomic function. This functional listing will be described in more detail in the next Section 3.3, where the encapsulated described functionalities are interconnected to an implementable decision unit that will be embedded in Chapter 4 into an embodied autonomous agent – a virtual robot.

3.2.1 The Embedded Mind – Top Level Considerations and Detailed Functional Combination

The following description of the psychoanalytical part of the presented model is the result of my four year long study concerning the possibility of describing the theories of metapsychology in a technically feasible and functional way. The model has been developed together with the project team ARS (Artificial Recognition System) including psychoanalytical advisors and resulted in several interdisciplinary publications and the interdisciplinary conference ENF [DFZ+09]. As stated in Chapter 1, first realizations following the bionic approach were already published in the late nineties. These findings, gained during the last decade form the basis for the psychoanalytically inspired model that will be presented in the following chapters.

Figure 3.3 shows the first layer of the top down design approach and roughly described the main functionalities of the three psychic instances. This top-level consideration is given by the metapsychological theory of psychoanalysis. Figure 3.4 shows a first attempt[10] for the bottom side of the model of the human psyche including the interconnections of the functionalities. It has been developed by psychoanalytical advisors together with engineers within the project ARS (Artificial Recognition System) and shows a first attempt to describe the deliberation process of the human psyche in a functional sequence. The model has been published in [DZ08] and [DFZ+09] and contains detailed functional units with their corresponding inputs and outputs and how they are interconnected. The functional modules (depicted as differently shaped squares) are described in Section 3.3 and the interconnections (depicted as the arrows between the squares) in Section 3.3.3 in more detail. The shown functional model is the basis for the top-down design approach described in the following sections. As a non-psychoanalyst, it is neither credible nor possible to create a top-down design of the human psyche by starting at the structural model. However, with both ends of the chain, the structural model of metapsychology at the top and the functional model derived from metapsychology at the bottom, it becomes possible to apply the top-down design technique to the model. The outcome is the missing link between the top and the bottom, namely the layers in-between that are necessary to describe the entire model.

Without a basic knowledge of the detailed functions, a top-down design would not be constructive since there are normally several ways existing of decomposing functionalities. As a modeling technique, a top-down design approach has the advantage to prove the completeness of the lowest layer and the implicitly included proof of a technically completely specified and comprehensive model. Therefore, the lowest layer's functionalities were grouped together with semantically similar functionalities. The resulting groups of functionalities are again grouped together, all with respect to two main concepts: the primary- and secondary process and the structural model. The latter is the goal of this

---

[10]The model is not claiming to be complete. It is a first description of the mental process that is necessary to make a technical modeling possible.

Concept and Model of the Decision Unit

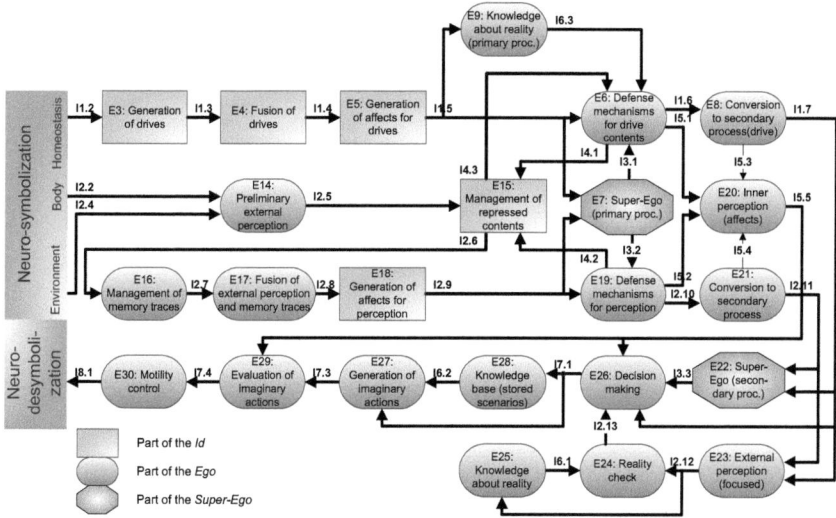

Figure 3.4: Functional Model of the Psyche Deduced from Psychoanalytical Metapsychology

reverse-engineering process and must not be confused with a bottom-up-design approach from scratch. In contrast to the bottom-up design, each sub-functionality is directly related to one and only one of the three instances at the top layer in the top-down design. The results of the described reverse-engineering process will be described in the following sections starting with Figure 3.5 from the top of the model. It claims to separate each of the three instances into further sub-functionalities according to a top-down design approach. It is important to state that the functional blocks that are contained in each of the instances are exclusive and therefore do not overlap in their functionality. This demand does not mean that there is no data exchange between the modules. Further, each functionality can be fully described with its sub-functions identified in the next layer. This postulation would infer the completeness of each layer's function. Although the model has been built with this demand in mind, it is not realistic to claim a complete definition from a technical point of view. Attention has been given to the, in discussion with psychoanalytical advisors identified as crucial functions in the human decision-making process. However, the model is in a development process and does not claim to be complete. Since the concept for description is a modular one, the presented version can be extended in a later review-process with additional functionalities.

Id - Layer 2:

Concept and Model of the Decision Unit

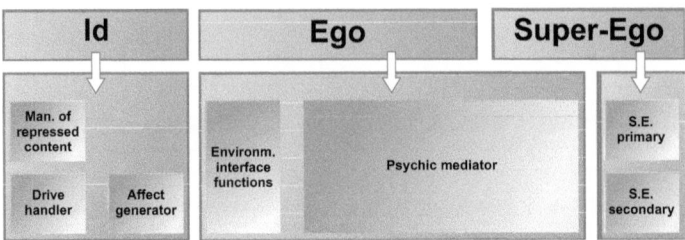

Figure 3.5: The Second Topographical Model - The Second Layer in the Top-Down Design Approach

Starting on the left hand side of Figure 3.5, the psychic instance of the Id is subdivided into three further blocks that are describing the functionality of the Id as a whole. As mentioned in Section 3.1.3, the Id is the origin of the psychic representative of the bodily needs formed as the drives. The module *Drive handler* contains the whole functionality that is necessary to generate and process drives. Since each thing presentation (and therefore each drive) is also connected to a corresponding affect, the functionality of generating affects and connecting them to thing presentations is consolidated in the module *Affect generator*. Finally, the functionality of the Id is completely[11] described with the module *Management of repressed content*.

Since the latter of the three introduced modules will not be divided into more sub-modules, the functionality of this module has to be described in the current layer of the top down design approach. Psychic content in the form of thing presentation and affect pairs have to pass several different filters (the defense mechanisms, described later in this chapter) before they can be converted into secondary process structures including the corresponding word presentation. When the psychic content is refused by these filters, they are not disappearing but still present in the psyche, waiting for a new possibility to become further processed. The module *Management of repressed content* is a collecting pond for the repressed contents coming back from the defense mechanisms. Additionally, it performs another functionality than merely storing these contents: According to the principles of primary process, contained tuples of thing presentations with their corresponding affects can be disconnected and reassigned to other counterparts. The main task of this procedure is to disguise restricted content in order to increase the probability of passing the filter mechanisms. Repressed contents are always striving for getting conscious (in the presented model where consciousness is not considered this means a conversion to secondary process

---

[11]Completely regarding the necessary specifications that are needed to build a first version of a psychoanalytically inspired decision unit for an autonomous agent.

structure) and in the case of a drive it represents the only possibility to get satisfied. In a technical consideration, besides the two functionalities of storing and rearranging repressed contents, it is important to prioritize these contents with respect to other contents that have there origin in actual homeostatic or environmental perception. The reason is the ability of stored, repressed content that can – under certain conditions – suppress the actual bodily or environmental sensations. This prioritization has also been sustained or changed during time according to metapsychology: *"Thus the maintenance of a repression involves an uninterrupted expenditure of force, while its removal results in a saving from an economic point of view."* [Fre15b, p. 151].

Ego - Layer 2:
The instance of the Ego has two main functionalities. First it is responsible for *psychic mediation* between the other two instances as described later in this section to meet the demands of drives as well as environmental and social rules. The psychic mediator includes all deliberative functions (primary process as well as secondary process) that are not part of the preprocessing of the perceived sensations in the Id, described above. This is the main function of the Ego but it requires incoming sensor data and the possibility to alter the environmental conditions by activating the available actuators. Therefore, it is secondly responsible for the bidirectional interaction with the environment that can be identified in the functional block *Environmental interface functions* that are the interface to corresponding sensors and actuators and will be described in Section 3.2.2.

Super-Ego - Layer 2:
Albeit the organizational form of primary or secondary process, the Ego, and therefore all perceptual and deliberative processes are directly or indirectly influenced by social rules. These rules were learned by the individual especially during childhood. The *Super-Ego* actively supports the primary- and the secondary processes of the Ego by evaluating current situations and giving positive feedback in the case of kept or negative feedback in the case of violated Super-Ego advises. It can be decomposed into two further functional modules: The *Primary advisor* and the *Secondary advisor*.

The *Primary advisor* encourages the Ego in antagonizing repressed content and influences the filtering functions of the defense mechanisms. It provides knowledge for the decisions what drive contents or perceptions are allowed or forbidden to be converted to the secondary process and how drives can be deformed or changed. Therefore, the *Primary advisor* module has to be provided with some information about the current situation, containing homeostatic, bodily and environmental information.

Additionally, the Super-Ego influences the secondary processes of the Ego. This functional part will be called the *Secondary advisor*. It's contents are word and thing presentations and it influences the decision-making process that takes place in the organization of the secondary process. Similar to the *Primary advisor*, it has to be provided with information of the actual situation, but due to the terms of the secondary process in a more abstract way that is based on concepts of the word presentations.

In technical terms, the Super-Ego as a whole, containing the *Primary advisor* and the *Secondary advisor*, will be treated as an enhanced knowledge base that is not only able to retrieve knowledge in the form of Super-Ego rules but is also aware of the current situation and retrieves relevant rules on its own. The purpose of these Super-Ego functionalities can be compared to the 'normative behavior' described in [SMFL06][12]. It influences the decision-making process on the two different processing levels (primary and secondary) to meet the demands of socially and learned behavior necessities. It further supports and is a key component for ethical reasoning as described in [AA07]. With this component, agents become able to estimate the impact of their taken actions on surrounding and affected individuals.

3.2.2 Functional Structuring Applying the Top-Down Design Approach

Whereas the functional modules of the Super-Ego and the *Management of repressed content* in the module Id are completely described in Section 3.2.1, the other modules have to be decomposed in an additional third layer. This section will describe the functional parts of the Ego and the *Environmental interface functions* of the Id in its most detailed part. To describe the total functionality of the module *Psychic mediator*, a fourth layer will be necessary and described in Section 3.2.3. Figure 3.6 shows the third layer of the top-down design approach. The arrows are indicating that the functional modules at the beginning of the arrow are decomposed into the sub-functions the arrow is pointing to. The arrow has here the 'contains'-functionality, such as $A \longrightarrow \{B, C\}$ means that the function A contains the sub-functions (or can be decomposed into) B and C.

Id - Drive handler - Layer 3
Starting on the left hand side, the module *Drive handler* contained in the Id can be decomposed into two further functions. The first functional module *Drive generation* composes

---

[12]However, Scheve et al. are using SONAR/MULAN, which is a concept that uses Petri nets to implement their model of multi-agent structures. For this work a complete different approach (the Top-down design approach) is taken because of the complex structures of the human mind, which is beyond the descriptive possibilities state-diagrams as in Petri nets are offering.

Concept and Model of the Decision Unit

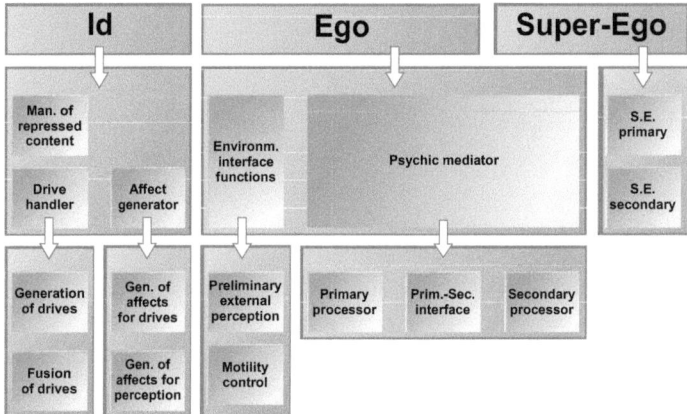

Figure 3.6: The Second Topographical Model - The Third Layer in the Top-Down Design Approach

a drive in the form described in Section 3.1.3. Based upon the already known patterns provided by the memory trace structure, bodily processes are transferred into psychic processes. This module has the functionality of mapping the tensions originating in a variation of the homeostasis to the corresponding thing presentations, which are the psychic representation of the drive. The second functional module of the *Drive handler* has been identified as the *Fusion of drives*. The generated thing presentations for the occurred drives are strictly separated and are connected with weighted associations of affects to the corresponding pairs of opposites within this module. With these two sub-functions, the module *Drive handler* is considered as sufficiently described. Both sub-functions can be considered as leaves of the tree structure and will not be decomposed in a higher, functional granularity

Id - Affect generation - Layer 3
According to Section 3.1.3, each perceived thing presentation has to be assigned with a corresponding affect that represents the quantity of the sensation. This pair can either represent drives or bodily and environmental perceptions. The functional block *Generation of affects for drives* attaches the corresponding affect to the thing presentation that represents the drive. This affect together with the thing presentation is forming the drive. The affect itself is – in the case of a drive – the psychic representation of a corresponding bodily tension. The *Generation of affects for perception* has the same purpose as the above described *Generation of affects for drives* with a different functionality. The affect repre-

sents an associated impact on the individual. A positive value of the affect indicates an already experienced and therefore associated reduction of tension. A negative value indicates an increase of bodily tension. The affect is always connected to a thing presentation that qualifies it and therefore gives the affect the corresponding meaning. Therefore, the module *Generation of affects for perception* searches for one or more associated tuples of thing presentation and affect. They are representing an experienced drive satisfaction or dissatisfaction or other associated perceptual thing presentations.

Ego - Environmental interface functions - Layer 3
When the complete psyche is seen as a central processing unit between bodily sensors and actuators, the sub-functions of the *Environmental interface functions* of the Ego are receiving the sensory data first and hand over the actuator commands to the bodily actuators. The *Preliminary external perception* is the sensory part of the environmental and bodily connection. The word *cathexis* is used in psychoanalysis to indicate that memory traces are activated (or for directing 'psychic energy' to memory traces as it is also found in psychoanalytical literature). The module *Preliminary external perception* performs the cathexis of memory traces due to incoming perceptual symbols. The technical demand to this module is to identify predefined patterns that are representing the memory traces when the corresponding perceptual symbols are perceived. This module therefore converts the perceptual symbols generated by the neuro-symbolic model to thing presentation, the information structure of the psychoanalytical model. The *Motility control* does the opposite work and converts psychoanalytical information structures (thing- and word presentations) into motility control commands. In this way, the corresponding actuators are triggered and the environment as well as the body including hormones and sensor-adapting actuators can be influenced.

Ego - Psychic mediator - Layer 3
As described in Section 3.2.1, the *Psychic mediator* module is the core module for deliberation. The primary and secondary process are the two operation modes of this module and has been defined in detail in Section 3.1.3. The psychic mediator is decomposed in the *Primary processor*, the *Secondary processor* and additionally in a third functional block that holds functionality that is not clearly assignable to the former two: The *Primary- Secondary interface*. Already on this level of the top down design, the functional sequence of the deliberation can be described: Incoming perceptions that are evaluated are processed in a primary process way of organization within the *Primary processor*. The result has to be transformed into a secondary process organization, which is performed by the *Primary- Secondary interface* and its functionality. This results in a data stream of asso-

ciated affects, thing- and word presentations of different informational contents. The word presentation is the only part that can be further processed in the *Secondary processor*. Due to the complexity and diverse functionalities of each of the three modules, it is necessary to further decompose the functionality of the Ego in the fourth and most granular layer of the proposed model.

3.2.3 Functional Description of the Lowest Layers

The previous Section 3.2.2 reached the finest granularity of the description in this work for the Id, the Super-Ego and the *Environmental interface functions* of the Ego. The most important part for decision making has not been described in a sufficient detail. Figure 3.7 shows in addition the missing fourth layer, where the main functionalities of the decision-making process are shown. Again, the arrows are indicating that a functional module in a higher layer can be decomposed to the sub-functions the arrow is pointing to. For example, the functions of the secondary process can be decomposed to the functional modules *Perceptual preprocessing*, *Deliberation* and *Secondary knowledge utilizer*. The following subsections are describing the functionalities of each of the three blocks of the psychic mediation in more detail.

3.2.3.1 Primary processor

The primary processor can be seen as a first switching point in the deliberation process. Presuming a subjective perception of the environmental and bodily sensing according to experienced knowledge, the decision, which perception is allowed to be processed in the primary decision is taken. All functional modules in the primary processor unit are working on the basis of the primary process-like organized data.

Subjective perception

The *Preliminary external perception* is converting perceptual data into the corresponding thing presentations. These thing presentations are the direct representation of the environmental data in the psyche. Such a thing presentation would not have any meaning because it is in no relation to anything. The module *Subjective perception* associates the perceptual thing presentation with repressed content and information that is already associated to the type of actual content of the perceptual thing presentation. Regarding a technical implementation the *Subjective perception* module has to search in a primary process way for repressed and previously experienced thing presentations that are associated

Concept and Model of the Decision Unit

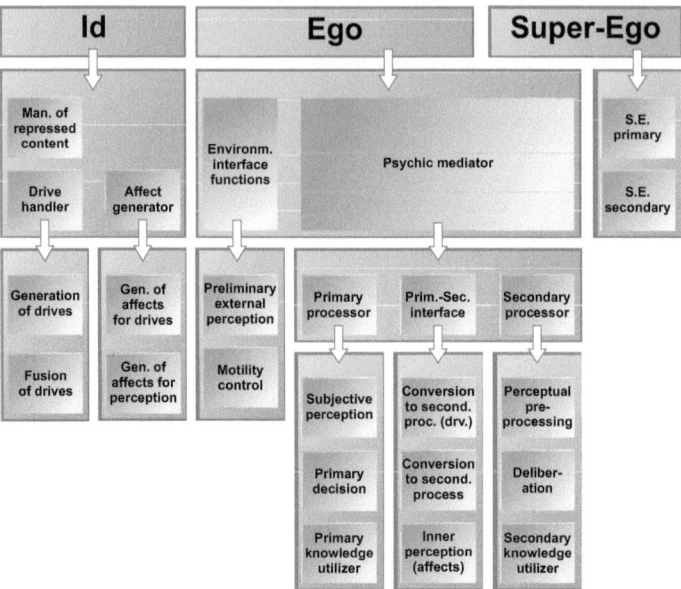

Figure 3.7: The Second Topographical Model - The Fourth Layer in the Top-Down Design Approach

with the actual perception. As the incoming and first completely unrelated perception can be changed or distorted in this process, the module has also the functionality of error correction or signal adaption.

Primary knowledge utilizer
Within the *Primary processor* (Figure 3.8), two necessary types of knowledge can be identified. First, the incoming perception in the form of thing presentation together with former repressed content has to be stored to be retrieved in the further deliberation process and in future. This functional module can be named as *Management of memory traces* and uses the memory trace functionality, as described in Section 3.1.3.

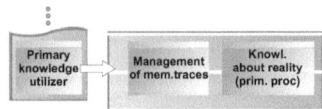

Figure 3.8: Primary Knowledge Utilizer

With this functionality, thing presentations and groups of thing presentations can be stored, retrieved, and associated to each other. Second, a *Knowledge about the reality (unconscious)* is necessary to determine what is possible within the reality and what is impossible according to the already learned information. The output of this functional module does not depend on the current environmental situation (the module 'Knowledge about the reality (conscious)' depends on the current environmental situation and will be described in the *Secondary processor*) but on drive contents. It checks whether a satisfaction of the drive is possible or not. This functionality corresponds to the psychoanalytical reality check. An example is a child's wish for a sexual relationship with its mother. In contrast to the *Super-Ego* that holds only social rules and restriction, the *Knowledge about the reality (unconscious)* holds the information that a relationship is simply (physically) not possible. This module can be seen as a basic world model repository with very abstract, semantical rules and with respect to occurring drive contents.

Primary decision

With the affectively evaluated and subjective perception of the environment, the body and the homeostasis, including all associated memory traces, the *Primary decision* (Figure 3.9) decides what parts are allowed to be further processed, what parts are repressed for a possible later influence and what parts are fended. The *Primary decision* module can be further split into the *Defense mechanisms for drive contents* and *Defense mechanisms for perception*. Whereas the former exclusively deals with homeostatic occurrences in the form of drive related thing presentations the latter is responsible for actual information extracted from the rest of the bodily perceptions and the environment.

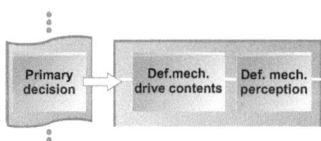

Figure 3.9: Primary Decision

The *Defense mechanism for drive contents* module determines which drives will be allowed to be processed in the secondary processor according to the social constraints of the *Super-Ego* and the *Knowledge about the reality (unconscious)*. Besides the functionality of this filter function (let the drive representatives pass or repress it), the module can also alter the contents of the incoming drive representatives or disconnects the thing presentation from the drive of the associated affect. Changing the content of a drive representative means to mask or totally hide the origin of the drive representative. In [Fre38], Anna Freud describes different defense mechanisms that are able to change the content of these pairs. In [SSK97], they are summarized in a more compact way. In [Rie09, p. 20], fifteen different concepts are discussed also regarding a possible use in embodied, autonomous agents. The different types of defense mechanisms are not described or implemented within this work but the model allows a later implementation of them: by providing the drive representative the defense mechanisms are applied to and all necessary data from past experiences, the knowledge about the reality as discussed above and relevant Super-Ego rules. One of the defense mechanisms is repression, where contents can be repressed and are not allowed to be transformed into the secondary process. A repressed content is influencing related perceptual content and can pass the defense barrier when joining or adapting to such a related content. The quantity and quality of the original drive content is never changed entirely, although the repressed content managed to reach the secondary process. An implementation of a defense mechanism therefore has to hold the pair of a thing presentation and the affect (the psychic representation of the drive), and has to have the possibility of splitting this pair and searching for related thing presentations or affects that can be used as a carrier for these free 'radicals'. The results of this search as well as the amount of quantity of the drive (which is the attached affect) that is shifted to another thing presentation depends on the used defense mechanism. This means for the affect that it is either totally repressed, or partly attached to another thing presentation (a different quality of the drive representative). This presentation is able to pass the defense filter, or it remains as an unknown and unqualified quantity that is further processed as anxiety.

The *Defense mechanisms for perception* module has the same contingent of defense mechanisms that can be used. However, there is no *Knowledge about the reality (unconscious)* necessary to apply certain constraints given by the reality. Only the *Super-Ego* actively supports the *Defense mechanisms for perception* in its decision of filtering restricted content out of the perception stream for further processing. The conceptual functionality of the defense mechanisms can be seen as identical. The *Defense mechanism for drive contents* can technically be seen as a specialization of the *Defense mechanisms for perception* with an additional interface to the *Knowledge about the reality (unconscious)*.

3.2.3.2 Primary and secondary interface

The *Primary and secondary interface* is the interface that converts the output of the *Defense mechanisms* from a primary process structure to a secondary process structure. The main component that is added here is the *Word presentation* (already described in Section 3.1.3) – an additional and conceptual description form for the content of the pair of the thing presentation and the affect. This structure makes it possible to apply logical connections and to discover existing contradictions.

Conversion to secondary process (drive) and
Conversion to secondary process (perception)
The incoming pair of thing presentation and affect is representing either a drive or an external (bodily or environmental) perception. It is connected with an associated word presentation that fits as a secondary process concept to the incoming pair. The information of the associations between a thing presentation and a word presentation is held within the conceptual framework of memory traces.

Conversion to secondary process (affect)
This module is the key of affective reasoning. Repressed affects that are existing in the form of an unqualified quantity can be converted to the secondary process and therefore influence the decision-making process (e.g. in the form of an unbiased anxiety). Affects that were assigned to a thing presentation in one of the two transformation processes described above are also collected in this module and are influencing the decision-making process.

3.2.3.3 Secondary processor

After the perception of the homeostasis, the body and the environment, the association with memories and affects, the appliance of the defense mechanisms and the conversion to the secondary process structure including the association of corresponding word presentations, the logical but still affective reasoning process begins. The following three submodules of the *Secondary processor* are representing the functionalities of the human psyche that are working in the organizational form of the secondary process. Although the structure can be compared to the *Primary processor* – with an informational preprocessing, a decision module and an additional knowledge utilizer, the data structures and ways of processing are different and will be explained in the following paragraphs.

Perceptual preprocessing
The triples of thing presentation, affect, and word presentation that are representing drive contents or external perceptions have different intensities according to their quantity of the corresponding affect. However, the module *External perception (focused)* can shift the proportion between the different intensities according to the current situation and the current reasoning process to draw the focus of attention to a specific part of the perception. The module *Perceptual preprocessing* is shown in Figure 3.10.

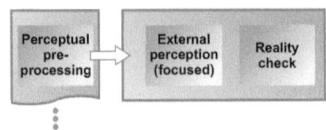

Figure 3.10: Perceptual preprocessing

One possible implementation would be to distinguish between different types of reasoning processes. It can be distinguished between their final objective to satisfy a drive content or a long term goals that is currently worked out. The implementation would have to provide a list of typically related perceptions, such as food that satisfies the hunger or an obstacles that have to be avoided when following a path to a destination. The module would boost the intensity of the typically related perceptions by a predefined value. With this focused and secondary process information about the perception and a semantic knowledge about relations in the environment, the module *Reality check (conscious)* provides information about permitted drive satisfactions and inflicted demands of the environment and the current situation. Again, the search for permissions and constraints is based on the secondary process and therefore on the contents and concepts of the word presentations.

Deliberation
The deliberation process (with its module shown in Figure 3.11) can be seen as a three folded process: The *Decision making*, the *Generation of imaginary actions* and the *Evaluation of imaginary actions*. Each of the listed steps can be seen as its own functional module. The *Decision making* module collects the generated representatives of drives (the drive demands), the information of the environmental and bodily perception (reality demands), and the information of social rules (the Super-Ego demands) and mediates between these three demands. And furthermore it considers the actual affective state.

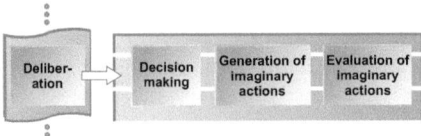

Figure 3.11: Deliberation

The drive representative that has the best opportunity to get satisfied without essential violation of social rules or reality demands is chosen. Because not only the best drive representation is concerned in the further decision process of the human psyche, an implementation has to prioritizes the drive representations according to their intensity, the amount of social punishment or praise, its degree of feasibility, etc. It selects the one with the highest resulting priority, which can be considered as a very rough approximation to the humans decision-making process. However, this oversimplification of a possible implementation is able to deal with the demands of the functional description and does not exclude the possibility of several decision processes in parallel.

The module *Generation of imaginary actions* is responsible to work out a plan to reach a satisfaction of the drive or any other longterm goal. It uses the input of a secondary process drive representative that has the best opportunity of satisfaction according to the *Decision making* module. This requires a knowledge-base of stored scenarios (described below) and action tendencies that are the components of the resulting plan. The different action plans are evaluated in the module *Evaluation of imaginary actions*, Then the selected plan is executed. Information from an episodic memory, where already experienced impacts to actions are stored, and the current affective state are influencing the selection for the best action plan. In [ST02, p. 281], Solms describes these two functional modules as follows:

"Thinking may be regarded as imaginary acting, whereby the outcome of a potential action is evaluated. This is achieved by running the envisaged action programs while motor output is precluded (inhibited). Acting without acting is thinking (imaginary acting). Inhibition is therefore the prerequisite and the medium of thought." [ST02, p. 281]

The psychoanalytical theory in this area of the model does not give an exact definition of the functionality of logical thinking, the creation of imaginary action plans or the evaluation regarding the impact of the planned actions. It simply assumes and requires its existence. For a possible implementation there have to be two constraints considered: First, the action plan always follows the previously selected goal that should be achieved. Second the evaluation has to consider the current affective state and previously experienced causalities to predict a probable impact. In Chapter 4 these modules will have to perform a logical means ends reasoning in order to be able to cope with these demands. It will be shown that the demands from the psychoanalytically side can be met, although implementation methods from Artificial Intelligence will be applied. Further concepts of implementations of this module may partly use psychologically (not psychoanalytically) inspired theory.

Secondary knowledge utilizer
The sub-functions of the *Secondary knowledge utilizer* is shown in (Figure 3.12). As one part of a semantic memory, the module *Knowledge about reality (secondary process)* holds lexical knowledge about functions, causalities and properties of the reality. The semantical associations are also managed within the network of memory traces. The knowledge is used

Concept and Model of the Decision Unit

to perform the reality check as described above in the module *Reality check (conscious)*. It has to provide knowledge about the possibilities in a certain situation.

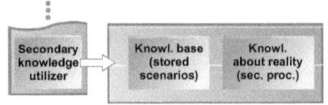

Figure 3.12: Secondary knowledge utilizer

As a simple, functional implementation, the module would take the information of the current situation in the form of thing presentations, word presentations, and affects and has to retrieve necessary, possible and explicitly prohibited actions that can be taken. In contrast, the module *Knowledge base (stored scenarios)* does not hold semantical and abstract rules, but already witnessed experiences – episodes – including the initial conditions and the impacts to the individual and the environment. With this knowledge, it becomes possible to generate and evaluate action plans as described above. Again, a simple technical implementation would take the current situation and start a search of all past episodes with the same initial conditions. Such a functionality is e.g. used by Ho and Dautenhahn in [HDN05] for navigating an autonomous agent within an unknown terrain. In [RLD+07] and [DGLV08], the episodic memory model from Tulving ([Tul83]) and Baddeley ([Bad97]) is applied to autonomous agents, as described above in Section 2.6.

With the above given description, the top down design approach has reached the finest granularity of functional decomposition that is needed for the implementation of a computational decision unit in an autonomous agent following psychoanalytical concepts of decision making. Figure 3.13 shows the final tree structure of the top-down design that corresponds with the content of Figure 3.7. The pure functional description of the introduced modules and the hierarchical assembly of the modules that starts from the top layer as depicted in Figure 3.7 does not give any information of the horizontal interrelationships and the sequence of function calls of the particular functional modules. In Figure 3.4, the functional relations are shown, starting at the upper left side with the inputs from the sensory part and ending at the lower left part at the output for actuators. Whereas the model includes a detailed information for the most important functionalities defined in metapsychology, the next Section 3.3 will reduce the complexity of the overall model with respect to the formulation of a wish that is the basis for the further processing of the *Secondary processor* described above.

Concept and Model of the Decision Unit

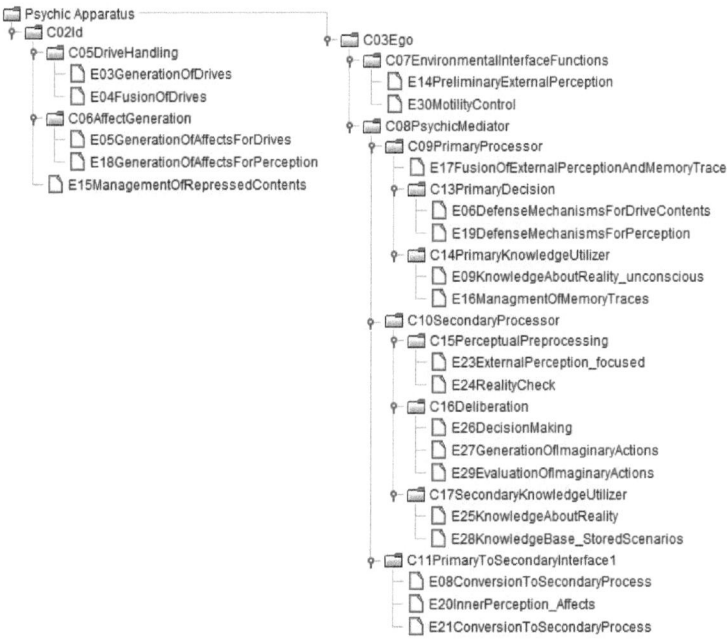

Figure 3.13: The Final Top-Down Design Approach Depicted in the Form of a Tree

3.3 The Structure of Psychic Processing – A New Approach in Computational Planning

The previous chapters provided detailed information about the function of each module starting from the top level of the used design approach and resulting in a detailed functional description of used sub-modules at the highest granularity. The following sections uses the detailed functional definitions and shows the interactions and interrelationship between the functional modules. Starting from the homeostatic, bodily and environmental input streams, the call-sequence of the functional modules will be discussed that finally leads to an output-action of the system. However, for this discussion the set of functions will be reduced to a minimum with respect to the generation of a wish, the main connection point between model and implementation. A 'work-flow of the artificial psyche' is presented that shows the main functional sequence. It discusses the advantages and disadvantages of describing a highly parallel and distributed process like the psychic reasoning in a quasi-sequential appearing way.

3.3.1 Minimum Requirement Analysis for Structural Planning

Metapsychology identifies a functional framework of the human psyche that was the basis for the functional top down description in Section 3.2. The described structures, functional units and interrelationships are used in the following to improve current concepts and their implementations of planning in the area of Artificial Intelligence. The main connection between the described psychoanalytically inspired model and concepts from cognitive science as well as implementation methods from Artificial Intelligence is seen in the psychoanalytical construct of the *wish* that has been described in Section 3.1.3 in detail. In the area of Artificial Intelligence and autonomous agents, the term *desire* has become an important term as shown in [JW06]. Desires are also a crucial part in the BDI-Framework [Bra87] and its implementations [GI89] as described in Section 2.4. The advantage of using the desire as a central key issue is that thereby, a computer program like the decision unit of an autonomous agent turns from a classical 'task oriented' to a 'goal oriented' agent. At first view this particular change may not seem to be a big advantage but when considering the environment is the real world *"[...] where chaos is the norm, not the exception"* [GI89] the advantage becomes more clearly. A system that only executes a sequence of commands without any knowledge about its goal (which is defined by the current desire) requires preprogrammed exception-handling routines to continue proper working. A goal-oriented system, like a BDI system, only has to detect the exception. Since the system still has the information about its actual goal and an actual world model it can immediately restart to plan the next steps - an implicit recovery from failures. The psychoanalytical view offers a theory for generating such a wish, according to the actual situation of the agent (as argued above, it includes the homeostatic, bodily, and environmental information), and for a further processing and handling. With respect to an implementation, it has to be discussed what are the minimal requirements, what minimal components are necessary and what functionality has to be implemented in minimum to meet the specifications and deal with constraints of the introduced model.

To select a wish the agent needs detailed information about its homeostatic values. The wishes (former drives with an attached word presentation) of an individual are reflecting its actual, homeostatic state. In order to be able to select one drive, also environmental and bodily information have to be considered. Besides the generation of drives, the decision unit decides whether evoked drives and perceived environmental or bodily information is further processed or repressed. Besides a variety of possible mechanisms (described in Section 3.2.1 as the *Defense mechanisms*) the psychic instance *Super-Ego* supports the decision in filtering the mentioned data structures and their content. The combination of drives and environmental information in combination with subjective associations represents the generated wishes and has to be transformed into the secondary process structure, where logical ordering can be applied. With the generated information of the wishes, the wish deliberation starts: First, a deflector has to be applied that selects the most urgent demand. This can be done in a first implementation by simply prioritizing each possible wish with respect to the actual context. To provide an output of the system, a mechanism has to be installed that generates the possible plans that lead from the actual position to the satisfaction of a wish. This can be generated by using logical definition languages and reasoning frameworks as long as they are providing the possibility to integrate different, user-defined types of constraints (for example a secondary process ordering) and evaluation systems (for example an affective evaluation system for further reasoning). Second, the generated plans to achieve a certain goal have to be evaluated in order to determine the best one, considering pleasure, energy effort, minimum arousal of negative affects, etc. To realize the described functionalities, the basic functions of organizing and associating content in a primary and secondary process way are necessary. Within the model, each piece of information therefore has to be enveloped in one of the three basic objects: affects, thing presentations, or word presentations. In technical terms, these parent classes have to implement specific interfaces that enables primary or secondary process handling of the content. The different instances of the classes are the basic data types that are used for inter-functional communication. The templates of these instances are the global concepts of already known thing- and word presentations with the corresponding affect. They are the parts of the basic knowledge of the agent and have to be stored and retrieved within a global accessible functional module that manages all memory traces. Although semantic, episodic and other types of memory are necessary within the model, the memory types of modules that are used in psychological theory (see [Tul83], [Bad97], and [ST94]) to distinguish between the organization of the content, cannot be assigned to a specific functional block in the introduced model. The memory structures depends on what information is created, accessed or altered in all of the functional modules as introduced in Section 3.2. A classification whether the content of thing- or word presentations are semantic, episodic, or other types of memory systems will not be made because most of the entries within the knowledge-base are assigned to and associated with several different memory systems. Section 3.2 only gave a functional description of each module, following the top-down design approach. In the next Section 3.3.2, the functional sequence of the complete model will be discussed, starting with the sensory inputs of the model and ending at the actuator controlling output.

3.3.2 The Sequential Coherence of Psychoanalytical Functionalities

Developing a psychoanalytically inspired decision unit for an autonomous agent requires in particular three types of definitions. First, it has to be defined what data types are necessary, which was already done in Section 3.1.3. Second, the basic functionalities have to be clarified in Section 3.2 by applying the top down design approach to the structural model of metapsychology. The most detailed functions were shown in Figure 3.4 and were the basis for structuring the functional blocks into the described layers. The arrows between the functions show a first functional sequence that will be described in more detail in the following chapter. From this detailed functional model some functional closely related modules will be combined to one super-module to provide a better overview. Although these functions are located at different layers of the top-down design and some cannot even be assigned to the same psychic instance, they are sequentially connected, meaning that the output of one functional module is the input of the next module. In Figure 3.14 the combined set of functions is shown. The functional modules have inputs and outputs, where the processed data is received or sent to the next connected functional module(s).

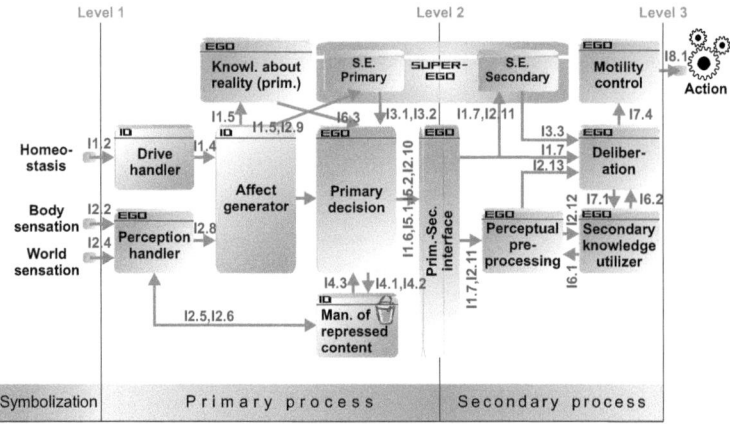

Figure 3.14: Modeling the Psychoanalytical Processing Sequence

The shaded rectangles in Figure 3.14 are representing the functional modules including their name and the psychic instance (*Id*, *Ego*, and *Super-Ego*) they are part of. The psychic instances are the highest level of the top-down designed model. The arrows between the modules are indicating a singular or bidirectional communication between the modules.

The main information flows from the left to the right hand side. *Level 1* is the borderline between neurologically inspired symbolization and the psychoanalytically inspired decision unit as shown in Figure 3.1. The interface requires already symbolized information about the homeostasis, bodily-, and environmental sensations that are transformed into symbols with semantical meaning as described in [VLBD08]. *Level 3* on the right side denotes the borderline between the psychoanalytically inspired decision unit and the generation of motor commands. The interface is sending information out of the decision unit and transmits the produced high level action commands that will be decomposed to specific motor control outside of the decision unit. In Chapter 4 action commands like *move forward*, *collect energy* or *attack* will be used as these high level commands. Again, in Chapter 4 the high level action command *move forward* will be transformed to the forces that are applied to the wheels of a simulated two-wheeled autonomous agent. *Level 2* splits the sequential model into two parts: The *primary-* and *secondary process*. As described in Section 3.1.3, all information within the area of the primary process structure is following specific rules for organization. An occurring data between *Level 1* and *Level 2* is encapsulated in the combinations of a *thing presentation* and an *affect*. They are organized and associated according to the specified rules. Between *Level 2* and *Level 3*, the data is additionally consisting of *word presentations* and follows the specific rules of the *secondary process* for organization and association.

The following part describes interrelationship between the functional blocks and show the information flow. The functional sequence of Figure 3.14 is designed to realize it in the decision unit of a simulated (virtual) embodied agent in a time discrete computer simulation. Sensory information is collected in each single simulation step of the discrete simulation. The time between two simulation steps can be considered as constant within the simulation, although the time of the complete calculation of the processes can vary. After the sensor data is collected, but still in the same simulation step, the input data for homeostasis is processed by the functional block called *Drive handler* and the input data for the sensations of body and world are processed by the perception handler. Both functional blocks are providing the next module – in this case the *Affect generator* – with an input that is sequentially further processed and so on. When the last functional module, which is the *Motility control* has received and processed its input values, it produces the output of the decision unit. However, this all happens in one simulation step, which means that the system is halted until the decision unit produces a corresponding output to a given input. The reasoning process virtually takes no time and this is important for the relevance of a further simulation. It is clear that a sequential handling can never be compared to the highly parallel processing activities of the human brain. But when the sequentially called functions are processed in one single point in time, it would be (at least theoretically) possible to realize a cooperative multitasking system with a sequential core that is fast enough to appear like a parallel one. These simulation aspects should just give a first remark on the reason of the sequential ordering and should clarify that it is not assumed that the psychic apparatus of the human is working sequentially. Additionally to the call hierarchy, the input and output data that is transferred between the modules according to the arrows will be described in more detail. The naming follows the functional top-down design as defined in Section 3.2.

The *Drive handler* is discussed first due to its importance for the perception of a homeostatic imbalance. The input information of this component consists of symbols containing the information of the quality of the part of the homeostasis (which represents the actual state of the body parameters like the stomach fill level or the blood sugar) as well as the quantity of the deviation of the representing value. The *Generation of drives* maps the organic processes into psychic processes and creates an instance of a thing presentation[13] that represents the quality of the homeostatic value within the psyche. The attached quantity remains but can be shifted to other drive representatives as defined in the *Fusion of drives* module. The output of the drive handler therefore is a list of thing presentations where each represent the quality of a drive and an attached quantity. This output is passed to the *Affect generator*, described later in this chapter. The perception handler is more complex than the drive handler, because it includes three basic functional modules. First, the *Preliminary external perception* transforms sensory processes from the body and the environment into psychic processes, similar to the *Generation of drives*. Therefore, a constellation of symbolized sensory values are transformed into instances of the corresponding thing presentations. Only perceptual constellations that are completely unknown are forming new memory traces that contain new thing presentations. However, these new data-sets are always derived from similar information that already exists. The generated thing presentations are then sent to the *Management of repressed content* that is able to alter selected thing presentations (as described below in more detail). The altered instances of thing presentations (and possibly combined affects) are then stored in the module *Management of memory traces* for a further primary or secondary process use. Finally, the *Subjective perception* associates the thing presentations with related thing presentations. With this process, the perceived data in the form of thing presentations are attached with a semantic meaning for the individual that is used in the further processing

---

[13]The thing presentations themselves can be seen as the pattern or templates that defines such sensory constellations and are available within the entire net of memory traces. When a sensory constellation matches one of those patterns, a certain instance of the thing presentation is created.

sequence. Additionally attached thing presentations can be for instance similar objects or thing presentations that are closely related to the current situation, which is representing the actual context. The output information of this module that is the input for the affect generator is similar to the *Generation of drives* namely a list of thing presentations representing the quality of the sensation and the quantity that denotes the strength of the stimulus or personal involvement.

The generated thing presentations indicating the sensation of homeostatic, bodily and environmental sensors are still free of any emotional evaluation. The module *Affect generator* therefore has the functionality to evaluate the incoming perception and connects the thing presentations with a corresponding affect. In terms of the drives, the affect is generated by carrying the quantity of the sensation from the homeostatic origin over to become the value of the affect. This value of the affect can be seen as the amount of reluctance the corresponding homeostatic imbalance is resulting in. For perceptional thing presentations the affect alone would be of no significance, because it is just a value without any meaning. The thing presentation of the perceptional sensation has to be connected with another thing presentation that holds the information of the quality of a drive and a corresponding affect for the quantity. A short example explains this necessity better: The perceptional sensations of food are psychologically represented as a thing presentation. The perceived object food would satisfy the drive that is related to a grievance of the stomach. Therefore the perceived thing presentation for food has to be attached with a thing presentation that represents the drive with the stomach system as its origin and an affect. This affect is the expected value of satisfaction for the corresponding drive, the expected release of drive tension when the perceived object 'food' is consumed. Since a perceived object can be the representative drive object of several drives, also several combinations of thing presentation and affect can be associated. The output of the module is the affective, emotionally evaluated perception and is relayed to the modules *Knowledge about Reality (primary process)*, the *S.E. Primary* of the Super-Ego, and to the *Primary decision* module.

The former two (*Knowledge about Reality (primary process)* and *S.E. Primary* of the Super-Ego) can be seen as decision support units for the primary decision. Depending on the current situation, the module *Knowledge about Reality (primary process)* delivers primary organized information on what is possible and what is not[14]. According to the incoming and affectively evaluated thing presentations the output is formed to deliver only the relevant information to the *Primary decision*. The same functionality is executed by the *S.E. Primary* of the Super-Ego, but the guidelines are considering only social constraints.

---

[14]A closer description of the functionality of this and all other modules has already been given in Section 3.2

Additionally to a list of relevant social constraints, this part of the Super-Ego is also able to generate qualified affects that are complimenting the individual for avoiding the violation of Super-Ego rules or afflicting it when the rules were violated. The resulting output is forwarded to the *Primary decision* unit that includes the functionality of the *Defense mechanisms* for both, the drive contents and the perceptual contents. Provided with the affectively evaluated perception and the corresponding rules that define the possibilities and constraints of the current situation, this unit has to decide whether the perceived information is allowed to pass to the next higher level. Contents in the form of thing presentations and affects, which are, according to the existing defense mechanisms, not allowed to pass this gate can be either split apart to be reassigned to other thing presentations or affects and become able to pass the censor of the defense mechanisms or are repressed and therefore redirected to the *Management of repressed content*. The output of the *Management of repressed content* is transmitting a list of thing presentations and affects of repressed contents. Thing presentation and affect do not have to be connected necessarily together. The output of the 'Primary to Secondary Interface' is transmitting content that has to further processed. The *Management of repressed content* collects and stores the repressed content and permanently tries to reassign parts of this content to new, incoming perceptions to retry a possible pass at the defense mechanisms. The passed information of the defense mechanisms, which is the output of the 'Primary decision' unit is then transformed to the secondary process organized data in the module *Primary to Secondary Interface*. Here, the thing presentations and affects are connected with a corresponding word presentation that applies a certain concept to the perceived thing presentation. All further processes can use this new information structure that implies a semantically higher processing of the data.

Within the *Perceptual preprocessing* module, the bodily and environmental perception are represented by combinations of word presentations, thing presentations, and affects. The quantity of these perceptual sensations are represented by the affect and can be amplified or suppressed according to the current focus of attention. The focus of attention can have several origins, e.g. the final objective of an actual wish. Whereas the described functionality corresponds to the already described module *External perception*, the module *Reality check*, which is also part of the 'Perceptual preprocessing' adds relevant information of permitted drive satisfaction and inflicted demands of the environment to the output stream. This information comes from the *Secondary knowledge utilizer* and its functional module *Knowledge about reality (secondary process)* that offers semantical knowledge.

The output of the 'Perceptual preprocessing' is therefore a, according to the current focus of attention, prioritized list of perceptual information and an appropriate list of semantical rules. It is redirected to the *Deliberation* module. The three inputs of the deliberation module are lists of associated word presentation, including the perception, and corresponding associations and constraints: The first input represents the drive representatives that have been approved by the 'Primary decision' and become wishes on this level. The second input is the information about the body and environment, affectively evaluated and associated with subjective and semantic knowledge. The third input comes from the *S.E. Primary* of the Super-Ego that again delivers social constraints just as the unconscious part does but provides secondary organized information in the form of conceptual word presentations and their associations. The *Deliberation* module first has to select the most relevant wish that occurs, with respect to the constraints of the *Super-Ego* and the *Demands from the reality*. This selected wish, including all information attached to it is then forwarded to the module *Generation of imaginary actions* that searches for possible ways to fulfill the wish and therefore to satisfy the underlying drive(s). It is supported by the functional module *Knowledge about stored scenarios* that is part of the 'Secondary knowledge utilizer' and retrieves known episodes that already led to certain changes in the environment due to past actions. These episodes are connected together to generate the imaginary action that leads to the fulfillment of the wish. The output, a list of action plans in a structured formation of word presentations is finally forwarded to the module *Evaluation of imaginary actions*, where each prepared plan is evaluated and the best one is selected. This plan is then forwarded to the *Motor control* system that is responsible for the proper execution of the semantically high level action-routines.

The sequence of the identified functions that are executed in the psychoanalytically inspired decision process is designed to take place in each single time-step of a simulation as it will be described in the implementation details of Chapter 4. A change of the situation in any time-step therefore influences the decision-making process at once. According to the currently executed actions and the prioritization of goals that are trying to satisfy drives and fulfill wishes, also the behavior of the system may change at once. Suppressing a permanently action-changing behavior is part of the functionality of every module in order to avoid instability and oscillations. However, the module *Deliberation* is the last instance and is responsible to avoid or – in certain situations – produce such behavior.

3.3.3 Interface Specification of the Functional Modules

The sequence described above offered an overview of the execution sequence of the functional modules. Figure 3.14 gives a comprehensive view by showing functional containers within the top-down design instead of showing all functional modules in the lowest layer. At the beginning of this chapter, Figure 3.4 showed the execution sequence of all functional modules in the lowest layer. The following paragraphs will now deal with the interfaces between the functional modules of the lowest layer. The interfaces are enumerated in Figure 3.4 with an 'I', followed by two digits. One example is 'I1.3' for the interface between the modules *Generation of drives* and *Fusion of drives*. This enumeration is used in the following to identify the corresponding interface without referring to the corresponding modules and their names.

Table 3.1 gives a comprehensive view of the data transmitted through the specific interfaces. To avoid unnecessary specifications of transmitted data, the specification of the interfaces begins with the output of the system. Backtracking along the execution sequence, the interfaces from the former functional modules are defined until the interfaces of the three different inputs of the system are reached. The interface specification is confined to the possible output information of the simulated, embodied, virtual agent that will be described in Section 4.1. The impacts of the defined actions of the interface 'I8.1' will also be shown in the same chapter.

Starting with the possible actions that can be sent to the agent's neuro-desymbolization, *I8.1* transmits action symbols that are executed by the corresponding actuators of the agent after neuro-desymbolization.

Nr.	Content type	Description
I8.1	Action symbols	Symbols that represent action commands and their respective parameter. Example: MOVE_FORWARD(Speed)
I7.4	Action plan	The selected action plan consists of a sequence of word presentations that represent the sequence of actions to be taken. Example: Move forward (WP), stop (WP), take object (WP), ...
I7.3	List of action plans	The list holds word presentation meshes containing the action sequences. Example: Plan 1 (WPM): 'Run to object', Plan 2 (WPM): 'Walk zigzag to object', ...
I5.5	List of current feelings	These feelings are former affects that can now be described with two word presentations - one for the quality, one for the quantity. Example: Anxiety (WP) and High intensity (WP of affect)

Table 3.1: (continued)

Nr.	Content type	Description
I6.2	Planning information	Contains complete plans (WPM) or plan fragments (WPM or WP) that were previously stored in the knowledge-base of stored scenarios.
I7.1	Perception	Transfers the currently selected wish (WPM) and a list of environmental perceptions (WPM)
I2.13	Perception + Reality information	Contains currently perceived information (WPM) of the environment and corresponding rules (WPM) that meet the demands of reality
I6.1	Reality rules	Depending on the current situation, the interface returns reality rules (WPM) that could be violated by satisfying the actual drives. Example: Cannot eat more than capable (WPM).
I2.12	Perception (focused)	Word presentation meshes (WPM) represent the current perception. They contain the information about the object (WP) and the corresponding quantity of the sensation (WP). This quantity has been shifted within the module E23.
I3.3	Super-Ego rules	Depending on the current, social situation, the interface returns Super-Ego rules (WPM) that could be violated by satisfying the actual drives.
I1.7	Wishes	The homeostatic perception of drives is contained in the form of wishes (WPM). They contain the *Drive target* (WP), the intensity of the affect (WP), and corresponding *Drive objects* (WP's).
I2.11	Perceptions (body and environment)	Word presentation meshes (WPM) of the subjective perceived information from body and environment. Example: Object 'Cake' (environment), Object 'Pain' (body).
I5.4	Associated feelings of bodily and external perception	The feelings caused by the perceived objects are collected and transferred.
I5.3	Associated feelings of wishes	The feelings caused by the current drives are collected and transferred.

Table 3.1: (continued)

Nr.	Content type	Description
I5.2	Unqualified affects (perception)	Transfers affects which are no longer connected to a corresponding environmental or bodily thing presentation. These affects will result in the feeling of anxiety.
I5.1	Unqualified affects (drives)	Transfers affects that are not connected to a corresponding, thing presentation of a drive. These affects result in the feeling of anxiety.
I2.10	Subjective perceptions	A reduced list of thing presentation meshes that contain the thing presentation of the perceived object (TP), a corresponding affect, and associated attributes (TP).
I1.6	Drives	The list contains the remaining pairs of opposite drives (e.g. nourish and bite) after the defense mechanisms. Each single drive (TPM) contains the drive target (TP), the affect, and associated drive objects (TP).
I3.1	Super-Ego rules for drives	A list of thing presentation meshes (TPM=TP's+A) that represent rules that have to be considered.
I3.2	Super-Ego rules for perception	A list of thing presentation meshes (TPM=TP's+A) that represent rules that have to be considered.
I4.1	Repressed drives	The components of a repressed drive (drive target (TP), drive object (TP), affect) either together or in part through this interface.
I4.2	Repressed perception	The components of a perception (object (TPM) and corresponding affect) are repressed either together or in part trough this interface.
I4.3	Repressed drive contents (retry)	Transfers the repressed components of a drive (object (TPM) and corresponding affect).
I6.3	Reality demands	A list of thing presentation meshes (TPM=TP's+A) that represent reality rules that have to be considered.
I2.9	Subjective perception	A list of thing presentation meshes that contain the thing presentation of the perceived object (TP), a corresponding affect, and associated attributes (TP).
I2.8	Subjective, perceived object	A list of pairs of thing presentation meshes (TPM, containing the currently perceived object) and an affect.

Table 3.1: (continued)

Nr.	Content type	Description
I2.7	Perception and attached, subjective contents	A list of pairs of the 'objective' perception (TPM) and an associated memory, including the affect (TPM+A).
I2.6	Perception and attached, repressed contents	A list of pairs of the 'objective' perception (TPM) and an associated repressed content, including the affect (TPM+A).
I2.5	Perceptual thing presentations	A list of perceived, unevaluated thing presentations.
I2.4	Perceptual (neuro-) symbols body	A list of symbols (techn.) describing the current bodily perception.
I2.2	Perceptual (neuro-) symbols environment	A list of symbols (techn.) describing the current environmental perception.
I1.5	Drives	A list of pairs of opposite drives (e.g. nourish and bite). One single drive (TPM) contains the drive target (TP), the affect, and associated drive objects (TP).
I1.4	Drive pairs and affect candidates	A list of *pairs of opposite drives* (TPM) and their corresponding *affect candidate*. The drive consists of the *drive target* (TP) and several *drive objects* (TP)
I1.3	Drives and tension	On the one hand, a list of drives (TPM, containing of target (TP) and objects (TP's)) are transferred. On the other hand, the current qualities and quantities of homeostatic deviations are transferred.
I1.2	Organ tension	A list of symbols representing a homeostatic deviation or tension on the corresponding organ.

Table 3.1: Interface Specification of the Introduced Model, Depicted in Figure 3.4.

Together with the top down design and the functional description provided in Section 3.2, and the described execution sequence from Section 3.3.2, the interface specification is completing the description of the introduced model. This is the basis for the considerations in Chapter 4 when realizing the functional modules and the introduced psychoanalytically inspired functional model.

3.3.4 Discussion of Expected Advantages and Possible Limitations

To complete the considerations regarding the introduced model for a decision unit that mainly follow the basic concepts of metapsychology, the model should be discussed with respect to advantages and possible bottlenecks in the implementation. As mentioned in Chapter 2, a wide variety of models for decision units of autonomous agents exists and an appreciable part of them is also based on psychological models. One of the main reasons for the decision to model and implement a new decision unit architecture is that many existing solutions are focused on one specific problem. An example is the memory storage system that seems to be the core of several architectures (SOAR and ACT-R are strongly focused on the problem of memory storage and retrieval). The functionality of memory is naturally an omnipresent component, because nearly every function within a decision unit needs access to stored information. Nevertheless, it must not be seen as the core of the decision-making process. It merely stores and retrieves information.

The introduced model therefore tries to focus on each part of the chain in decision making without preferring single parts. The applied top-down design as a tool supports such an individual considerations. The resulting model provides a functional description, starting from the very beginning of how symbolized sensory data must be processed and combined, to the very end of how motor-control commands have to be generated and processed. The description seems complete with regard to the typical units of an artificial decision unit. The introduced functions described in the deepest layers of the top down design need to be discussed further during the implementation regarding their specific functionality.

As the model has specifications and constraints on each layer in each functional module, an implementation following the given specifications should be possible in principle. As a main advantage, the architecture clearly focuses on the integration of drives but also requires a complex body that produces these drives. Furthermore, the emphasis lies on the process of evaluation and several adequate filtering mechanisms. The evaluation process is done by affects, but also by a preliminary attachment and association of further information that is relevant for the following filtering processes. Each process of data preparation and reduction reduces the search-space for the next module or preliminarily adds concepts that can reduce the search space. Compared to the BDI-Framework (Belief-Desire-Intention), the introduced model not only generates desires (the corresponding term for the wish) but also adapts and provides the beliefs of the system. The intention would be the simple product of the beliefs and desires, but a strong relation between the reality, the desires and the constraints is automatically included.

Although no specific evidence has been offered regarding the processed content of information, the occurring data types that hold the content have been described in detail. Together with the concept of primary and secondary process organization, a specification of the type of associations and how these associations can be established has been provided. The described *compare operators* for thing presentations and word presentations that work either primary or secondary process-like organized are the essential component in building new associations. Finally, the constraints of these methodologies of comparison have to be applied to the logical part of the reasoning. Affective evaluations and possessive drive demands have to be considered as well as social or environmental constraints. However, psychoanalysis does not offer concrete specifications on how the logic in logical concepts is generated, handled, applied, or processed. From the point of view of psychoanalysis, this learnt functionality simply exists in the sane human psyche of an adult and is discussed in more detail in cognitive psychology, e.g. in [Bes99, p. 398ff].

The following Chapter 4 will describe a possible implementation of the introduced, psychoanalytically inspired model of a decision unit. It focuses on the question whether Freud's model of metapsychology is sufficiently defined to implement and to operationalize it. Whereas the following chapter only focuses on the content of the decision unit, it will be applied in Chapter 5 to an autonomous, embodied agent that is embedded in a virtual environment within a simulator. Not the content but the resulting behavior of the decision unit will be the focus of Chapter 5 and the corresponding results will be presented in Chapter 6.

4 Implementation in Embodied Agents

Different implementations of decision-making units for autonomous agents are available in the open source sector as well as in the commercial sector. The examples, already given in Section 2.4 are – besides of logical planning – partly focusing on the structuring of information that is held in the decision unit (especially ACT-R and Soar) on the one hand and on the evocation of actions with respect to given goals on the other hand (e.g a desire in the BDI-framework or a goal in Soar as depicted in [GPP+99]) on the other hand. These concepts are partly using methodologies that have been defined in psychology. Memory management and especially the realization of episodic memory is a good example for the exchange between psychological models and their technical implementation. The theory of Tulving [Tul83] and Baddeley [Bad97] have been used as the foundations for several realizations of artificial episodic memory, as described in [DGLV08]. The following sections describe the way from the technically formulated and psychoanalytically inspired model described in Chapter 3 to the realization of these concepts with respect to an implementation of a decision unit for an embodied autonomous agent (called ARSi09/Lang) situated in an artificial, simulated environment. Although the model is very different to already existing cognitive architectures because of the usage of psychoanalytical concepts only, similarities in the implementations will be outlined. These similarities start at the definition for the interfaces of the decision unit described in Section 4.1 but can also be found again in the extended logical reasoning core of the agent. A main task of this chapter is to distinguish between the areas where the defined model gives sufficient information for an implementation and where the model still needs either a more detailed, psychoanalytical specification or additional theory from other research areas.

4.1 The Embodied Agent as Implementation Platform

Before starting to implement a new decision unit ARSi09/Lang for an embodied, autonomous agent, the platform has to be specified that runs the decision unit. Several standards do exist for the communication between an executing platform and the contained decision unit. One such interface definition is *Player* that is applied especially in robot control environments together with the robot simulator called *Stage* ([GVH03] describes both terms). In this case, a clear separation between the robot's body that includes all available sensors and actuators and the decision unit is eligible because the decision unit is often run on an external computer. The communication between the robot and the computer that runs the decision unit is established using wireless or wired transmissions. This concept has one main advantage: Since the decision unit is totally decoupled from the underlying hardware and only depends on the used interfaces (which would be in this case defined in *Player*) the same decision unit can be run on a different platform (another robot or other environment) and vice versa the platform can be directed by different decision units, which allows significant comparison as well.

With respect to the example of *Player* and a realized robot-decision unit the development process for the decision unit is also decoupled from a certain hardware. The hardware layer lies below and the corresponding interfaces are enabling data exchange between different layers. However, before defining such an interface, the requirements to the containing environment have to be discussed. For the model as it is described in Chapter 3 and especially in the Section 3.3, it is mandatory to distinguish between the three different types of sensory input containing the homeostatic, bodily and environmental information. Therefore, the agent's body that contains the decision unit also has to provide the sensory data for homeostatic, bodily, and environmental processes that are generated by the corresponding available sensors. In the following paragraphs, the presumed information that is forming the content of the interface for the simulated, embodied agent is described. More detailed information of the available sensors and actuators that are used in the simulation with respect to the tasks of the agent is given in Chapter 5. In the following, a few examples are listed.

Homeostatic Information
Energy level, hormone level, body temperature, ...

Bodily Information
Body part positions, body part temperature, average current of motors, ...

Environmental Information
Visual, acoustics, tactile (bump, surface sensitivity), olfactory, ...

Additionally, the interface also has to pass and deliver action commands from the decision unit to the corresponding actuators or at least to the corresponding action command dispatcher. Typical control information for actuators and their actions are listed below.

Actuator Information
Two wheeled motion, tentacle (to hold an object), energy consumer, facial expression regulator.

The platform requirements to the underlying, simulated hardware[1] are therefore defined. The following implementation has been realized using the object oriented, structured, imperative programming language Java from Sun Microsystems[2]. Different open source multi agent simulation (MAS) environments (three selected MAS's have already been discussed in Section 2.3) as well as decision units for autonomous agents (discussed in Section 2.4) have already been implemented in Java. The reason for using Java to realize the decision unit is the implied advantages of an object oriented programming language and the broad usage of Java in the academic and open source sector, especially in multi agent based simulations.

To realize such an interface in an object oriented programming language, every instance of an agent also has to instantiate a decision unit that is a subclass of the base class for all implemented decision units. Figure 4.1 shows the main concept of the interface between the agent and the decision unit. On the left hand side, each information about the above described homeostatic, bodily and environmental processes are passed throughout the interface class `clsSensorData`.

This container class `clsSensorData` holds one list of internal (homeostatic and bodily) and one of external sensor data. The class `clsBaseDecisionUnit` therefore stores the incoming sensor data by the external call of the function `update()` and also implements the functionality that is necessary to communicate action commands back to the agent, using the interface `itfActionProcessor`. Each specialization of the base decision unit therefore gets the current sensoric data by accessing the contents of the field `moSensorData` and stores action commands by accessing the functionality of the field `moActionProcessor`. The exact content of the sensor- and actuator-information classes depend on the corresponding

---

[1] In fact the whole project including the agent and its environment is simulated. It is therefore only spoken metaphorically when calling these components hardware. However, the decision unit has been designed to be flexible enough to be processed on a real world robot. The only limitations are given by the processing power the actual implementation requires.

[2] The official homepage can be found at `http://java.sun.com/` (accessed on the 20th Aug. 2009)

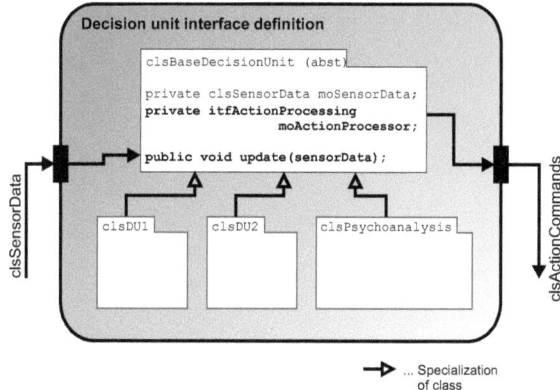

Figure 4.1: Diagram for the Interface to the Decision Unit ARSi09/Lang of the Autonomous Agent

sensor and actuator. No limitations are made here, except that each class that represents sensor data has to extend the base class clsDataBase that can be held by the containers of the interface class. The same procedure is valid for the action commands that have to implement the interface itfActionCommand.

The information first has to be symbolized outside according to the neuro-symbolization model described in Section 3.1.1, because only the transferred low level sensory data from the attached sensors is passed through the interface. These generated perceptual symbols can then be used as an input for the psychoanalytically inspired model and to generate corresponding thing presentations. However, currently no implementation of this model exists that can be used. Therefore, a first attempt of symbol generation is implemented as described in [RLD+07], [LBP+07] and [LBVD09] using predefined patterns called 'mental images' to match sensory information to semantically meaningful symbols.

A mental image is a kind of template that consists of a set of rules, defining the perception of specific types of symbols. These symbols can be very simple like the number of persons in a room or the temperature or humidity in a room or they can contain complex information like 'a meeting is taking place in the conference room'. Because of the generic way of the concept for defining image templates, the name and meaning of a symbol are abstracted in the further text as symbols s_1 to s_n. The perception module of such a system produces a constant stream of symbols. Every calculation step contains a subset (P) of the set of all possible symbols (S) including the elements s_1 to s_n, shown in Formula 4.1.

$$\begin{aligned}
S &= \{s_i \mid 1 \leq i \leq n \text{ and } i, n \in \mathbb{N}\} & \text{Possible Perceived Symbols} \\
P &= \{s_3, s_9, s_{17}, ..., s_m \mid m \leq n \text{ and } m \in \mathbb{N}\} \subseteq S & \text{Actually Perceived Symbols} \\
IT_1 &= \{w_3 \otimes s_3 \wedge w_{17} \otimes s_{17}\} & \text{Image Template} \\
W &= \{w_3, w_{17} \mid 0 \leq w \leq 1 \text{ and } w \in \mathbb{R}\} & \text{Weights of the Image Template}
\end{aligned} \quad (4.1)$$

Every existing definition of image templates (IT_1 is one example) must be compared with the currently perceived set of symbols (P). In the given example, the symbols s_3 and s_{17} must be perceived in order to detect the image template IT_1. Because these symbols are perceived (and therefore present in P), the image IT_1 is in the result set and includes the weighted match (w_3 and w_{17} are the weight factors) of the perceived symbols. The used operator '$\otimes$' returns either the corresponding weight or a weight of '0' when the symbol was not perceived. To calculate the total weight, the elements can be connected with a logical and '$\wedge$' or or '$\vee$' operator. To computationally define the content of one image template, a tree structure was created that holds the information of both, the necessary symbols and their weights within each image template. Figure 4.2 shows the three basic elements of this tree: image element (iE), image node (iN) and image leaf (iL).

Name	Symbol	Base
iE	○	-
iN	◆	iE
iL	★	iE

Figure 4.2: Basic Elements in the Image Template Definition

As a base class (labeled as *Base*) of all elements within the tree, the image element holds the following data. Any element contains a name and optional a description of the specific use for debugging and visualization. Further, any element – no matter if node or leaf – stores the information whether this element is optional or mandatory. Additionally to this information, the image node is equipped with the information about its child nodes. These can be further sub nodes as well as image leaves. It is also equipped with the Boolean composition (AND or OR) between these sub elements and a negation flag that concerns all sub elements.

An image leaf contains the specific information rather than the logical compositions of the nodes. It defines the type of the symbol that becomes part of the image template detection and the type of the compare-operator (==, ! =, <, <=, >, >=) used in the underlying compare algorithm. This value depends on the kind of symbol generated from the corresponding sensors, which can be for example an integer value (counter, temperature, ...) or a fuzzified value (freezing, cold, warm, hot, boiling in case of temperature), which is mapped to an enumeration.

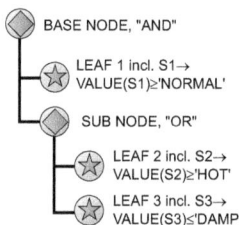

Figure 4.3: Example for a Generic Image Template Definition Accomplished in a Tree Structure

In Figure 4.3 an example is given for a generic image template definition visualized in a tree structure. The used symbols are defined in Figure 4.2. Described from bottom to the top, in this image template, either the value of symbol S_2 has to be equal or higher than 'HOT' (as a symbolic output for e.g. a temperature sensor - for what ever that means semantically) OR the value of symbol S_3 has to be equal or lower than 'DAMP' (as a symbolic output for e.g. a humidity sensor). With this lower part of the illustrated tree, the node of the image template is completely defined and matches, if the perceived data is within the defined range of values. The second node of the image template is matching, if the value of symbol S_1 equals or is greater than 'NORMAL'. The image template only matches fully, when both conditions – leaf 1 as well as the sub-node – are matching. This is defined by the logical operator 'AND' in the base node.

After comparison of the predefined image template with the actual perceived symbols, a value from zero to one must be generated that describes the quality of the match. To calculate this quality, a simple algorithm has been implemented. First, the number of elements within a node, containing the operator 'AND' are counted and summed up with the nodes containing an OR-operator. Applying this algorithm recursively through all branches of the tree, the total weight of the tree is calculated, independently of a match. In the example tree of Figure 4.3, the total weight is two - one for leaf 1 and one for leaf 2 or 3 or for both of them. In the next step, the same algorithm counts only leaves, which have a valid condition match. The number of matching conditions divided by the total weight of the tree gives the quality of the match. Referring again to the example depicted in Figure 3, the match would be 1.0 if leaf 1 and one or both of leaf 2 and 3 matches, 0.5 if leaf 1 but neither leaf 2 nor 3 are matching or only leaf 2 or 3 are matching. The match would be 0 if none of the leaf rules meet the conditions. Table 4.1 shows these possibilities including the full and the zero matches.

Match	L1	L2	L3
1.0	X	X	X
1.0	X	X	-
1.0	X	-	X
0.5	X	-	-
0.5	-	X	X
0.5	-	-	X
0.0	-	-	-

Table 4.1: Possibilities of matches in the example image template

In the current implementation, every element has the same weight. In a future implementation, an image element can be extended by a weight that denotes the importance within the rule tree. The algorithm that calculates the match of the image has to be slightly adapted to the given weight in each node in this case. Dornes describes the human process of perception in [Dor04, p. 64 ff], of comparing the current perception to a set of templates that have been previously learned or, in this technical realization, predefined. By applying the concept of image template recognition, a higher semantic level of symbolization is reached.

To put the described interface and generation into the big picture of the embedded decision unit ARSi09/Lang of the agent, the basic information flow of a decision unit, using the notation described in [JW06] can be applied: Through the interface that delivers data to the agent, the agent can access the *perceptual input system* that provides primitive representation of the agent's environment or situation. With this data, the agent has to build up *beliefs* that are representing its individual and most likely incomplete world model. The world model that may also include the bodily state of the agent together with predefined urges are evoking so called *desires* (in the notation of this work, they are equivalent to the used term *wishes*) that are the basis for further actions. The fulfillment of the most urgent desire is then transformed into the *active goal* that has to be reached. A reasoning unit is then responsible for selecting feasible sub-plans and assembling a *plan* that leads to the achievement of the goal. The generated plan includes *actions* that are relevant to its active goals and have to be finally executed by activating the *output systems*. These actions can be seen as the initiative activity to the environment.

The described information flow of [JW06] makes no claim to be complete, but it is applicable to any decision unit of an autonomous agent. This information flow, shown on the

Implementation in Embodied Agents

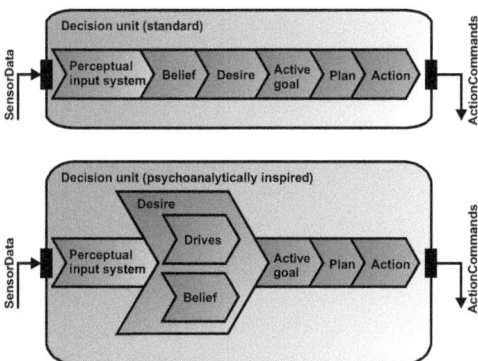

Figure 4.4: Basic Information Flow of the Decision Unit of an Autonomous Agent

top of Figure 4.4 also takes place between the above described input- and output interface, where the generation of perceptual symbols can already be seen as a part of the perceptual input system. However, in the psychoanalytically inspired model for the decision also the beliefs are already influenced by desires, which is shown in the bottom part of Figure 4.4. Again, the notation of Jones was used to emphasize on the principle structure. The psychoanalytical terminology for a desire would be the wish.

With these prerequisites, the introduced model for a decision unit can be provided with the necessary, symbolized data and has also the possibility to react in a given environment with the use of several actuators. The following sections describes the implementation of the core model using the given implementation platform as a basis.

4.2 Transforming Metapsychology to Implementation

The core of the implementation of ARSi09/Lang consists of the underlying implementation fractions that are permanently used in most of the functional modules described in Chapter 3. The complexity of the implementation resulting from these different functionalities can be reduced, by identifying common and therefore reusable data structures and concepts. In the following sections, a realization for the four most common concepts regarding information representation, rule bases, and logical reasoning is introduced.

4.2.1 Utilized Data Structures

The psychic representation of perceived information is, according to Section 3.1.3, held by the metapsychological constructs of affects, thing presentations, and word presentations. In a first step, the content of created perceptual symbols as described in the last chapter have to be mapped to the corresponding thing presentations and attached affects or word presentations. This process applies the content to the empty frame of the metapsychological frames. Figure 4.5 shows the class diagram of the data structures within the ARSi09/Lang implementation. The different arrows are using the UML-notation[3] for class diagrams specified in [UML09a, p. 129 ff] and summarized in Appendix .

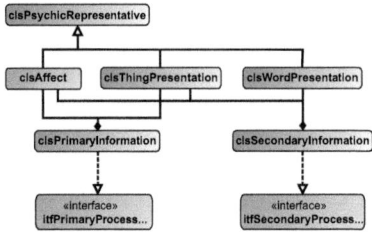

Figure 4.5: Defined Classes for Data Structures and their Interrelationship

To be able to handle each type of the three psychic representatives (depicted in the second line of the diagram), each of them are extending the super-class `clsPsychicRepresentative`. However, according to the introduced model in Section 3.2 the thing presentation is combined at the very beginning of the functional sequence with the corresponding affect. The combination between these two representatives is the actual processed data structure. The `clsPrimaryInformation` is designed to hold both psychic representatives, the affect as well as the thing presentation. This class has to implement the interfaces for primary process functionality, and each instance[4] can be accessed, associated, organized, and processed by functionality defined in the primary process. The different interfaces will be described in the next Section 4.2.2. The `clsSecondaryInformation` contains the word presentation and the `clsPrimaryInformation`, which itself contains the affect and the thing presentation. It is the main information structure, used in the functional models

---

[3]The Unified Modeling Language (UML) as specified in [UML09a] is a standardized general-purpose modeling language for software engineering. The standard is available on http://www.omg.org/spec/UML/2.2/ (accessed on 12.2009), the web-site of the corresponding consortium 'Object Management Group (OMG).

[4]To avoid a multiple meaning of psychoanalytical and technical terms, the term 'instance' indicates an instantiation of a class. This instance must not be confused with the term 'psychic instance', which refers to either the Id, Ego, or Super-Ego.

within the area of secondary process between Level 2 and Level 3 as depicted in Figure 3.14. The clsSecondaryInformation also has to implement the defined functionality of accessing, associating, organizing, and processing because it implements the interface of the secondary process. The functionality of this interface differs according to the specification given in Section 3.1.3 from the implementation of the primary process in ARSi09/Lang. The introduced design of class inheritance forces the developer of new primary or secondary information to provide the functionality required by either the primary or secondary process. This standardized concept is further used in the entire ARSi09/Lang implementation of the functional model by each functional unit depending on its actual location.

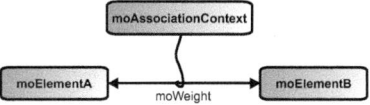

Figure 4.6: Association Between Psychic Representatives

Although the creation of the knowledge-base of the agent is not the main topic of this work, it is essential to realize connections between related psychic representatives or memories. As mentioned in the introduction of this chapter, several theories of storing and retrieving already experienced information exist where the association between two or more information elements play a central role. To be able to define such relations, a weighted, contextual relation element was designed, which does not claim a psychoanalytical background at all. It connects, and therefore contains, two instances of psychic representatives having the same type. It can connect a thing presentation with one or several other thing presentations or it can connect a word presentation with one or several other word presentations. In addition to the simple information of being connected, the connection can be weighted. Processes that are searching for related psychic representatives can use the weight to distinguish between a tight or loose connection. With this feature, it is possible to create a weighted graph and perform a search of the four closest related objects. As the relation depends on the context of the current situation, the association allows the storage of a third psychic representation that contains this context. This additional attribute for the association can be used for the above mentioned search algorithm to reduce the search result for associated psychic representatives. Only those that fit into the current context are considered at the search. This oversimplified functionality of an association between psychic representatives is used within the further implementation of ARSi09/Lang and is not psychoanalytically inspired. However, the next section describes the process of associating information based upon psychoanalytically concepts and uses the described implementation structure for these associations.

4.2.2 The Association Framework Linking Information

Within ARSi09/Lang psychic representatives in the form of thing and word presentations attached to a corresponding affect are represented as `clsPrimaryInformation` and `clsSecondaryInformation`. Both classes have to implement the assigned interfaces of the primary or secondary process functionality as depicted in Figure 4.5. The interface named `itfPrimaryProcess...` and `itfPrimaryProcess...` denote that there are several interfaces starting with the same prefix. The following sections describe the interfaces, their required function headers and their corresponding implementation details.

Although the implemented functionality differs between primary and secondary process, the defined interfaces are the same, namely:

- itf[Primary|Secondary]ProcessComparable
- itf[Primary|Secondary]ProcessComparableSpecific
- itf[Primary|Secondary]ProcessAssociation
- itf[Primary|Secondary]ProcessStorage
- itf[Primary|Secondary]ProcessRetrieval

Where [Primary|Secondary] stands for either primary or secondary. Starting with the interfaces for primary processes, a comparison whether two thing presentations can be marked as identical or not is the key functionality in organizing information. Either two clsPrimaryInformation can be compared to each other or the contained thing presentation is compared to a specific thing presentation. The latter does not consider the attached affect for the comparison. The comparison of the thing presentation follows the concept, described in Section 3.1.3: The implemented compare operator detects a correlation as soon as one attribute of the thing presentation is identical. For example two different objects that are both red would be considered as identical in a primary process organization.

The compare operator only searches for similarities of two thing presentations by iterating and comparing each of the attributes and detects an identity of the objects as soon as one attribute is identical. The compare operator is the basis for associating primary information. As similarity is one criteria, creation is another. Here the same moment of the creation of two psychic representatives forms the association. Two thing presentations that are always appearing together are closer related than two thing presentations that are never appearing together in the information stream of the perception. Thing presentations appearing in the same context are also closely related with each other.

Finally, the interface for storage provides the functionality of holding data that has to be accessed on a later point in time. It ensures the implementation of the storing method that takes a primary information as a parameter and calls automatically the association interface to reorganize the weighted graph of information. The retrieval interface provides the functionality for accessing the stored data and can be seen as the front end of the memory trace net as described in Section 3.1.3.

The interfaces of secondary processes are the same as the primary process interfaces but require a different implementation since the main data type is changed from the class clsPrimaryInformation to the clsSecondaryInformation. The main difference between the two types of information is the compare operator. It logically works as a real compare operator used in many programming languages including *Java*. First of all, the information object described by the word presentation included in the secondary information has to be of the same type. This means that two word presentations first of all have to have the same underlying concept. Otherwise, the compare operator cannot be applied. To use a physical example, an intensity of electric current can never be compared to an intensity of the electrical voltage. In the primary process, this would be possible, because both are entities e.g. for the electric potential energy. A realization in *Java* is easily possible because the base classes of an instance can be easily determined. When both objects have the same super-classes, the compare operator has to compare the content of each relevant attribute. When every attribute is the same, the operator signals a congruency, which is in fact not just a similarity. With these concepts of associating information the following section describes the mechanisms that are necessary to realize a search and filtering mechanism.

4.2.3 Implementing Rules, Searching, and Filtering Mechanisms

In the described framework of Chapter 3, modules are defined that have the functionality of a knowledge-base. They contain valid rules for different situations and provide an additional search functionality. A part of the Super-Ego functionality uses exactly this methodology. According to the current context, valid Super-Ego rules have to be retrieved. These rules are influencing search- and filtering mechanisms of other functional modules. In the model, the functionality of repression of the defense mechanisms is for example influenced by these rules. This circumstance makes it necessary, to provide a rule-base that is able to select a set of rules according to an input set of rules. For a detailed description, again the interaction between the functional modules *Super-Ego* and *Defense mechanisms* will be discussed. Both modules are supplied with information about the current situation and implicitly also the current context. According to the current situation, the Super-Ego has to reduce the set of stored social rules to a subset of rules that are only relevant in coherence to the actual situation, the individual is in. The above described context aware association between psychic representatives can be used to first filter the contents according to the relevant context. This reduced subset of rules is then forwarded to the defense mechanisms, where it is determined whether perceived information is being allowed to get to the secondary process or has to be split or repressed. Therefore, each Super-Ego rule has to be applied to the incoming psychic representatives. In the case of a matching Super-Ego rule, the combination of the psychic representative and the applied rule have to search for a corresponding rule that defines the defense action. A simple rule for a defense action would be:

Psychic Representative **AND** Super-Ego Rule of Denial **LEADS TO** Action(Repress Psychic Representative)

For the implementation of such rule bases within thing and word presentation meshes (according to [ZLM09]), different technical concepts can be used. The most simple implementation is a plain list of rules. In this approach, each psychic representative has to be compared to all defined rules as depicted left hand in Figure 4.7.

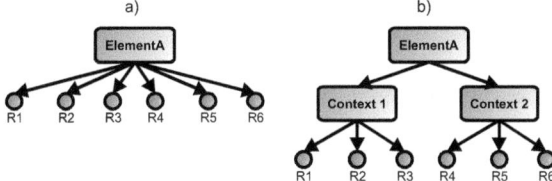

Figure 4.7: Rule Trees for the Different Approaches a) Breadth First Search b) Informed Search

With the use of the information about the current context, it is possible to add an intermediate layer into the rule tree and reduce the search space to the rules that are associated with the current context. The rules therefore are assigned to one or more defined context labels that are the first search criteria in the rule tree. A further possibility to build and organize knowledge-bases is the usage of the RETE algorithm, which is for example used in the the open source rule engines Jess[5] or the Jadex Rule Engine as part of the Jadex BDI Agent System or Soar (the latter two have been described in Section 2.4). Rete (described in closer detail in [For82] and [Doo95]) is an efficient mechanism for solving the difficult 'many-to-many matching problem' that is usually occurring when defining and accessing a rule base. The Rete algorithm supports forward chaining and recent developments also include backward chaining and other optimizations. For a higher performance of the search the second possibility for the matching algorithm has been implemented in ARSi09/Lang using the context as a label for several rules.

---

[5]http://herzberg.ca.sandia.gov/jess/ - accessed 28th August 2009.

4.2.4 Employed Concepts and Implementation of Causal Planning

One approach to create a plan that is leading from a current situation of the agent to a desired goal is to predefine subgoals in a knowledge-base and use a causal reasoning algorithm like the data driven method 'forward chaining' or the goal driven method 'backward chaining' to create a complete plan. Jadex (described in Section 2.4) uses a means-ends reasoning algorithm [Woo00, p. 21ff] that searches for the sub-plan (including actions that are changing the environment) that brings the system as close as possible to the goal. In the next planning step the means of the system are updated, which are representing the world model including the prediction of the changes caused by the planned action. With the new world model, the algorithm recursively repeats the search for new sub-plans until the goal can be reached.

However, within this work it is assumed that the system already knows any possible plan to reach any generated goal from any position. Neither learning nor planning are considered because the generation and selection of a wish that triggers the planning algorithms are the focus of this work. Thus, the possible actions, scenarios, and goals had to be limited in the simulated environment to avoid a huge and probably incomplete database of plans that define the best possible actions to reach a defined goal. The planning has been designed in two phases: First, the current scenario has to be recognized in a way that the system has to categorize the current beliefs and the current wishes. Second, a corresponding plan has to be selected that provides the actions that are leading from the current situation to the satisfaction of the wish, which is actually the goal.

The described concept of Section 4.1 only deals with a single moment in time. Every image template and the resulting match do not consider changes during time. By adding the value of time, a new step in the hierarchy is made, containing the perceived data in the past. A scenario is defined as a sequence in time of several recognized images that are perceived. By looking at common sequence diagrams, it has been decided to use the concept of state charts to represent such scenarios. From the beginning to the end of a scenario recognition process, several circumstances may occur. For instance, there may be more than one possibility of events that have to be perceived by the image template recognition. Different paths have to be covered within the definition of a scenario process. It is necessary to make global abort conditions possible, either caused by a timeout or another event that triggers the abortion of the scenario recognition and resets it. Figure 4.8 shows the four basic elements of a scenario definition and their purpose: starting scenario state (SCB), ending scenario state (SCE), scenario state (SC) and scenario transition (ST).

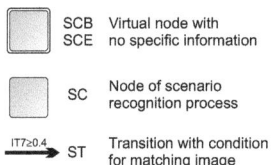

Figure 4.8: Basic Elements of Scenario Definition

The start and end states only have a virtual meaning in the system. All scenario recognition processes are initially set to the begin state, waiting for the first transition condition. As the end state is reached, the scenario recognition process reaches the end of its lifetime and does not include any further information. The scenario states between the start and end state are indicating the process of the scenario recognition defined by their position. Each scenario state (except of the end state) holds a list of transitions. These transitions specify the condition to switch to the next state. The match of a selected image template must meet the specified condition. For the example of the transition condition shown in Figure 4.8 the image template number 7 must have a perceived match higher than 40 percent. Figure 4.9 shows a generic but complete scenario template definition. In this case, the scenario recognition process will be triggered when the image template (IT) number 1 is perceived with a match of at least 60 percent. The current state is set to the state S1. This state contains two different transitions. The first transition leads to state S2 as soon as IT 2 is perceived with a match of hundred percent. The second transition would lead to the state S3 when IT 3 is perceived with at least 80 percent. With a match of at least 70 percent, IT 4 closes the path and the recognition process gets into the state S2. The final condition for a complete scenario recognition is met when IT 5 is perceived with a match of at least 50 percent.

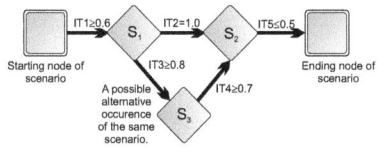

Figure 4.9: Generic Scenario Template Definition

The definition of both, the image templates and the scenario templates, have to be defined in an XML structured file[6], especially designed for the image data and represent one part of

---

[6]XML stands for Extensible Markup Language.

the knowledge of the system. Images or scenarios that are not defined in this database will not be recognized. Based upon a direct mapping between a recognized scenario including an implied wish and the best plan that leads to a goal, a plan is executed. The implementation of the plan in ARSi09/Lang uses the described process for scenario recognition but extends it with the possibility to define actions in addition to purely passive perceptions. One phase or sub-goal of a plan is finished if all defined actions are successfully executed and necessary information is perceived that are the preconditions for the next sub-plan.

The more complex the environment, the body, the homeostasis, and the possibilities of actions are, the more numerous are the necessary plans that may or may not lead to a goal. In a future implementation, a more complex and symbol based reasoning unit has to be used to define and create causal plans on demand, as it will be described in Chapter 7. Otherwise, the manual definition would lead to gaps in the problem space. However, the above described implementations will be used in multiple functional modules of ARSi09/Lang that will be described in the following chapter.

4.2.5 Global Class Framework, Synchronization Aspects and Sequencing

The implemented model is designated to run as the reasoning unit of an autonomous agent. It therefore has to be provided with the sensoric values of the agent in the form of neuro-symbols as described in Section 3.1.1 and also needs the possibility of controlling the agent's actuators. The implementation of ARSi09/Lang is designed to run in a time discrete simulation environment. For the model this means that the whole process beginning from the first functional block that buffers the current sensory input data to the output that is connected to the controlled actuators has to be run in each time step. Within the simulation environment, a specific routine (described in detail in Chapter 5) is responsible for calling the decision unit of each agent in every simulation step. Figure 4.10 exemplifies the oversimplified information flow of the decision unit with the use of the main modules. First of all, the content of the box is the actual functional chain that has to be executed within each simulation step. The `while(1)` at the top of the box is the indicator of the polling mechanism provided by the simulation environment.

On the left hand side, the interface to the sensory symbol generator as described in Section 4.1 has to be provided with an input to the contained functional modules (schematically named A to D). During the single simulation step it has to be ensured that the processed values of the incoming sensor data are not changing hence an input buffer has to be

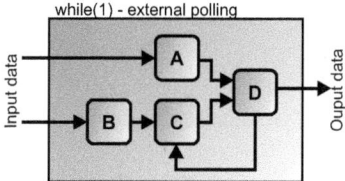

Figure 4.10: Functional Sequence of the Information Flow

used. However, the multi-agent simulator that halts the simulation of the environment (and therefore prevents changes on the input side) during the reasoning processes of the agents. This also assures that each agent is provided with the same information about the environment without an interference of previously executed reasoning processes of other agents. Focusing on the reasoning unit of a single agent and with respect to Figure 4.10, the input data is accessible for the functional modules A and B. A command processor now ensures the execution of the correct order of the functional flow. Since module D needs an input from both paths – A as well as C followed by B – the command processor routine executes the functional modules in the following order: A - B - C - D. Because there is no dependency of within the two paths, a valid order would also be B - C - A - D. The output information of A and C is the input information for module D that is executed after the described two paths. Its output is the final output of the oversimplified, modular reasoning unit and as described above and consists of motor-action commands.

Module D also shows a typical problem that can occur during the information flow: a feedback loop. In this example, the output of module D is fed back as an input for module C. Such loops can cause problems in the functionality, because of possible infinite loops of calling functions (e.g. when method X calls method Y that is again calling method X). Such infinite loops are resulting (depending on the programming language) e.g. in an overflow of a stack that holds the function calls. To avoid this problem, each function is called by the command processor only once per simulation step. In the case of the information feedback between module D to C this means that module C that is called the next time in the next simulation step, where new sensory data has to be processed, can process and access the output of module D only in the next simulation step. The information is stored within an input buffer to guarantee the access to the produced information of module D. The two described mechanisms (the command processor that calls the functional modules in the correct order and the buffer functionality that handles feedback information) are guaranteeing a synchronized information flow. Two communication partners (sender and receiver) in the model are synchronized if they are in the same context of the protocol that handles the communication. Compared to an asynchronous model, the sequential, synchronized call hierarchy implies the problem that if one functional module cannot finish its calculation (this can be caused by a recursive call or a deadlock), it would stop the complete system. The implementation of each module has to be free of such deadlocks.

A time delay of an information that influences the behavior of the corresponding feedback-influenced function exist and has always the value of one simulation step. Within a simulation, the impact of such a delay can be reduced by decreasing the time between two reasoning cycles to a minimum. For the simulation time it is a simple task, because the simulation process that changes the environment can be easily paused by not processing the changes. In a real world environment, the advantages of this approach would depend on the performance of the reasoning process of an agent. Because the system is designed to run in a virtual, simulated environment, these demands can be met.

The next chapters describe the implementation of the main functional modules of ARSi09/Lang according to Figure 3.14. Within the implementation, the information flow is controlled by a command processor that follows the above described concepts.

4.3 Realization of the Primary Process Functionality

According to Figure 3.14, the primary process includes the functional modules between Level 1 and Level 2. The following sections describe a possible ARSi09/Lang-implementation for the core functionalities in the primary process with respect to the psychoanalytically inspired model described in Chapter 3. The three main modules discussed here are the *Drive and perception handler*, the *Management of repressed content* and the *Defense mechanisms* and focus on their interactions to the other modules.

4.3.1 Drive and Perception Handling

Starting at the sensed, homeostatic tensions, the module *Drive Handling* has to transform information about organic processes regarding the homeostasis into information that is the basis of further, psychic processes. By using the matching algorithm, described in Section 4.1, predefined constellations of homeostatic values (the drive sources) can be summarized and identified as one or more drives. Depending on the deviation of the different homeostatic values, the total quantity of the drive can be determined. Each drive has to be associated with the aim of the drive (this information includes specific actions that are capable to potentially reduce the internal tension [LP73, p. 21]) and the object of the drive (this information includes the object that is able to tentatively reduce the tension). The calculated quantity of the drive is also transferred to the affect generator, which is, according to Figure 3.14 the next functional unit in the information flow.

The module *Perception Handling* uses the same matching algorithm to create thing presentations out of the sensory data from the environment. However, compared to the generation of drives, additional functionality has to be implemented. One reason is that in contrast to the drives, the pure external perception does not have any meaning to the individual. The drive-content 'eating' for example already has a subjective meaning to the individual, the perception of an apple in the form of a thing presentation does not. Therefore, perceived thing presentations that are including information of the environment or the body (which must not be confused with the homeostatic values, which are actually responsible for the drive generation as described above) first have to be associated with further, individual information.

The first step in individualizing external perceived information in the form of thing presentations is to assign corresponding categories of drive contents to the environmental thing presentations and associate them with already repressed content. This mechanism is described in the next Section 4.3.2. Second, the module *Management of memory traces* stores the produced information and updates the weights of already existing associations according to the described association concept in Section 4.2.2. The third functional unit is the *Subjective perception* that attaches subjective associations to the thing presentation. This association attaches on the one hand semantically closely related thing presentations (according to the current context that will be discussed in more detail in Section 4.4) but on the other hand also missing parts of the perception that are usually appearing at the same time. The implementation uses the already described framework for association and performs a breadth-first search in the weighted tree of associations with the actual perception as the root of the search. Since the information has not been transformed into secondary process organization, the association is done using the primary process organization as described in Section 4.2.2. The search is finished, when there are no associations left on the reached depth that have a weight higher than a certain threshold. Figure 4.11 shows the weighted graph of the search space for associated thing presentations.

The thing presentation TP_A represents the currently perceived information and therefore the root of the search. The edges of the graph are labeled with their weight and context ($W_{1...4}$, $C_{x,y}$). The actual weight, shown in Equation 4.2 for the search algorithm is the product of the association's weight (W_{assoc}) and the matching of the stored context with

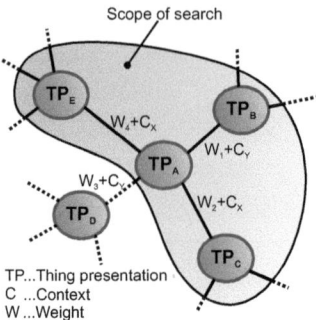

Figure 4.11: Breadth First Search of Associated Thing Presentations and the Scope Within the Threshold of a Given Weight (=1/Cost)

current context (Match(Context of association, Current context)).

$$W_{act} = W_{assoc} * Match(C_{assoc}, C_{curr}) \quad \text{Actual Weight for Search} \quad (4.2)$$

In the implementation of ARSi09/Lang, the algorithm searches for those associations that have a certain context-entry and retrieves a list of thing presentations that are within the scope of the search (Figure 4.11 shows the scope of the search that includes the result-set of associated thing presentations). The multiplication of the associations weight with the current context match emphasizes the importance of associations that are in the same context, but may also return thing presentations in the result set that are associated with a very high value of the association's weight although the are not in the same context. This can also be seen as a preliminary error correction, if parts of the perception are missing that are usually appears together. The output of the module *Perception Handling* is a weighted list of recognized thing presentations that are representing the current information from the perception. Each thing presentation optionally includes an association with another thing presentation and/or an affect attached from the *Management of repressed content* and a weighted list of associations to related thing presentations and affects from the *Subjective perception*. This result set is transferred to the module *Affect generation*.

The *Affect generation* finally converts the quantity of the drive that is representing the tension of the corresponding organ or drawback of homeostatic values to an affect. This affect is associated to the thing presentation, which is representing the quality of the drive. In the implementation, a new class `clsAffect` is created that holds the value of the described tension. In the case of environmental perception, the corresponding affects of the perceived thing presentations are results of the subjective associations that are describing the subjective meaning of the thing presentation to the individual. The consumption of an apple for example satisfies the drive related to the content to eat. Thus, every object that can have a certain impact on occurring drives needs to be associated with a `clsPrimaryInformation`. It is representing the drive that can be satisfied including its quality in the form of a thing presentation and its quantity in the form of an affect. The association is already made in the module *Subjective perception*. Within the *affect generation*, these primary information are identified and organized within an additional list. Therefore, the output values of the modules *Drive handler* and *Perception handler* are supplemented with a further list that holds the information of the corresponding affects.

4.3.2 Primary Decision and Repressed Contents

The *Primary decision* module is consisting of the two modules *Defense mechanisms for drive content* and *for perception*. The module is divided into two sub-functionalities because they work with different information. However, the basic functional mechanisms that are repressing or filtering the information that becomes transferred into secondary process information are the same for both modules. Both modules have to decide, whether a psychic representative of drives or perceptions can pass – and therefore finally become converted into secondary process information – or not. In the latter case, the content can be repressed and forwarded to the module *Management of repressed content*, where the deposited content is influencing future perceptions or divided into its single components to repress either the thing presentation or affect.

In order to select the psychic representatives that have to be examined by the defense mechanism, knowledge about the reality and social rules from the Super-Ego have to be considered. The described implementation realized in ARSi09/Lang uses an oversimplified concept for these types of rules. The drive contents can be categorized into four categories that are derived from the sexual drive. They can be ascribed to the human's early development phases: oral drive contents, anal drive contents, phallic drive contents and genital drive contents as described in Section 3.1.3 in more detail. According to the current situation that includes the current context, the *Knowledge about Reality (primary process)* and the *S.E. Primary* of the *Super-Ego* are delivering recommendations to repress contents that can be assigned to a specific type of drive content. First of all, both modules have to have access to the current situation. This is provided through the net of memory traces that holds this information. Second, the categories that are not allowed (in terms of Super-Ego rules) or simply not possible (in terms of the reality knowledge) in a situation have to be predefined within the basic knowledge of the agent. The restrictions are weighted and multiple entries (up to all four categories) are possible. These 'forbidden' categories are the output of the implementation of the two modules. They are representing the filtering criterion of the defense mechanisms. Drives or perceptions are repressed if the drive contents match with one of the prohibited contents.

```
public void defenseMechanism
        ( clsPsychicRepresentative poPsyRep, clsScenario poScen )
{
    if( checkMatching( moRealityKnowledge.getProhibits(poScen), poPsyRep ) )
    {
        repress(poPsyRep);
    }
    if( checkMatching( moSuperEgo.getProhibits(poScen), poPsyRep ) )
    {
        repress(poPsyRep);
    }
}
```

Listing 4.1: Pseudo-Code of Defense Mechanism

Within the implementation, a certain threshold has to be exceeded. The pseudo-code shown in Listing 4.1 depicts the basic idea behind the implementation in ARSi09/Lang. The function `defenseMechanism()` requires two parameters. The former represents the data that has to be evaluated and the latter represents the current situation. First, the function checks if there are forbidden drive contents in the module *Knowledge about reality (primary process)* and compares if there is a coverage within the current psychic representative that represents the perceived data. In a positive case, the psychic representative is repressed. The same is verified with the prohibitive rules from the *Super-Ego*. The ordering of the execution of both modules is irrelevant due to the disjunction of the construct: A psychic representative is repressed if either the Knowledge about Reality or the Super-Ego or both are providing a matching prohibition.

After the description of the implementation of the defense mechanism, the module *Management of repressed* will be described. Figure 4.12 shows this module, which has to cope with several different requirements. To distinguish clearly between the different functionalities, three main modules are defined as depicted in Figure 4.12.

The first functional unit has to receive the psychic representatives (containing a thing

Implementation in Embodied Agents

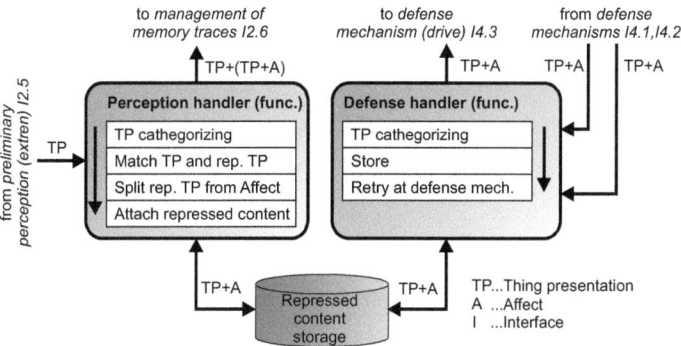

Figure 4.12: Implementation Units of the Management of Repressed Content

presentation and an affect) that are repressed by the *Defense mechanisms* and categorizes this data according to the drive content (oral, anal, phallic or genital). This categorization is predefined within the implementation, so each psychic representation has to be assigned to at least one of this categories. The already repressed content has to be sent again to the *Defense mechanisms* to retry if the content can pass the defense caused by a change of the situation. The repressed and categorized content has to be stored to be accessible in the next simulation step. The storage functionality of categorized, psychic content can be seen as the second functional unit. The third functional unit takes current thing presentations from the body and the environment and categorizes their content also according to the drive content. The categorized sensory thing presentations are then matched with the already stored repressed contents with respect to the same category. In the case of a match, the repressed content is attached to the incoming thing presentation. At this point, the matching and therefore selected, repressed content consisting of an affect and a thing presentation can optionally be split and only one part (the affect or the thing presentation) can optionally be attached to the incoming thing presentation. The exact mechanisms and criteria of splitting these contents are currently not defined within the project group and were therefore not defined in Section 3.2.1 and are not be considered within the implementation in ARSi09/Lang. Thus, the output of the model is a list of thing presentations that are connected to repressed contents of the same drive content category. This attached content is influencing the further functional mechanisms up to the defense mechanisms, whether they are successfully passing the defense mechanisms in a new iteration or not.

In the final functional module of the primary process, the *Primary to Secondary Interface*,

Implementation in Embodied Agents

each psychic representative in the form of a thing presentation and affect that is held by the class `clsPrimaryInformation` needs to be transferred to a class `clsSecondaryInformation` that is additionally holding the corresponding word presentation. Within ARSi09/Lang, the corresponding word presentations are predefined within the knowledge-base of the primary to secondary interface. Therefore, the module creates a new instance of the class `clsWordPresentation` and initiates its content with the information that is retrieved by a predefined list of associations between thing- and word presentations – an ordinary one-to-one matching. In the next step, the module creates a new instance of the class `clsSecondaryInformation` and assigns the affect, thing presentation, and word presentation to the corresponding attributes of the instance. With this new structure, the operations of the secondary process, including the associations between word presentations that differ from the primary process, becomes possible.

4.4 Realization of the Secondary Process Functionality

The reduced information of perceptual thing presentations are representing drives or perceived environmental objects. They are associated to related thing presentations. This set of information is the basis for further, secondary process functionalities. *Perceptual preprocessing* and *Deliberation* can be seen as the main functional units in the range of the secondary process. Their specific functionalities and interaction with additional units within ARSi09/Lang will be discussed in the following sub-sections.

4.4.1 Perceptual Preprocessing

Similar to the *Perception handler* in the primary process, the module *Perceptual preprocessing* has to attach additional information to the incoming data that is necessary for further processing. This incoming information contains instances of the class `clsSecondaryInformation` with its main attribute for the secondary process: the word presentation. Previously associated information using primary process organization that is following the pleasure principle is now achieving a different meaning. Not only with respect to the current situation (as it has been described in Section 3.2.3 in the module *Subjective perception*) but also with respect to the current wish of satisfying a certain need, the perceived homeostatic, bodily, and environmental information is re-evaluated. Section 4.4.2 is describing the meaning and the generation of the wish in more detail. In this additional evaluation, information that is closely related to the current context and to the current wish is higher prioritized than information that is neither context- nor wish related. Within ARSi09/Lang, the same mechanism as described in Section 4.3.1 is used though, a different data basis results in different associations: the association between word presentations in a secondary process organization. The scope of the search as depicted in Figure 4.11 that is representing the result set of the subjective perception for a certain thing presentation is not the same result set as it is in a search for the corresponding word presentation in the secondary process. Logical associations like negations, disjunctions or conjunctions can be embedded in the associated word presentations. With these possibilities, additionally knowledge concerning confinements of the reality is attached to the incoming word presentations by the module *Reality check (conscious)*. The information about permitted drive satisfactions and inflicted demands emerging through the environment and the current situation are organized in the form of rules. In the case of the discussed implementation, these rules are reduced to weighted and proposed action tendencies from the range of minus one to plus one. The limit *plus one* stands for a possible and acceptable action tendency whereas *minus one* stands for a totally impossible action tendency within the current situation.

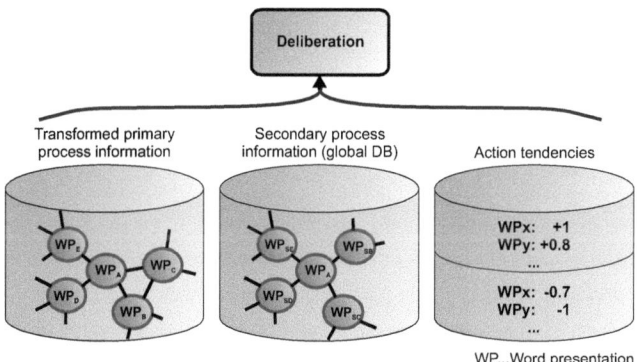

Figure 4.13: Output Data of the Functional Unit *Perceptual Preprocessing*

Figure 4.13 shows the databases that are generated by the *Perceptual preprocessing* and forwarded to the *Deliberation module*. The first database contains the search result of the module *Subjective perception* where the thing presentations have been converted to word presentations and become processable within the structure of the secondary process. The module is labeled as *Transformed primary process information* because the associated data has its origin in the primary process but has been converted to the secondary process in the module *Primary to Secondary Process Interface*. The second database shown in Figure 4.13 is labeled *Secondary process information* and represents the result set of word presentations that are closely related to the perceived word presentations. The *Deliberation module* can access associations via the globally available database of memory traces, represented in the module *Management of memory traces*. It has to be stressed that the associated word presentations of the secondary process information (WP_{SB} to WP_{SE}) are not the same as the associated word presentations of the primary process information (WP_B to WP_E), due to the different compare operator that was used for the association algorithm. The third database consists of a weighted list of action tendencies in the form of word presentations that are representing either recommendations or prohibitions. They have their origin in the check regarding violations of social rules or rules of the reality. These three databases are forwarded to the next functional block, the *Deliberation* that is described in the following sub chapter. With the perceptual preprocessing, the information again is filtered with the functionality of the focus of attention but gets also more semantic meaning with the additional information about action tendencies.

4.4.2 Deliberation - Generating the Desire to Plan

Human deliberation is permanently influenced by processes that are never entirely conscious or purely unconscious. According to Freud *"the Ego is not master in its own house"* [Fre17, p. 143], which impressively denotes this circumstance. The Ego may not have access to every single part of the generation of a wish[7] that lies in the corresponding satisfaction of drives. It is still able to perform a specific action, which is a basic difference between an animal and a human being: the inhibition of drives [ST02, p. 282]. It is one of the main functionalities, the module *Deliberation* is responsible for. Based upon the information provided by the module *Perceptual preprocessing* as described in the previous chapter, and supported by additional social prohibitions from the *Super-Ego*, the module *Deliberation* first has to select one of the rising drive-demands of the primary processes, which are called wishes in the secondary process part.

---

[7]It has to be emphasized that the drive that has passed the primary process mechanisms and has been converted to the secondary process, including a corresponding word presentation, is referred as a wish within the secondary information processes.

To select one of the active wishes for further planning, the following components have to be considered:

- *Intensity of the wish* - This component is based upon the drive tension that has been converted to secondary process data.
- *Focus of attention* - It is based upon already selected wishes that have to be satisfied. New or other wishes become therefore less important.
- *Reality check* - Determines whether the actions that have to be taken to satisfy the wish are possible within the current environment or not.
- *Super-Ego recommendations* - Counts the number of social rules that have to be violated (results in a -1) or that are respected (results in a +1) to satisfy the wish.

The first selection criterion, the intensity of the wish that arises from the tension of the drive throughout the primary process was already discussed. The focus of attention is, as described in the former chapter, a product of the current context and the currently activated wish. Each perception that is closely related to one of these two contents is amplified in its intensity. It is also amplified for drives that have already been selected. Thus a currently active wish with the process of satisfaction still in progress, automatically gets a higher intensity than other arising wishes.

If the satisfaction of a wish is closely related or simply implies an action that is violating a demand of the reality (the list of action tendencies that are restricted in the corresponding situation have already been discussed in the previous chapter) the evaluation process is decreasing the intensity of the wish. If the reality check contains rules that would be met by applying an action sequence that is necessary to reach the goal of satisfying the wish, the evaluation increases the intensity of the wish.

Prohibitive Super-Ego rules are handled in the same way. Each rule that would be violated if an action tendency implied by a certain wish is executed, the final intensity decreases. It is the criteria for the selection of the wish that has to be satisfied. Rules that are respected by necessary applied actions are increasing the intensity. Equation 4.3 shows the single components of the prioritization.

$$W_{prio} = (W_{intensity} * W_{focus}) + \\ + \sum Act_{reality}[-1, \ldots, 1] + \sum Act_{social}[-1, \ldots, 1] \quad \text{Prioritization of a Wish} \tag{4.3}$$

The prioritization of the wish is the sum of the intensity of the wish multiplied with the factor representing the focus of attention and the both sums of necessary but restricted actions that are prohibited by the demands of the reality and by social rules. Figure 4.14 shows the impact of a change within one of the components in Equation 4.3.

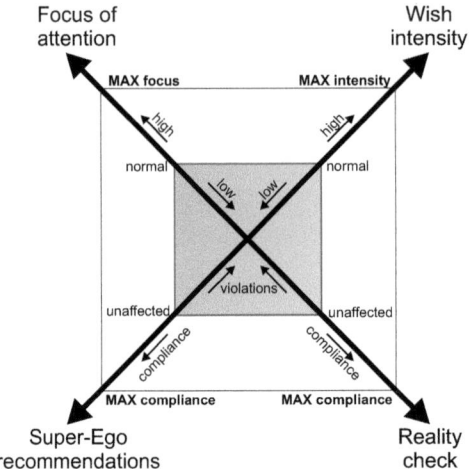

Figure 4.14: Geometrical Method to Determine the Prioritization Value of a Wish

The four orthogonal axes represent the four components of the evaluation for the wish priority with each of them having their own origin in the middle of the axis. A wish of a normal intensity that has no corresponding entry for one of the other three components and therefore neither positive nor negative impact would result in the 'norm-shaped' square. The corners of the square are the current values of the components. When a value of a component changes, the shape also changes and the area of the quadrilateral (the polygon with four points) either increases or decreases. The area of the shape can be seen as the prioritization of the wish.

With the goal to fulfill a selected wish, plans have to be made to reach this goal. The module *Generation of imaginary actions* is responsible for the generation of such plans and closely cooperates with the module *Knowledge about stored scenarios* that represents the plan library. In a first implementation, the database is predefined and fixed in ARSi09/Lang. For each wish – which can be seen as the selected desire and therefore the goal in terms of Artificial Intelligence – one or more plan(s) exist that can be used by the agent. The module *Generation of imaginary actions* actually does not generate imaginary actions in this implementation but submits a search request to the module *Knowledge about stored scenarios* to retrieve already stored plans that are leading to the fulfillment of the wish.[8] The plans that are retrieved by the plan library contained by the *Knowledge about stored scenarios* are using the concept of the complex event processing mechanism described in Section 4.2.4.

Two main functionalities are implemented, using this concept. A scenario recognition process detects the current scenario the agent is situated in. Like plans, scenarios have to be predefined and loaded within the module *Knowledge about stored scenarios*. When the transition conditions of a current state of the scenario recognition process are met according to the perceived sensory data the next state is achieved that has different transition conditions to reach the further next state. When all states of the stored scenario have been recognized, the scenario is fully detected. The information of the current scenario is an information that exceeds one simulation step because changes on the input of the system (homeostatic, bodily, or environmental) are necessary to toggle through the states of the scenario. A successfully recognized scenario influences the further processing of several modules of the primary as well as the secondary process. The output of these modules is depending on the recognized scenario that is representing the current situation. The influenced modules are: *Subjective perception, Knowledge about Reality (primary process), S.E. Primary*, both instances of the *Defense mechanisms, External perception, S.E. Secondary, Reality Check, Decision making*, and the described *Generation of imaginary actions*.

The next functionality realized within the module *Generation of imaginary actions* that uses the concept of complex event processing is the plan-generation and execution. Additionally to the transition conditions that are necessary to trigger the scenario recognition to switch to the next state, a definition of actions can be given within each state. A plan therefore includes a passive and an active component: The passive component is – like in the scenario recognition process – the transition condition that holds the set of necessary perceptual changes to switch to the next state and the active component is a list of actions that are executed when a new state is reached. With this concept, it becomes possible to define conditioned action sequences that are leading to the fulfillment of a goal based upon perceived information. One example would be a robot with an energy level that falls below a certain threshold. Supposing the robot has the absolute coordinates of the position of the desired energy source and its own position, the robot first has to turn towards the direction of the energy source. The first state includes the action command of *'turning'*. Using the information of its compass, the transition condition from the current to the next

---

[8]This oversimplification has been made because the two topics planning and learning are not defined in Chapter 3 and not part of the main focus of the work. However, possible implementations of these modules in ARSi09/Lang that are using models from cognitive science will be discussed in Chapter 7.

state would be achieved with the correct orientation. When the next state is reached, the robot stops rotating because the action command defined in this state is *'move forward'*. The length of the chain of events and actions can be as long as the scenario or plan requires it. Furthermore, a plan does not necessarily has an expire-date. Within a state, it is possible to define a maximal time until the state either falls back to the last state or the whole plan is canceled. The measured time is represented by simulation steps within the simulation. With respect to [Sha09] it has to be stated that the implementation of the plan library is not claiming to provide general intelligence to the agent. Since the rule-set has to be predefined in ARSi09/Lang, the intelligence only lies in the definition of these rules and does only support an event triggered behavior that again influences the perception and therefore the actions of the agent. It can be seen as the generator that stimulates the previous functionalities in the described model and the corresponding implementation does not conflict with the psychoanalytical demands described in Chapter 3. This first implementation of ARSi09/Lang shows the usage of the input- and output data interfaces and realizes the described module specifications. It now becomes possible to implement certain functions by using other – already existing or new – implementations, to compare them with the presented minimal implementation and to discuss certain differences.

With this definition and implementation it becomes possible to realize short term goals as well as long term goals, representing the plan to achieve a certain goal. Before executing the plan that leads to a wish-satisfaction the suggested plans have to be evaluated first. The functional module *Evaluation of imaginary actions* is processing the suggested plans and selects the best plan to be executed by the last module within the chain: the *Motility control*. For this evaluation, each state, each action, and each transition is represented by a corresponding `clsSecondaryInformation` including the Word presentation and an Affect. The affect denotes the level of gaining pleasure or displeasure for any of the listed components of the plan. A first implementation of the evaluation algorithm considers only the *"gross agent pleasure" (GAP)* that is achieved during the execution of the plan within one single agent. The evaluation according to the GAP[9] is currently neither considering the impact of taken actions to other agents as suggested in [AA07] and described in Section 2.5 with the *Total net pleasure* nor an optimization according to necessary energy, time, distance, etc. Following the simple concept of egoistic plan-evaluation, the agent selects

---

[9]The acronym is following the term *"Gross national happiness" (GNP)* that is a measurement of the quality of life in monarchy of the Bhutan

the plan with the most positive sum of affect-values P$_{pleasure}$ as shown in Equation 4.4.

$$P_{pleasure} = \sum Affect_{State}[-1,\ldots,1] + \sum Affect_{Transition}[-1,\ldots,1]+ \\ + \sum Affect_{Actions}[-1,\ldots,1] \quad \text{Total Pleasure of the Selected Plan} \tag{4.4}$$

This methodology offers the possibility of further implementations for the three modules described in this section (the *Deliberation*, the *Generation of imaginary actions* and the *Evaluation of imaginary actions*) but depicts the demands from the psychoanalytical side. Especially these three modules illustrate that methods from Symbolic AI can be applied and would increase the quality of causal reasoning. The next Section 4.4.3 depicts the starting-points and integration of an already implemented reasoning unit.

4.4.3 Uniting Demands of the Model and Implementation

The described computational framework ARSi09/Lang of the model are first attempts to realize the psychoanalytical concepts within the decision unit of an autonomous agent. As long as the implementations are meeting the psychoanalytical specifications given in Chapter 3 and the specifications of the defined interfaces described in Sections 4.3 and 4.4, the modules can be implemented as well by using other technical methodologies and concepts. One example can be given for the discussed three modules within the containing module *Deliberation*, consisting of the already mentioned functional modules *Decision making*, *Generation of imaginary actions* and *Evaluation of imaginary actions*. The main functionality of these modules is to select the most urgent wish of the list of currently arising wishes, generate plans to reach the goal of satisfying this wish, evaluate the generated plans, and select the best one for the current situation to execute it. The described flow of functionality perfectly matches to the Belief-Desire-Intension (BDI) Model already described in Section 2.4. Jadex, described in [PBL03] is one open source implementation of the BDI architecture and offers a means-end decision making based upon the three components, the beliefs, desires, and intentions. It will be used for a reference implementation in the following discussion of integrating existing BDI implementations. However, the current implementation does not integrate Jadex or other BDI-implementations but implemented the necessary functionalities above described from the scratch on in Java. For further implementations, such an integration would increase the performance of the decision unit of an agent.

When integrating a BDI architecture it has to be provided with three different types of information to enable a proper planning (e.g. through means-end reasoning). The first knowledge-base is considered with the term *beliefs* and represent the knowledge of the current environment including past and therefore episodic percepts and actual percepts originating in the current sensor data. The module *Decision making* within the introduced model is supplied with instances of *Secondary knowledge* that holds the information of the currently available sensor data from the environment. As long as each possible instance of a *Secondary knowledge* can be assigned to a specific symbol within the BDI implementation, the systems beliefs can be updated. Since the symbols of the BDI framework are identified with a unique identifier in the form of a string, it is possible to connect both systems together providing an attribute in the *Secondary knowledge* instance that holds the name of this instance. The amount of different *Secondary knowledge* instances that represent environmental information has been held as small as possible and they are predefined. Within the definition phase, it is therefore necessary to give each template of an instance a meaningful name that can be used for the transformation process. The same approach can be used with respect to the desires of the BDI implementation. The introduced model provides a generated list of wishes in the form of instances of *Secondary knowledge*. As long as the templates for the instances provide an attribute that holds a meaningful name in the form of a string, the transformation can be easily made from a psychoanalytically inspired data-type to the BDI terminology. With the third component, the plan library, it has to be guaranteed that each atomic part of the predefined and used episodic plans can be attached to one or more affective values in the form of *Secondary knowledge*. One approach of integrating such affective values into a logical reasoning BDI system has already been shown in [Lor08]. Based upon these values, the best plan has to be selected - a functionality that can be reached in the Jadex-Framework by using the provided interface of Reaction Deliberation as described in [PBL05]. Finally, the atomic parts of the selected plan from the BDI framework has to be transformed from the BDI terminology back to an instance of the psychoanalytically inspired *Secondary knowledge* to trigger certain actions of the agent.

The brief introduction of another possibility of implementing the psychoanalytical inspired functional modules shows the advantage of the strict modularity and the well defined interfaces of the framework: Each module can be considered by its own as long as the specifications of the interfaces, namely the input- and output data and the functionality that has been specified with respect to psychoanalysis are met. The BDI implementation of Jadex is one example that can meet the specifications of the three described modules.

Whereas the current Chapter 4 discusses the agent's reasoning unit and supposes embodiment to support the reasoning unit with sensor data and possibilities for actions, the next Chapter 5 discusses the aspects of situatedness of the agent. Not the embedding of the reasoning unit into the agent, but the embedding of the agent into an environment will be the main topic with respect to creating a virtual environment that is the basis for evaluating the quality of the psychoanalytically inspired reasoning unit. With the current status of the realized implementation ARSi09/Lang, it is possible to run an an autonomous agent. Except of social aspects and an agent-to-agent communication, each functional module has been realized in a first version of implementation.

5 Simulation of the Situated Agent

The purpose of a situated, embodied, and proactive agent as discussed in the previous Chapter 4 is to influence the kind of environment the agent is situated in in order to accomplish several predefined goals. Different types of agents are operating in different environments. An agent therefore needs adequate sensors and actuators to interact with the environment. The differences between the demands of specific agents become clear when categorizing agents in software agents, virtual agents or real world agents. In the following chapter the psychoanalytically inspired reasoning unit operating within a virtual, embodied agent is situated into a virtual and simulated environment to test the performance of the designed reasoning unit. The used simulation environment that bases on the multi-agent simulation platform MASON (described in Section 2.3) will be described in detail. The simulation platform is necessary to set up the virtual environment and to situate the agent into the environment where different tasks can be performed. It will be the basic framework to verify the performance of each implemented module of the reasoning unit in ARSi09/Lang, the performance of the agent's reasoning unit, and the total performance of multiple agents. Chapter 6 will use the introduce simulation framework in order to discuss these performance measures.

5.1 Simulation Environment

Changing the focus from the reasoning unit of the autonomous agent to the situatedness of the agent (as described in [Rie02]) means to place the agent into an environment that allows interaction. The following sections are describing the realization of the simulation environment. This environment is designed to supply the reasoning unit with sensory data as well as to provide a platform that enables the implemented reasoning unit to operate within the environment. After a description of the global demands to the simulation platform for the virtual agent, the used elements of the MASON simulation platform are described. Based upon the MASON framework the realized agent simulation architecture is described. Entities including the agent with the psychoanalytically inspired reasoning unit can be generated, situated and simulated. The design concept of strictly separating the simulated environment, body (origin of organic values), brain (symbolization), and psyche (the decision unit) are first discussed. Finally it is described how the reasoning unit is embedded in the setup.

5.1.1 Global Demands, Complexity, and Selection Criteria

The main reason for choosing an embodied, virtual agent within an artificial environment is the close connection between body and decision making. The functionalities of the psychoanalytical model of the introduced reasoning unit are also influenced by homeostatic values from the body. Identifying and defining the body of a virtual but nevertheless robot-like agent and comparing it with specific parts of the human body is more plausible than doing so with software agents. Also agents that are equipped with a 'body' that is totally different to the human body are hard to be adapted presumed in the psychoanalytically inspired concept. An agent for this case would have a body that is for example not able to move as it is the case with a building. With respect to this demand of the psychoanalytically inspired model, it has been decided to realize a multi-agent simulation environment where the situated and embodied agent is able to move around as humans do in a real world. This circumstance, and the additional assumption that the agent's sensor ranges are limited in their distance includes a powerful pre-selection of the possible input data. This is a filtering mechanism humans share with real world robots that are not connected with a so called 'omni-vision camera' that is mounted above the agent's environment. According to R. Brooks in [BBI+98] this 'out-of-the-box' filtering mechanism in conjunction with the capability to move and therefore adjust or orientate the sensors have an essential advantage: they decrease the demands to the reasoning unit and further correspond to a real robot. This statement is valid for two main components of the reasoning unit, the symbolization and the memorization. The former reduces the effort because the symbolization unit only has to cope with a maximal amount of sensations. The latter refers to the possibility of movement and reduces the necessary capacity of the agent's world model repository. Details of already perceived objects can be regained by simply direct the sensor range back to the object situated in the environment instead of storing each perceived detail just in case. To provide the opportunity to perceive sensory information, the simulation environment has to be enriched with other entities than just one agent. Multiple instances of agents equipped with the psychoanalytically inspired reasoning unit are necessary to evaluate the social and affective components of the model. Furthermore, simple entities without reasoning units like energy sources or obstacles have to be provided to perform the tasks that will be described in Section 6.2.4. For the evaluation, world boundaries were defined to limit the agent to a certain area where the objects of the test are concentrated. With these demands it is necessary to fix the number of dimensions the virtual environment should be designed with: a two-dimensional or three-dimensional world. In an investigation with respect to self-awareness of embedded agents, Dobbyn and Stuart are summarizing in [DS03] the main consideration for a two-dimensional virtual environment:

"..., there does not seem to be any good reason for believing that a three-dimensional world has any special properties that will guarantee the emergence of self-awareness; it is just as plausible to posit the idea of an animate inhabiting, and extended in, an eight-dimensional world: provided with appropriate sensory, proprioceptive and actuating capacities, the animate's body would have virtual extension in such a higher-dimensional virtual space." [DS03]

According to them, the fact that the body of the agent is a virtual one, plays the same minor role as the fact that the environment only has two instead of three dimensions. The only main difference would be the amount of necessary sensors and actuators to be able to interact with the third dimension of the environment and as a result the amount of sensor data that has to be processed in this additional degree of freedom. However, due to the missing third dimension it has to be considered that conclusions drawn from a two-dimensional environment must not be automatically assumed as valid in an environment with a third dimension.

With the gained experiences of the simulations described in [DZLZ08] a strict separation between the engine that calculates impacts of actions applied by agents to their environment and the agent and the agent's actuators themselves is mandatory in the design. Otherwise the design principle of embodiment according to [PIG06] would be violated by extending the functionality of the agent and its circumference. Therefore, the simulation platform has to provide the possibility to distinguish between the agents' data processing cycle and the calculation of virtual, physical impacts to the environment including other agents. Furthermore, a framework that already handles physical impacts would be preferable to a framework that only supports the possibility. Such a physics engine would handle applied forces and their impacts to different shaped objects with a certain weight and a certain friction.

Additionally to the pure simulation, the possibility of the visualization of both, the simulation environment including all visible entities and the internal values and processes has to be offered by the framework. The former is essential to test and evaluate the behavior of agents in certain, predefined situation during the simulation run. The latter is used to evaluate internal values like a simple energy consumption up to complex values of affects or wishes of the psychoanalytically inspired reasoning unit of the agent.

The basic demands to the simulation platform are clearly heading to a multi-agent simulation environment as they have been described in Section 2.3. Since simulations of groups of agents also have to be realized, a lightweight simulation environment without unnecessary overhead in timing, processing, or visualization had to be selected with respect to have more calculation time for the agent's reasoning process. The multi-agent simulation platform MASON, already described in Section 2.3 meets the above described demands and has been selected as the basic platform for the simulation environment of the agent, described in the following sections.

5.1.2 Customizing the MASON Environment as a Basic Platform

The main goal of the created simulation environment was to place the proposed model into a simulated, embodied, robot-like agent that is able to interact with a simplified two-dimensional environment as it is shown in Figure 5.1. The simulation is based on the fast discrete-event multi-agent simulation library MASON, a Java-project developed by the Georg Mason University described in Section 2.3. It provides, amongst other simulation possibilities, a framework for handling and scheduling multi-agents within a two-dimensional environment and also supports two-dimensional object collision handling by integrating an implemented, efficient and lightweight two-dimensional physics engine.

Figure 5.1 shows a screen-shot from the visualization of the simulation. Within the world boundaries, where agents cannot pass, different entities were randomly placed. Obstacles are objects that are static and cannot be moved by agents. The displayed cake is the energy source that can be consumed by the agents. There are two different types of agents displayed. The RemoteBot only contains the virtual body of the agent, including sensors and actuators, but does not contain a decision unit. It can be controlled via dedicated keys on the keyboard for testing purpose. The agent with the ARSi09/Lang-Implementation uses the decision unit described in Chapter 4. The simulation bases upon the provided MASON-example '2D-Bots' that uses the integrated, two-dimensional physics engine. The

Simulation of the Situated Agent

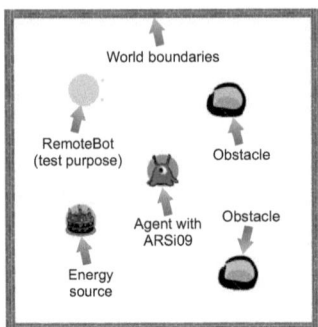

Figure 5.1: The Virtual Environment of the Agents with Randomly Placed, Exemplary Objects

MASON simulation environment basically distinguishes between two interfaces that will be discussed in more detail with the following interface names: `Steppable` (the name of the interface) and `Portrayal` (a class name). Besides the necessary functionality for handling objects and events during the simulation, these two keywords are essential for customizing the simulation environment.

The interface definition `Steppable` provides only one method that is called by the simulation framework in every step, as long as the object registers at the responsible scheduler. So, every agent has to implement this interface and the corresponding method `step()` to be invoked automatically and therefore become the opportunity to start its reasoning process. Contrary, the class `Portrayal` is the base class for each visible entity that is located within the virtual world. One class that implements the `Portrayal`-Interface is already part of the physics engine: `PhysicalObject2D`. Each element shown in Figure 5.1 is derived from the `PhysicalObject2D` and has a shape, color, name, is handled by the physics engine and provides the possibility to be inspected. Inspecting objects in MASON means to visualize their attributes in an additionally provided inspector window, called a *MASON inspector*. When an object with the `Portrayal`-interface is selected by a double-click (and it provides the necessary inspector functionality) its values can be either displayed by the standard MASON inspector or by a customized inspector. The standard *MASON inspector* iterates automatically through the public attributes of the selected instance of a class by using the *Reflection*-functionality supported by Java[1]. A customized *MASON inspector*, as described

---

[1] The functionality of the provided classes of the namespace *java.lang.reflect.** offers the possibility to access attributes and functions of any class in a generic way by iterating through a list of attributes and methods. With this functionality it is e.g. possible to access attributes of certain names and types during runtime rather than being only able to access them when the attribute name is know during the software-development. This functionality will be used and demonstrated in Section 6.2

above and in Section 2.3, is the second possible choice when visualizing the attributes of a selected entity. Since the MASON-framework already retrieves the selected object as well as a corresponding *JFrame*, which is the base class for any visualized windows in the Java-framework, a custom control can be easily designed by the programmer. With respect to the physics-engine, it is distinguished between all `PhysicalObject2D` whether they are stationary objects, meaning that they cannot be moved, or mobile objects. The described excerpt of the class framework of MASON together with the classes generated to meet the described demands of the agent-simulation can be seen in Figure 5.2. The UML-notation[2] for class diagrams specified in [UML09a, p. 129 ff] and also depicted in the Appendix is used to show the relationships between the declared classes within the implementation.

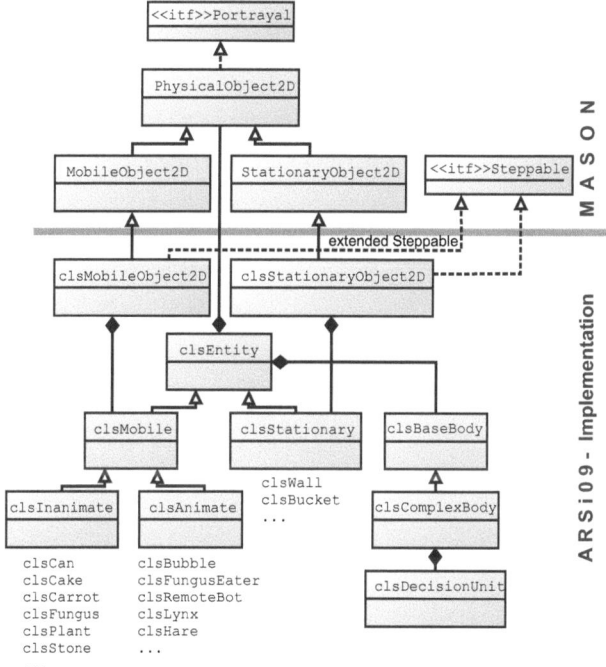

Figure 5.2: UML-Diagram of Visible Entities within the Simulation

The class structure on the upper side of the diagram represents the MASON-internal ob-

---

[2]The Unified Modeling Language (UML) as specified in [UML09a] is a standardized general-purpose modeling language for software engineering. The standard is available on http://www.omg.org/spec/UML/2.2/ (accessed on 12.2009), the web-site of the corresponding consortium 'Object Management Group' (OMG).

jects. It is shown how the MASON-framework has been connected with the necessary entity classes of the psychoanalytically inspired multi-agent simulation ARSi09. The basic interface classes between the MASON-framework and the ARS-PA-Simulator are depicted below the border between these two namespaces: `clsMobileObject` and `clsStationaryObject`. These classes are wrapper-classes and therefore directly derived from the corresponding MASON-classes. They override the functions necessary to be able to alter the attributes of both physical objects. This procedure avoids changes in the source code of the original MASON-classes and keeps the possibility alive to update to a new version of MASON. Furthermore, the two classes are implementing the interface `Steppable` and therefore called in each simulation step. This `Steppable`-interface is additionally extended within the `clsMobileObject2D` to realize the following sub-steps within one simulation step:

- *Sensing* - Updates the values of the external sensors according to the current object locations.
- *Update Internal State* - Manages the internal (bodily) system of each entity.
- *Processing* - Triggers the reasoning unit that accesses data gained within the former sub-steps.
- *Execution* - Applies the requested changes via the implemented actuators to the environment.

In the multi agent simulation, every existing agent's interface-function *Sensing* is called. When all agents processed their function for updating the sensor data, the next function *Update Internal State* is called for each agent. This procedure is done with all of the four functions of the agent. This adaption of the MASON-scheduling process is necessary to avoid unwitting manipulations of agents by already taken actions of agents that were called first. Here MASON only allows to specify a linear or random ordering method. Further it is possible to group entities and determine the sequence of scheduling. The special marked interface arrow within Figure 5.2 between the class `clsMobileObject2D` and the interface `Steppable` denotes this special implementation detail. This completes the interface classes between the MASON-architecture and the ARS simulation architecture and ensures a proper integration in both, the simulation's schedule and the simulation's visualization and physics engine.

5.1.3 Implemented Entities and their Class Framework

The creation of a new entity within the simulation automatically creates its corresponding `PhysicalObject`, enforces an implementation of the `Steppable` interface and registers both of them at the corresponding MASON functionality. Figure 5.2 shows the customized class hierarchy of the possible entities within the simulation's customized framework. The class diagram is graphically separated into MASON-specific classes and classes that have been created within the scope of this work. The agent-class that will be the host for the psychoanalytically inspired reasoning unit is here represented by the class `clsBubble` at the lower end of the picture. It extends (beneath the other classes listed below) the `clsAnimate`, which again extends the `clsMobile`. The latter directly holds the reference to the wrapper class of the physical object within the MASON framework. The differentiation between *Animates* and *Inanimates* is useful since inanimates do not contain sensors, actuators, or a reasoning unit. *Stationary* objects are objects that are fixed within their position and cannot be moved, such as the simulation world's boundaries. The simulation can be easily extended by creating a new class that extends one of the described base classes: `clsInanimate`, `clsAnimate`, or `clsStationary`.

In the following, the class hierarchy of a typical agent – e.g. an instance of the class `clsBubble` – have to be described. The entrance point to investigate the specific structure of the entities is defined within the base class of all entities, the class `clsEntity`. It contains the attribute `clsBaseBody`, an abstract class that encapsulates every functionality that is not covered within the MASON framework. An entity can be initialized with a certain type of body. Basically three types were implemented within the simulation that are extending the `clsBaseBody`, the simple-, the meat-, and the complex-body. The `clsSimpleBody` is just an implementation of the base body and does not support any further functionality. The `clsMeatBody` contains virtual *'flesh'* that can be consumed by other agents to gain energy. It has been used to simulate the classic 'predator and prey experiment' to investigate the swarm behavior within two groups, as e.g. shown in [TNH+06]. In the described simulation this type of body takes over the role of simple energy sources and to consume them is therefore the agent's primary goal to survive within a given scenario.

The following section will discuss the compounding of the class `clsComplexBody` that is contained by the agent. Figure 5.3 shows the components that are held by the complex body. The three classes that are responsible for the bodily processes are the agent's internal 'signal generator' and are representing the internal milieu, the virtual organs and the hormonal and nervous communication network of the agent. A closer description of these systems that are not within the focus of this work are given in [DTM+09]. The classes `clsInternalIO` and `clsExternalIO` are containing a list of sensors and actuators. During the initialization of the simulation it is possible to determine what internal or external

161

Simulation of the Situated Agent

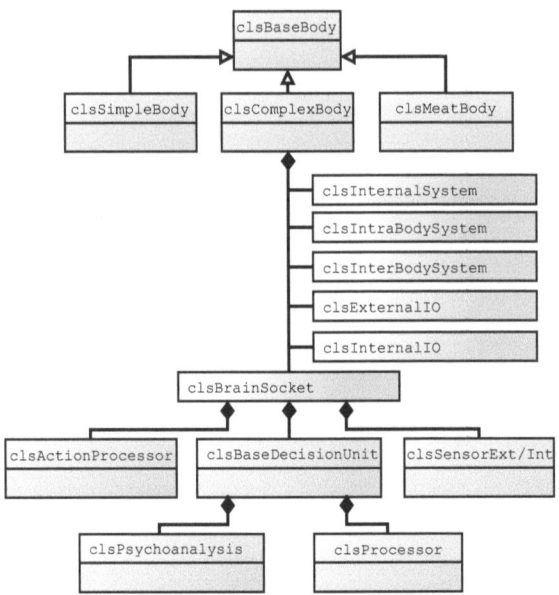

Figure 5.3: UML-Diagram of the clsComplexBody Containing the Psychoanalytically Inspired Decision Unit

sensors and actuators are contained and therefore supported by the agent. Section 5.1.5 gives a detailed overview of these systems. Finally, the complex body of an entity contains a class `clsBrainSocket` that is the host class of the decision unit. An entity within the simulator is designed to be a highly configurable and modular system regarding sensors, actuators and most important the decision unit. To be able to compare the psychoanalytically inspired decision unit to implementations using other methodologies, e.g. of classic Artificial Intelligence, it became necessary to define an interface that receives the complete set of sensor data, forwards it into the decision unit and forwards action commands that are originated in the decision unit to the corresponding actuators as shown in Figure 4.1. The above described classes, depicted in Figure 5.3, are contained by the class `clsComplexBody`. They are not visually represented within the core simulation field. Such internal classes do not have a corresponding portrayal- or physical object class and are not considered by the physics engine. However, these internal classes are responsible for data processing and the creation of actions that can influence the physical values of the physical representations of agents. With these implementation details, the basic framework and the possibilities of creating (virtual-)physically represented entities has been described. The following section shows the connection and interaction between the environment, the body, and the reasoning unit. The main possibilities, the situated agent has to interact with the environment are presented.

5.1.4 Situatedness and the Agent-Environment Interaction

One of the core issues within the simulation is to situate the agent in order to provide the possibility of sensing and changing the nearby surrounding environment. To simulate and to provide the sensory data that becomes the basis for further decision making of the ARSi09/Lang decision unit, a communication between the simulation engine that holds every simulated object and the agent has been established. This communication is encapsulated within the sensors and actuators of the agent. To avoid deadlocks during global data access of an agent to e.g. data from the environment, each entity has an exclusive access to the container of the simulated environment. This enables direct access to the information available within the simulated environment. An example for data that has to be accessed during the sensing-phase of an agent is the position (in relative or absolute coordination - both is in principle possible within the simulation) of another agent that is within the sensor range.

Figure 5.4 shows the embedded, psychoanalytically inspired decision unit topmost within the simulation environment with particular respect to the communication between environment and decision unit.

The functionality of the brain socket is to provide a defined interface between the agent's body, including sensors and actuators, and the agent's decision unit. With this modular design, it becomes possible to use one and the same type of entity-body with different decision units. Starting from the lower side of Figure 5.4, the MASON simulator contains each instance that exists within the simulated environment including the agent entities. As already shown in the class diagram of an entity in Figure 5.2 and 5.4, the entity holds an instance of the agent's body. In the case of an agent that is used as the host of the psychoanalytically decision unit, this body is of the type clsComplexBody and so contains the classes that are responsible for the sensor- and actuator functionality. During the step-call of an entity, the internal sensors are directly fetching data from the internal system of the body. The same is the case with the external sensors that are directly accessing the necessary data from the environment. The brain socket is the fourth component shown in Figure 5.4 that is contained by the body. It receives the sensor data from the internal and external sensors, converts them into corresponding data

Simulation of the Situated Agent

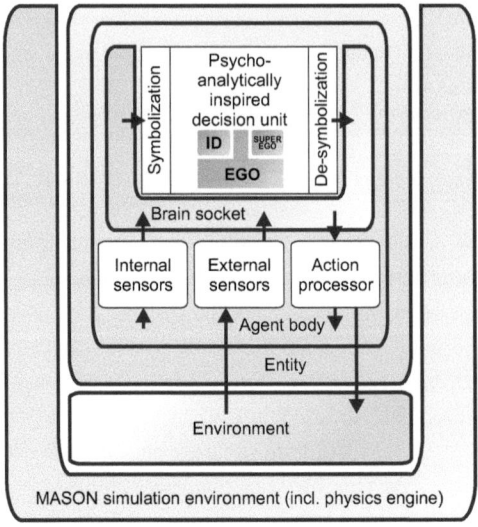

Figure 5.4: Modular Organization of a Situated, Embodied Agent

objects and forwards the list of data objects to the currently used decision unit. When the decision unit finished the deliberation-process according to the current sensor data, the generated action commands are passed through the brain socket into the internal and external actuator system, denoted as action processor. The specific actuators are again responsible to apply the certain changes directly to the entity's body and the environment. Although the action processor distributes the action commands and calls each actuator system, it is additionally responsible for detecting contradictory or exclusive actions-pairs. Further details in detecting these exclusive actions are described in [RLD+07] and [Roe07].

Figure 5.4 shows the modular organization with respect to a single agent. When considering multiple agents, the different functions (sensing, updating internal state, processing, executing) are executed sequentially for all agents and not only for one. According to the simulation steps described in Section 5.1.2 (sensing, update internal state, processing, execution), the sensor values for *every* existing agent (presuming a complex body) within the internal and external sensor systems are generated before the next step begins. The next state updates the internal states. Each step of the process is executed by every existing agent until the next sub-step is called by the command processing unit. Figure 5.5 shows the sequence diagram of the class representatives in UML notation for interactions in the form of sequence diagrams as specified in [UML09b, p. 459 ff]. The sequence dia-

Simulation of the Situated Agent

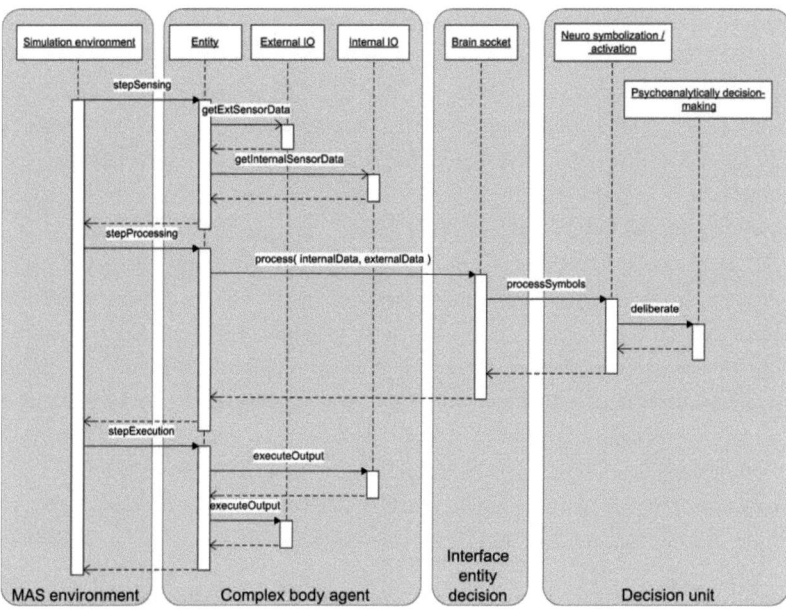

Figure 5.5: Sequence Diagram of the Deliberation Process of one Situated Agent During one Simulation Step (UML Notation)

gram only shows three of the four sub-step phases (sensing, processing, and executing) the internal state is not displayed within the diagram. The simulation environment sequentially calls the **stepSensing**-method of each entity in the first step. With the methods **getInternalSensorData** and **getExternalSensorData**, the entity triggers the available sensors that are collecting the necessary information from the simulation environment (this class interaction is not shown in the diagram). After the process of updating the sensor values, the entity reports the successful sensor update to the simulation environment. Between the end of **stepSensing** and the beginning of **stepProcessing**, the **stepSensing**-method of every other complex body agent is also invoked. Furthermore, the update of the internal state is executed, which is not shown in the diagram. After the update of sensors and the internal state, the simulation environment invokes the **stepProcessing**-method of the entity. This method is responsible for collecting the already stored sensor data and redirecting them to the brain socket by invoking the method **process**. The brain socket class converts the incoming data produced by the sensors in corresponding data objects that are defining the necessary interface between the brain socket and the decision unit and invokes the method `processSymbols` of the neuro-symbolization class. This module is supposed to generate corresponding symbols out of the sensor data. However, the sensor data generated by the internal and external sensors in the simulator are already on a high semantical level. The implemented symbolization process therefore only has to re-arrange the attributes of the sensor data classes to generate a symbolic level. The last part is containing the psychoanalytically inspired decision unit. It is invoked by a call of the method `deliberate` and gets the symbolic sensory data as input parameters. After the deliberation process, the generated output in the form of motor-commands are converted and redirected to the entity that stores the action requests. After completing the method `stepProcessing` of each other agent and entity, the simulation environment invokes the method `stepExecution` of the class entity that finally distributes the action commands to the internal and external actuators to apply the necessary changes in the environment (e.g. adding forces, changing properties of objects). After the execution of all sub-step routines, the multi-agent simulation framework handles the physical forces and applies them to the corresponding physical objects to prepare the system for the next simulation step.

5.1.5 Available Sensors and Actuators for Complex Agents

After this summary of one complete simulation step, starting at the simulation's core framework and including the environment, the body and the decision unit, the possibilities of such an agent will be described. The following paragraphs list the available sensors and actuators and their implementation.

```
public class clsExternalIO extends clsBaseIO {
    private clsActionProcessor moProcessor;
    public clsSensorEngine moSensorEngine;
    public HashMap<eSensorExtType, clsSensorExt> moSensorExternal;
    public clsEntity moEntity;
...
}
```

Listing 5.1: Definition of the class clsExternalIO

The extracted code segment in Listing 5.1 shows the basic assembly of the external sensor- and actuator class. The attribute `moProcessor` encapsulates the functionality of distributing and executing actions that have been triggered in the decision unit. The class `moSensorEngine` is a helper class for sensors that are aware of the presence of objects that are within a specified, entity-relative area, e.g the visual range of a camera. The attribute `moSensorExternal` contains all registered sensors of the entity. To access the list an enumerator was declared that serves as the key of the key-value-pair of the hash map. Finally, the attribute `moEntity` contains the pointer back to the containing entity and allows access to global, entity-related information.

The sensor system follows a modular designed in order to be easily expendable. In the current version of the system only the sensors that are necessary to realize the test-cases describes in the next section are implemented. These sensors types are:

- *Acoustics* - Simple, command-based communication between agents.
- *Bump* - Detects a physical collision to another object.
- *Ring segment area (RSA)* - Detects objects (type, color, size, count, ...) located within the area of a ring segment around the agent. It is the base class extended by the following sensors.
- *Eatable area* - Extends RSA and detects objects within the range of the agent's energy transfer.

- *Manipulate area* - Extends RSA and detects objects within the range of the agent's range of manipulating arms
- *Vision* - Extends RSA and detects all objects that are within the distance of the vision sensors.
- *Vision near* - Extends RSA and only returns objects in the first ring sector (close) to the agent.
- *Vision medium* - Extends RSA and only returns objects in the second ring sector, starting at the end of the first.
- *Vision far* - Extends RSA and only returns objects in the third ring sector, starting at the end of the second.
- *Position change* - Detects a position change that is not caused by a self-caused action and can determine e.g. the strength of an external hit.

Sensors like olfactoric (to smell other entities), tactile (distinguish between different surfaces) or radiation (a Geiger tube to detect radiant emitting objects) are also available but not necessary for the realization of the first use-cases. The internal sensors are measuring simple values of the energy, stamina, temperature and health. Especially the energy value is generated by a stomach system that holds different nutritious. This construct makes it possible to imply different meanings of different types of energy sources. Further, the internal sensor system contains the slow- and fast messenger system, whereas the former represents a simple realization of a hormonal system and the latter a simple realization of the agent's nervous system to communicate e.g. surface pain.

There are the following actuators available within the system:

- *Turn* - Applies an azimuthal force to the agent into the given direction.
- *Move* - Applies a radial force to the agent.
- *Eat* - Consumes objects that are within the range of the eatable area.
- *Pickup/drop* - Objects can be carried by picking them up.
- *Cultivate* - Objects within the manipulate area can be cultivated, e.g. to grow energy sources.
- *Attack* - Damages objects within the range of the manipulate area.
- *Excrement* - Empties the arrears left after the energy digestion process.
- *Sleep* - Switches off a subset of sensors and actuators to increase regrow of the stamina and health.

With the described sensors and actuators, the agent equipped with the clsComplexBody in principle fulfills the demands of a proactrive situated agent according to [Woo00]. An agent, equipped with the psychoanalytically inspired decision unit therefore can be situated with the above described implemented simulation environment. This section described the general framework of the multi-agent simulator, its main classes and interconnections. The demands raised by the need of simulating the psychoanalytically inspired decision unit were discussed and it was shown that the proposed simulation framework is able to cope with these demands. Due to a modular design of the implementation, it became possible to initialize different types of entities including agents with their own, specific sensors, actuators and decision units. The following Section 5.2 shows the global framework that is used to create different simulation setups that will be used to evaluate the functions of the implemented decision unit.

5.2 Setup and Initialization

The previous part of the chapter presented the general class framework of the simulation environment and the interactions between already instantiated classes. However, during the initialization phase, these classes first have to be instantiated by an automated loader process. This process is responsible for not only instantiating the required entities that are necessary for a certain setup of the virtual environment, but also has to fill the attributes of the newly created classes. The following subsections will describe the necessary loading procedure. It is distinguished between environmental information and information of the psychoanalytically inspired decision unit that has to be loaded.

5.2.1 Setup of the Environment

Situating the agents within the simulated environment requires a structured initialization phase within the simulator, where objects can be generically generated, initialized and placed within the two-dimensional simulation world as shown in Figure 5.1. For this reason, external configuration files in two different formats are used. Textual configuration files with key-value pairs are initializing the simulation-related objects and XML-files[3] are used to define the knowledge-base of the psychoanalytically inspired decision unit. The configuration files containing the key-value pairs are used to initialize the 'simple' attributes

---

[3]XML stands for Extensible Markup Language.

of each entity and its subclasses created within the environment. Simple values can be the number of entities of a certain type, the position in x-y-coordinates, its color, the affiliation to a team (to enable future social simulations), the list of available sensors and actuators of the entity, etc. Listing 5.2 shows an example of a property file, used for configuration.

```
entitygroups.0.entitygrouptype=BUBBLE
entitygroups.0.numentities=1
entitygroups.0.positions.0.pos_angle=0
entitygroups.0.positions.0.pos_x=100
entitygroups.0.positions.0.pos_y=100
...
field_height=200.0
field_width=200.0
worldboundarywalls=true
```

Listing 5.2: Key-Value Property File of the Simulation

With the `entitygroups`-keyword, the different types of entities can be defined. Within this example one entity of the type 'BUBBLE' is created. With the position key, the orientation and coordinates can be set. The second part of the exemplary listing defines the dimensions of the simulation environment and instructs the simulation framework to generate world boundaries that cannot be exceeded by agents. The textual key-value configuration file is loaded in the initialization phase into an instance of a HashMap that allows access to the value by providing the corresponding key. This instance, holding the complete configuration information, is passed as a parameter through every created instance of classes that are configurable. An agent, its 'complex body', each sensor and actuator are for example classes that are using the configuration information and can be accessed through the key. During the simulation, the 'Fast Entity Adapter' shown in Figure 5.6 allows additionally an adaption of the number of entities. Entities that are additionally placed via this dialog are randomly placed on the virtual environment.

The selection of different settings becomes especially necessary when simulating use-cases with the same agent but a different amount of objects that are representing the goal of the agent within a specific setup (a detailed description will be given in Section 6.2). In Figure 5.6 the entity adapter that is able to manipulate the values of the configuration file is shown on the left hand side of the screenshot. It contains the agent `BUBBLE` that will be the host of the psychoanalytically inspired decision unit. The agent accessible in the second line of the configuration dialog, called `REMOTEBOT` is not loaded within the displayed setup. The remotebot is intended to allow direct interaction during runtime and can be

Simulation of the Situated Agent

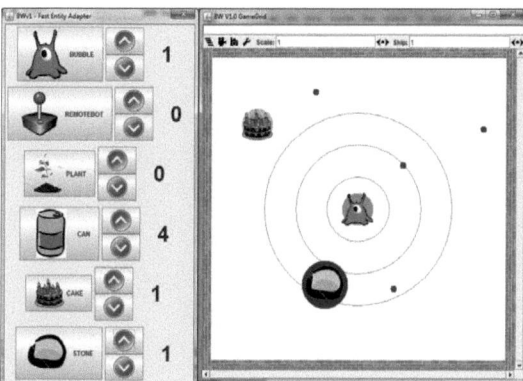

Figure 5.6: Screenshot of the Fast Entity Adapter to Change Setup Values and the Impact in the Simulation

directed by a human operator via predefined keyboard input (remotely controlled). The following objects are entities that are implementing a 'simple flesh' and can therefore be consumed by the agents to regain energy. A plant (not used within the displayed setup) additionally has the possibility of increasing its energy value when being 'cultivated' (an action that can be applied by the agent). The last type of entity that can be selected are stones, an instance of a movable object with a very high weight and therefore friction within the simulation. Moving stones would be highly energy-consuming for an agent.

5.2.2 Setup of the Decision Unit

With these configuration the virtual produced simulation environment including each entity can be sufficiently specified. Additionally, the decision units of the agents have to be initialized with a predefined knowledge. First, a mapping between internal and external sensation received by the corresponding sensors has to be defined. In Listing 5.3 a code snippet of the given definition within the used XML-file to define the mapping between drive sources and thing presentations that are holding the drive content are shown. The defined structure is used as an instruction set for the creation of thing presentations of the corresponding drives.

```
<?xml version="1.0" encoding="UTF-8"?>
<TPDrives xmlns:xsi="http://www.w3.org/2001/XMLSchema-instance"
   xsi:noNamespaceSchemaLocation="../xsd/ComplexEmotion.xsd">
     <TPDrive ID="1" name="eat">
```

```xml
<Description>definition of drive-sources</Description>
  <Drivecontent>EAT</Drivecontent>
  <DriveSourceList>
    <DriveSource SensorType="SLOWMESSENGER"
      ValueType="BLOODSUGAR" Ratio="0.6" ></DriveSource>
    <DriveSource SensorType="STOMACHTENSION"
      Ratio="0.4"></DriveSource>
  </DriveSourceList>
  <LifeInstinctList>
    <LifeInstinctRatio context="DEFAULT" oral="0.9"
      anal="0" phallic="0.1" genital="0"></LifeInstinctRatio>
  </LifeInstinctList>
  <DriveObjectList>
    <DriveObject type="PLANT" context="DEFAULT"></DriveObject>
    <DriveObject type="CAKE" context="DEFAULT"></DriveObject>
  </DriveObjectList>
</TPDrive>
  ...
</TPDrives>
```

Listing 5.3: Mapping Between Drive Sources and Thing Presentations of a Drive Content

In the listing, one drive definition is shown that completely defines the drive content 'eat'. The drive sources of this drive are represented by two different types of sensors, the *stomach tension* and the *slow messenger system* that includes the value of blood sugar. During the initialization phase, the implemented module *Generation of drives* of the psychoanalytically inspired decision unit is loading these values. During runtime, a thing presentation for the drive content 'eat' is created as soon as one of the two sensors are reporting a deviation of the homeostasis that results in a bodily tension. With respect to the module *Generation of affects for drives*, the ratio of both tension values are defined as a weight to calculate one single value for the quantity of the drive represented within the affect. For a further processing the categories of the life instincts (oral, anal, phallic, and genital) are assigned to the drive. This information is mainly used within the module *Defense mechanism for drive contents*. The values shown in Listing 5.3 are only for illustration (and not psychoanalytically evaluated) and vary in another context. In this example, only one context is defined – the default context. Finally, the *Drive object list* contains a list of objects, identified by their entity type name that represents "[...]the thing in respect of which and through which the instinct seeks to attain its aim (i.e. a certain type of *satisfaction)."* [LP73, p. 273]. This list of objects can also vary according to the current context.

Using these structures, the basic associations of the knowledge and functionality of the specific functional modules as described in Section 4.3 are predefined in external files. To determine the episodic context the agent is situated in, the described image and scenario recognition of Section 4.1, 4.2.4, and 4.4.2 have to be initialized with already perceived images and sequences of these images. The information is also defined within an XML configuration file according to the described rule tree and sequential definitions described in Section 4.1.

```
<TemplateImage ID="100" name="ESNear" fullMatchRequired="false">
    <Description>an Energy Source is in vision and eatable
                                sensor range</Description>
  <TreeRoot optional="MANDATORY" booleanOperator="AND"
                                                negated="false">
    <leafVisionSegment compare=">=" count="ONE">
      <sensortype>VISION_NEAR</sensortype>
      <location>FULLRANGE</location>
      <entitytype>CAKE</entitytype>
    </leafVisionSegment>
    <leafEatable compare=">=" count="ONE">
      <sensortype>EATABLE_AREA</sensortype>
      <entitytype>CAKE</entitytype>
    </leafEatable>
  </TreeRoot>
</TemplateImage>
```

Listing 5.4: Definition of the Template Image 'Energy Source Near'

Listing 5.4 shows the example definition for the image that represents the perception of a visible, eatable object (a cake) that is within the range of the eatable area. This template image is instantiated as a memory trace that represents an actual set of perceived information and appears during the decision process as soon as the predefined values are matching.

The structure in Listing 5.4 follows exactly the notation of the described rule tree of Section 4.1 displayed in Figure 4.3 and will provoke a match of the image as soon as an entity of the type CAKE is visible within the near vision range and also extends into the eatable area. With this construct it becomes possible to define certain events that are happening within

Simulation of the Situated Agent

the environment and are perceived through the agent's sensors. A probably reaction of the agent in case of hunger would be to consume energy from the energy source that is called 'cake' in this example. To determine sequences of detected *template-images*, *template-episodes* are stored that are connecting abstract images together and define predefined sequences in time. The scenario recognition process has to track the instantiated template images in the form of thing presentations within each simulation step to determine whether the process switches into the next state and either waits for the next event or is fully recognized. Listing 5.5 shows the definition of an episodic action plan. The structure is similar to the definition of a scenario, except the addition of actions. They have to be executed before recognized template images are considered as transition conditions to the next state.

```
<ActionPlan ID="1">
  <Name>searching and consuming energy</Name>
  <Context>SEARCHENERGY</Context>
  <EntryState>1</EntryState>

  <State ID="1">
    <ActionPlan>
      <Action ID="30" Priority="40" Source="MOTION" Name="Explore"
                                                  Params="PATTERN_8"/>
    </ActionPlan>
    <Transition>
      <TargetState>2</TargetState>
      <Condition>
        <TemplateImageId>102</TemplateImageId>
        <MinLevel>High</MinLevel>
      </Condition>
    </Transition>
  </State>
  <State ID="2">
    ...
</ActionPlan>
```

Listing 5.5: Definition of an Action Plan – similar to the Scenario Definition

Within this example, an agent that has decided to execute the presented plan is exploring the environment as long as the *Template image* with the specified ID (102) is detected. Then the scenario recognition switches into the next state, executes the defined actions and waits until the next template image is recognized. When the whole chain of causal links of template images is ran through, either the scenario is successfully recognized (in terms of a scenario detection without actions that have to be executed) or the plan has been executed (including each action defined within the plan).

This chapter gave an overview of the realization of the simulated environment. It will be used as the test platform for the developed decision unit modeled in Chapter 3 and implemented according to Chapter 4. With the implemented entities, physical constraints, bodily systems, and attached sensors and actuators, an interaction between the environment and the agent is provided. The following chapter uses the described simulation environment and its possibilities to set up environments with different tasks that have to be solved by the agents. These agents are equipped with the psychoanalytically inspired decision unit during the test runs performed in the next chapter.

> "The most difficult thing is the decision to act, the rest is merely tenacity. The fears are paper tigers. You can do anything you decide to do. You can act to change and control your life; and the procedure, the process is its own reward."
>
> [Amelia Earhart]

6 Results

Decision units for autonomous agents, which are processing information according to technical concepts inspired by the human deliberation process, are already existing. They are commonly based upon theories and models from psychology or the study of mental functions and behavior. The architecture developed and verified in Chapter 3 solely uses the theory of metapsychology as the basis for developed implementation concepts. This chapter discusses the performance of the implemented functional modules of the ARSi09/Lang decision unit as well as the performance of the embodied, situated agent with respect to environmental and internal, bodily performance indicators. To enable the possibility of measuring these values, the agent is situated within different environments – each of which designed to test the performance of different functionalities. Functional, quantitative, and behavioral criteria as discussed in Section 2.5 are measured by using a complex evaluation toolkit especially developed for the simulation environment described in Chapter 5. Finally, a comparison to classic AI decision-making architectures shows the main differences in the performance and behavior.

6.1 Utilized Evaluation Toolkit

To evaluate the performance of an agent within the running simulation, direct access to the defined performance measure has to be provided within the simulation environment. These visualized measures are the representative criteria for the success of an agent's behavior [RN03, p. 35]. As described in Section 5.1.2, the MASON framework already provides a mechanism where visualized agents within the environment can be selected. Selecting the agent, automatically opens a corresponding frame that can be used for visualizing the agent's internal values. Following the measuring criteria defined in Section 2.5, an evaluation toolbox was created. It allows the measurement of the three main types of criteria within the agent: entity information, bodily information, and information about the decision unit. Compared to Figure 2.16, this information is covering the two lower fields of the individual agent evaluation except the individual's behavioral check. The functional check of the complete decision unit and its submodules is provided by the use of a tree view, already shown in Section 3.2.3 (Figure 3.13). The evaluating agent has to be selected within the environment and the information about the decision unit has to be opened. According to the top-down design approach, the tree view contains each functional module of the proposed architecture of Chapter 3, starting at the psychic apparatus and ending at the finest granularity of functional modules. Selecting one of the module-items in the tree view shows the corresponding visualized measurements (in the MASON framework, these panels are called *inspectors*) of the corresponding functional unit. Each module's *inspector* is hand-crafted and designed to present the necessary information of this module. For the presented results in the following sections three different types of information are presented, all originating from these inspector classes. Data tables are visualized by using HTML[1] to present the static or textual contents. Bar diagrams are used to display the current value of different measurements, whereas charts are used to display the changes of these values, changing during time[2]. And finally, graph diagrams are used to display the associations between primary- or secondary information and the event processing chain to recognize scenarios and execute selected plans. Additionally, these panels are designed to be used to directly influence specific values of the agent (e.g. the current energy level or the priority of a plan)[3].

To allow an analysis of the global measurements – especially in a multi-agent-simulation – global inspectors are used. These inspectors are realized with the same visualization techniques as the single agent inspectors. A global set of measurements is provided that acts as a measurement container and can be used by any entity, especially agents. The global measurement inspectors are able to display the predefined values of either a specific team of agents or each agent. The number of reached goals per team is one necessary evaluation criteria for the performance of the agent's decision unit. The number of reached and consumed energy sources or other objects of the current goal can be depicted within these inspectors. An example from the literature is the collection of uranium ore in the

---

[1] Hypertext Markup Language (HTML) a markup language especially used for web pages. In this case, the visualized data is displayed within a control that is able to graphically display HTML source in the application's window.

[2] JFreeChart, an open source Java-library for charts under the GNU LGP Licence, has been used for implementation.

[3] JGraph, an open source Java-library to layout and visualize standard graphs under the GNU LGP License, has been used for implementation.

Results

fungus eater scenario described in [Tod82, p. 89] and will be described in detail in one of the next paragraphs. Additionally the internal values of the agent are considered – the drives that are representing the homeostasis of the agent – and are used as an evaluation criterion. An agent with least 'bodily' tensions during lifetime reflects the agent that copes best with the given goal to regulate its homeostasis either in terms of an optimal route to achieve the given goal or an optimal equilibrium between the given goal and the satisfaction of individual needs. The latter is subsumed as 'Total net pleasure', a performance measure as described in Section 2.5 to determine the well-being within the society of existing agents. Finally, the average life time of agents within a team is tracked and compared between the different teams using different implementations of the decision unit.

With these prerequisites of a principle performance measure and the possibility to visualize these performance measurements, the following sections are placing the agents – equipped with the developed psychoanalytical decision unit – into a predefined test environment. The agents are given several different goals that have to be solved by using a set of possible actions. The evaluation is done by applying the proposed evaluation toolbox during the runtime of the different simulations.

To simulate ARSi09/Lang – the implementation of the proposed concept for the decision unit of an autonomous agent – a virtual test environment has been designed. In the history of Artificial Intelligence, several models of the mind have been embedded into an artificial life simulation environment for measuring their performance. One of the first thought experiments, using virtual robots as hosts for developed decision-making units of autonomous agents was the 'Fungus Eater'-scenario, described in [Tod82, p. 89]. It is the archetype for the following considerations. Using the simulation environment, described in Chapter 5, the embodied, autonomous agent is placed into a virtual environment. Its main goal, to survive as long as possible, can be achieved by searching for objects that can be consumed and deliver energy to the agent. Within the different use-cases, the agent will be confronted with additional goals and receive enhanced possibilities to reach these goals. Although the simulation environment is completely virtual and abstracted from the real world, the used terms for intra-agent values and corresponding environmental objects, which are influencing these values positively or negatively, remain as anthropomorphisms[4]. In the further discussion the usage of anthropomorphisms is alleviating the description of interrelations between internal values, the goal of positively influencing these values, and the environmental entity or action that leads to satisfaction.

The goals of an agent can be categorized into explicit and implicit goals. Beneath the

---
[4]Applying human characteristics to non-human beings such as the proposed virtual agent.

main explicit goal to survive as long as possible, additional goals will be discussed within the use-cases. The ability to carry objects enables the agent to collect and cluster energy sources at a certain place with respect to a later lack of available energy sources. An agent that already formed an energy repository is able to avoid displeasure for a longer time. Further, the ability of nourishing energy sources comparable with plants, which can be harvested, gives the agent the possibility to decide to cultivate such energy sources and nourish them to satisfy long term goals instead of consuming them at once to satisfy just the current needs. Finally, the performance of the decision unit will be discussed with respect to applied cooperation within team agents. This task leads to a multi agent simulation and is used to show the statistical trends of the decision unit, as it is used. The goals of the agents are rather simple and the plans to reach these goals are already predefined. An agent, which is not initialized with the plans that are necessary to reach the goal within a discussed use-case, would not be able to complete the task. Learning and applying logical, semantic knowledge to generate a proper plan is not within the focus of this results section. However, the model has been designed to integrate such reasoning methods to increase the possibilities within more complex environments.

The implicit goals are already specified by the architecture of the psychoanalytically inspired decision unit. Gaining pleasure is the first and foremost implicit goal and is directly related to the further implicit goals. According to the model, parts of the lower tier of the decision unit are following the described *'pleasure principle'* (see Section 3.1.2) and are therefore permanently trying to increase the gained pleasure by satisfying internal, bodily demands. The actions that are necessary for their satisfaction have to comply with the corresponding Super-Ego rules. Each violation results in a loss of pleasure and decreases the corresponding measurement variable. A complied Super-Ego rule increases the total pleasure of the agent. Included in the predefined rule set of the Super-Ego are tendencies to cooperate with other agents in a certain context.

6.2 Simulation Results

The psychoanalytical decision unit ARSi09/Lang proposed in Chapter 3 combines implementation methods developed in the area of symbolic AI as well as in statistical AI. It defines a new concept for the functional interrelationship between the differently implemented functions using a modular approach and strictly specified interface definitions between these modules. The expected results have to prove two main requirements. First, it has to be verified if the psychoanalytical basis is consequently and completely defined

Results

to develop the decision unit of an autonomous agent. These results can be called the 'cognitive results'. Second, it has to be shown that the used concept is potentially capable of improving the agent's decision-making process in either filtering unnecessary and reducing perceived data or delivering more specific evaluation criteria enhancing goal-oriented tasks. The latter can be referred as 'engineering results'. The following sections will discuss both requirements by presenting corresponding performance measurements when placing the agent into a simulated, virtual environment. Although the agent as well as the environment are, compared to a robot that operates in a real world, extremely simplified the selected scenarios – subsequently denoted as use-cases – are designed to test the functionality and performance of the decision unit. They are simulating only the main problems an agent would be confronted within a real world application. After describing the main idea behind the use-cases, three different use-cases with increasing complexity of their goals are presented. A final discussion shows the impact of the increasing complexity and discusses the necessary enhancements that have to be taken for an application in a real environment.

6.2.1 Configuration and Impacts

The developed, functional model described in Chapter 3 mainly suggests a two-tier architecture, regarding data organization and processing. The concepts of the primary and secondary process that was already described in Chapter 3 was realized in the prototype implementation ARSi09/Lang of the model. Without a basic initialization of a main knowledge-base of the agent, the model is not able to generate an action. Because learning is not within the focus of the work, the system provides different storages containing the initial knowledge of the agent. These storages are centralized and accessible through an agent-global knowledge-base. The content of these different types of knowledge has to be predefined within the corresponding XML configuration files[5] and is read during the initialization phase of each agent.

The different knowledge-bases emerged out of the functionality of the introduced model. They are – in the first implementation of ARSi09/Lang– separated from each other. Multiple instances of one and the same object are therefore possible when they are represented in different types of memories. Due to the usage of one particular knowledge-bases in only one module, ambiguous data definition is currently avoided. In each of the following presented knowledge-bases, only two types of data structures are generated: primary and secondary information. So each knowledge entry is represented as a pair of an affect and a thing

---
[5]XML stands for Extensible Markup Language.

presentation for the primary information. In the secondary information it is extended to a triple of an affect, a thing presentation, and a word presentation.

The object semantic module loads and provides information that is automatically associated to the perceived primary information. In Figure 6.1, a screen-shot of the already loaded object semantics is shown. As reference object, the agent is able to perceive an energy source named CAKE and its associations are shown.

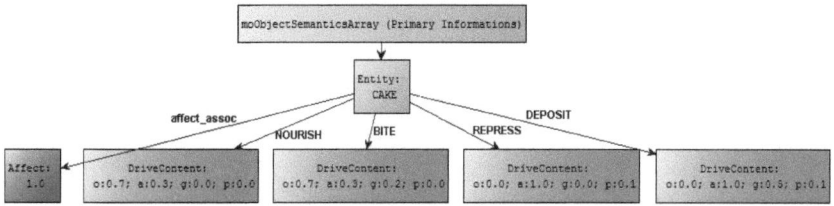

Figure 6.1: Excerpt Content of the Object Semantic Storage (Screen-shot of the Executed Simulation)

In this example, the object semantics knowledge-base provides one singe entry for an object, the entity CAKE. It is associated with two different types of objects. On the one hand, it is associated with the memorized affect across the association named by the system 'affect_assoc'. This entry allows a first estimation and evaluation of objects at the beginning of the system and reflects the agent's experiences with this object in terms of pleasure or displeasure. The object CAKE depicted in Figure 6.1, with a value of plus one therefore has the best evaluation an object can get because of the ranges from minus to plus one. Typically, these values would be altered and adopted during time when using a reinforcement learning module. The associations beneath the affect are associations to certain drive contents. The name of the associations represents the certain content that determines the corresponding distribution of the drive contents. Figure 6.1 shows four of these possible drive contents. It can be seen that within a context that is related to nourishing – meaning to consume energy – the distribution between the values of oral, anal, phallic, and genital importance is different to the three other possible distributions within the context *bite*, *repress*, and *deposit*. Depending on the current context of the system, the object semantic storage provides the corresponding drive content.

With this basic knowledge about perceivable objects, the agent can evaluate incoming sensory data in a very effective way with respect to the current situation. Only very basic types of evaluation are performed within the first modules of the described model such as the affect and the drive content categories as described above. The association with

Results

other objects, possible activities, impacts, or already experienced episodes is distributed within the complete model and consequently developed from module to module within the flow of information as described later in Section 6.2.4. The *Repressed Content Storage* is a necessary part to form the complete net of associations. During the agent's lifetime, the repressed content is permanently changing. Nevertheless, it contains also long term entries that were repressed during the development phase of the agent and permanently influencing the agents behavior. Unlike humans, the simulated agent does not 'grow up' and therefore needs to get initial values of repressed content. Figure 6.2 shows an excerpt of data within the repressed content storage of the agent during the simulation. It contains three entries of primary information (consisting of thing presentation and affect) that are representing the currently repressed content.

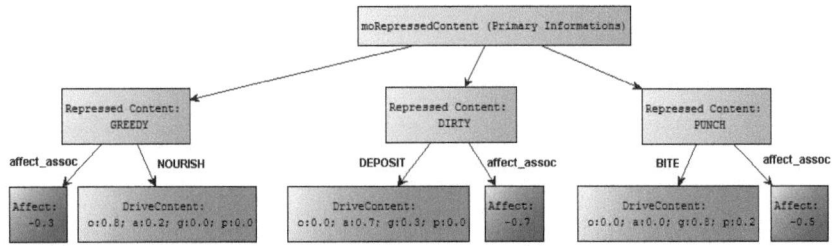

Figure 6.2: Excerpt Content of the Repressed Content Storage (Screen-shot of the Executed Simulation)

The similarity between Figure 6.2 and Figure 6.1 can be seen when observing a single entry of the repressed content storage. The entry basically consists of a primary information (GREEDY, PUNCH, and DIRTY within the figure) that is associated on the one hand with an affect and on the other hand with a drive content categorization under a certain context. This specific context is represented by the name of the association. The repressed content GREEDY at the left hand side here only defines a drive content categorization within a context called NOURISH. In the later discussion of data processing, the circumstance that both drive contents within the context NOURISH in Figure 6.2 and Figure 6.1 are very similar, will become of importance. Within the object semantics, the object CAKE is connected to a drive content category, which is very similar to the one of the repressed content GREEDY:

object semantics   CAKE: o:0.7; a:0.3; g:0.0; p:0.0;
repressed content   GREEDY: o:0.8; a:0.2; g:0.0; p:0.0;

In fact, these entries are giving the agent a personality by defining an already repressed content. In this case, it identifies the agent as a greedy agent. The corresponding affect, shown in the figure, is a negative affect and indicates displeasure. The meaning of displeasure or pleasure to the system is grounded on the internal performance-measures of the system, which are represented by *drives* and have to be predefined during the initialization phase. Figure 6.3 shows the definitions of the drives the system loads during startup. As described in Section 3.1.3, the system's *drives* are following the structure of the identified psychoanalytical structure. In the screen-shot, the visualized nodes are divided into two sets. On the left hand side, the two in this example existing drives assigned to the life-instinct (also called libido in psychoanalytical terms) and its associated components are shown. The right hand side consists of the opposite drives assigned to the death instinct.

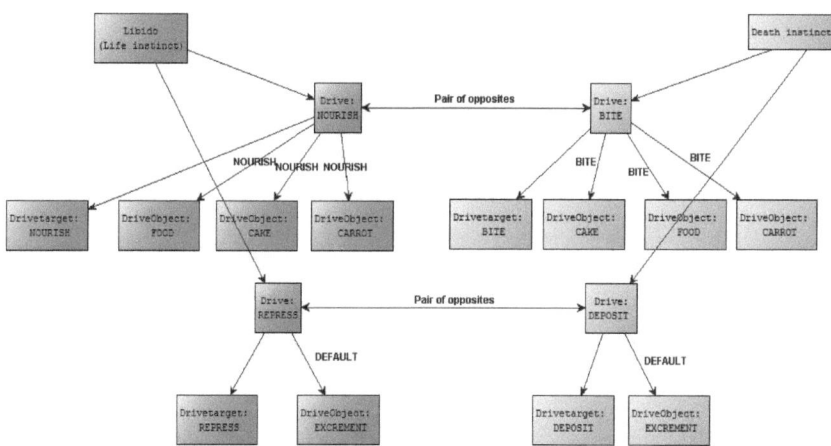

Figure 6.3: Definition of Pairs of Opposite Drive and their Components (Screen-shot of the Executed Simulation)

To briefly describe the outcomes, the pair of opposite drives NOURISH (assigned to the life instinct) and BITE (assigned to the death instinct) will be discussed. In the figure, the life instinct contains two further drives. The drive, responsible for nourishing is one of them. Each drive has an assigned drive target and one or several drive objects. The drive target assigned here is 'to nourish', which implicitly defines the types of action that has to be aspired. The drive objects are the objects that are necessary to satisfy a certain drive. The system holds this information in a flat list of objects that are not hierarchically assigned to each other in this first implementation. The drive objects FOOD, CAKE, and CARROT are corresponding virtual objects that can exist within the simulated environ-

Results

ment. The arrow description denotes the context in which this association is valid. The drive that is responsible for nourishing is also connected to an opposite part, its death instinct component. This is the drive responsible for biting, the aggressive component of nourishing. Even though, these are different drives, the drive objects are the same objects within the pairs of opposite drives. Figure 6.4 shows additional information for the drive definition that is loaded and visualized within the simulation at runtime.

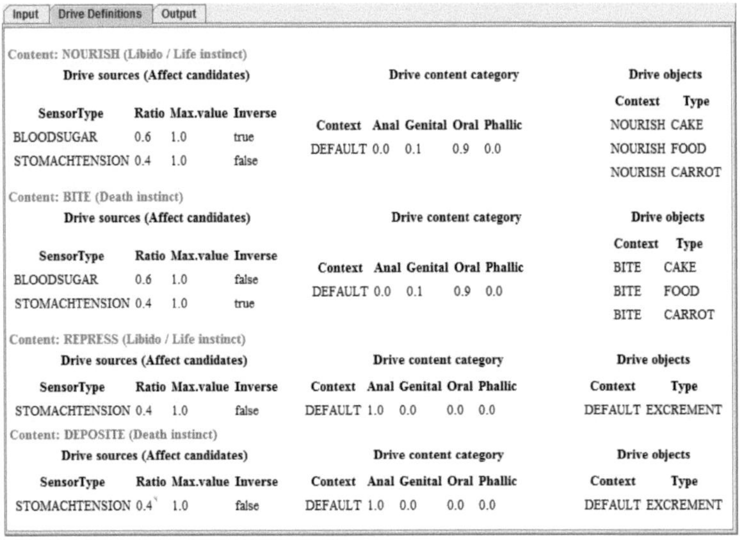

Input	Drive Definitions	Output							
Content: NOURISH (Libido / Life instinct)									
Drive sources (Affect candidates)				**Drive content category**				**Drive objects**	
SensorType	Ratio	Max.value	Inverse	Context	Anal	Genital	Oral Phallic	Context	Type
BLOODSUGAR	0.6	1.0	true	DEFAULT	0.0	0.1	0.9 0.0	NOURISH	CAKE
STOMACHTENSION	0.4	1.0	false					NOURISH	FOOD
								NOURISH	CARROT
Content: BITE (Death instinct)									
Drive sources (Affect candidates)				**Drive content category**				**Drive objects**	
SensorType	Ratio	Max.value	Inverse	Context	Anal	Genital	Oral Phallic	Context	Type
BLOODSUGAR	0.6	1.0	false	DEFAULT	0.0	0.1	0.9 0.0	BITE	CAKE
STOMACHTENSION	0.4	1.0	true					BITE	FOOD
								BITE	CARROT
Content: REPRESS (Libido / Life instinct)									
Drive sources (Affect candidates)				**Drive content category**				**Drive objects**	
SensorType	Ratio	Max.value	Inverse	Context	Anal	Genital	Oral Phallic	Context	Type
STOMACHTENSION	0.4	1.0	false	DEFAULT	1.0	0.0	0.0 0.0	DEFAULT	EXCREMENT
Content: DEPOSITE (Death instinct)									
Drive sources (Affect candidates)				**Drive content category**				**Drive objects**	
SensorType	Ratio	Max.value	Inverse	Context	Anal	Genital	Oral Phallic	Context	Type
STOMACHTENSION	0.4	1.0	false	DEFAULT	1.0	0.0	0.0 0.0	DEFAULT	EXCREMENT

Figure 6.4: Definition of Pairs of Opposite Drive, Including Drive Sources and Life Instinct Ratios (Screen-shot of the Executed Simulation)

Beneath the drive objects that are already shown in Figure 6.3, two further parameters are displayed. The drive sources are representing the sensors that are able to measure the tension of the 'artificial organs'. In the case of nourishing, the system uses the inverse value of the blood sugar to sixty percent and the stomach tension to forty percent for the generation of an *affect candidate* that will be converted together to the affect of a drive in the corresponding module *Generation of affects for drives*. The maximum value defines the highest possible occurring value of the corresponding source sensor. Similar to the object semantic storage and the repressed content storage, the drive content categories are also assigned to each specific drive with respect to a certain context. The values used within this example are not reflecting psychoanalytical findings and were used for test purpose only.

Results

With these basic information, the predefined knowledge that is necessary for the primary context is almost set. Within the secondary process, three different types of storages are defined that are now discussed in more detail. Because of the secondary process, the data shown in the following diagrams are no *primary information* anymore as in the previous diagrams, but are representing *secondary information* that consists of the triple *word presentation, thing presentation, and affect*. Due to the difficulty of describing thing presentation with words, within the following diagrams only the content of the word presentation and its corresponding associated affects are shown. The first knowledge-base that has to be discussed is the template image storage as shown in Figure 6.5.

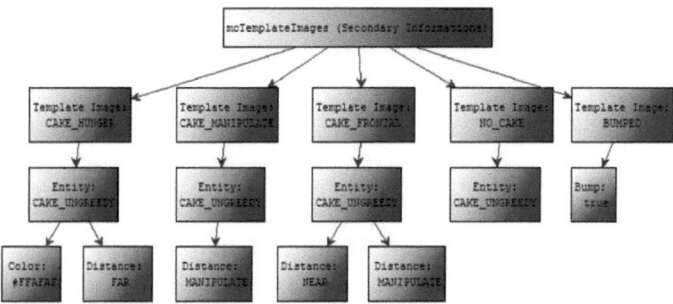

Figure 6.5: Definitions Within the Template Image Storage (Screen-shot of the Executed Simulation)

In Section 4.1 a method was introduced to detect particular occurrences of groups of sensor information by using the concept of mental images. Following this method, the system has a predefined set of images that are permanently compared to the current stream of perceived secondary information. In Figure 6.5, an excerpt of five different template images is shown. The most simple one consists of only one sensor entry like the template image BUMPED. With the corresponding algorithm, this abstract image matches to hundred percent when the agent bumps into an obstacle. Also negations are possible as it is the case with the template NO_CAKE. Only when no object of the type CAKE_UNGREEDY is visible, this template matches to hundred percent. The negation is not shown within the visualization. The remaining template images represent more complex specifications on the object CAKE_UNGREEDY. As an example, the template image named CAKE_HUNGER only matches if the object CAKE_HUNGER is perceived within the far distance and has a reddish color. The type of logical operator (in this case an AND composition) is not shown within the figure. To detect sequences in time and define sequences of actions that have to be performed, the system also holds predefined scenarios and plans as shown in Figure 6.6.

185

Results

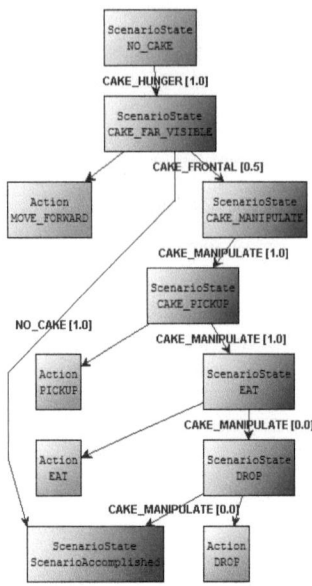

Figure 6.6: An Example Definition within the Template Plan Storage (Screen-shot of the Executed Simulation)

While scenarios (according to the described definition in Section 4.2.4) are only passive definitions of perceptual sequences, plans are also including actions that have to be performed first until the state of the plan can be switched to the next state. In Figure 6.6, an already loaded and visualized plan is shown as an example: It has the purpose to navigate the agent to an energy source and consumes the energy. The arrows between the scenario states are representing the transition conditions and are named with the template image that has to match. Figure 6.5 already showed the corresponding contents of the template images. The number within the brackets is indicating the quality of the match, where a 'one' stands for a complete match and 'zero' for no match. Within this example, four of the seven scenario states are containing an action that has to be performed until the corresponding transition conditions are checked. The execution of the plan will be discussed in Section 6.2.4. The scenario ends within the final state named *'ScenarioAccomplished'*.

With the predefined knowledge-base described in the past section, the agent is able to assign a predefined association to perceived primary information that are influencing the further processing. Additionally, different secondary information can be subsumed into new concepts that are also represented in the form of secondary information. They form the basis of sequential perception and acting. In the next subsections, the influence of the described initial data will be shown and the output of the functional modules within the different parts of the model will be presented.

6.2.2 Input Data Generation

The psychoanalytically inspired part of the model, introduced in Chapter 3 has two inputs. One input receives symbols that are reflecting the current deviation from the homeostasis. Grievances of internal values with their origin in particular organs or hormonal systems are provided via corresponding symbols to the psychoanalytically inspired decision unit. The second input receives symbols from the environment as well as bodily information produced by the agent. The following section discusses the results of the data generating process when perceiving such symbols.

Starting at the homeostatic information, bodily tensions of the simulated organs of the agent and their value are provided by the corresponding internal sources. The blood sugar level would be one example from the human body, which influences our urge to consume food. The agent described in Section 5.1.3 has such a system implemented. In machines, these values can be compared to the current energy level, free disk space, free processor or network resources. Figure 6.7 shows a screen-shot of the output data of the module *Generation of Affect for Drives* as described in Section 3.2.2. The complete data structure that represents the homeostatic deviations for further processing is created.

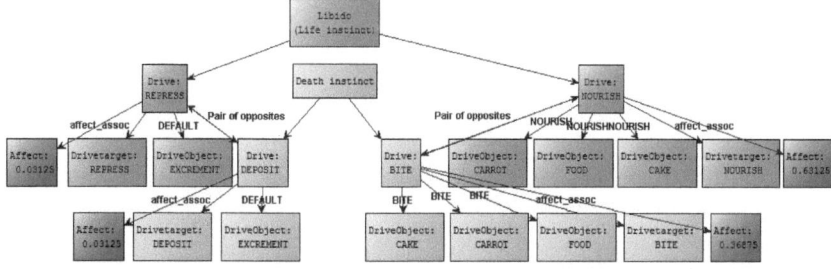

Figure 6.7: The Output of Module *Generation of Affect for Drives* After Preprocessing (Screen-shot of the Executed Simulation)

As described in the last section and shown in Figure 6.3 the pairs of opposite drives are predefined and their relation between homeostatic deviations and their affect are following

Results

the predefined associations shown in Figure 6.3. These definitions, together with the functionality in the modules *Drive handler* and *Affect generator* are forming the final output, displayed in Figure 6.7. These instances of thing presentations are representing pairs of opposite drives, and their associated drive target and drive objects. This loaded structure is static during runtime. The only variable component, additionally to Figure 6.3 that is associated to each drive is the affect. The value of the affects are additionally displayed in a chart form. A screen-shot is shown in Figure 6.8(a).

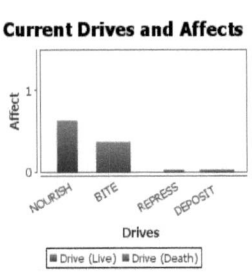

(a) Current Affect Value Display (Screen-Shot)

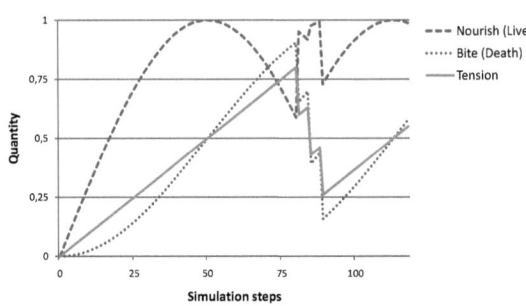

(b) Affects of *nourish* and *bite* and Organic Tension During a Time Span

Figure 6.8: Runtime-Inspector of Drives and Their Affect Values

The bars are visualizing the opposite drive pairs (*nourish* and *bite*, *repress* and *deposit*) as already depicted in 6.3. The value itself is the current quantity of the affect. Figure 6.8(b) shows the time diagram of the pair of opposite drives *nourish* and *bite*. During runtime, the virtual blood sugar level decreases in relation to the driven effort of currently executed actions. Therefore the drive *nourish* increases. At the same time, the drive *bite* increases but in the beginning not as fast as its counterpart. The more the organic tension increases, the more dominant becomes the affect of the aggressive component *bite*. The first reduction of the tension after the libidinous component reached its maximum is generated because of an initiated consumption of energy by the agent. It happened around the eightieth simulation step. A few simulation steps later, the agent repeats his action for further two times. The currently implemented transfer function that determines the ratio of the aggressive and libidinous part is a circular function that produces the plot in Figure 6.8(b).

The second type of input to the system captures environmental and bodily information. These symbols have to be transformed into thing presentations and associated thing presentations within the module *Preliminary external perception*. The symbols that are generated

Results

by the implementation of the sensor engine and the neuro-symbolization (both described in Section 4.1) are passed into the implementation of the psychoanalytical model. They are instances of classes, using the reflections functionality from Java together with a predefined mapping table makes it possible to generate thing presentations automatically. Figure 6.9 shows the generated perceptual thing presentations of an agent without any perceivable object in its vision area.

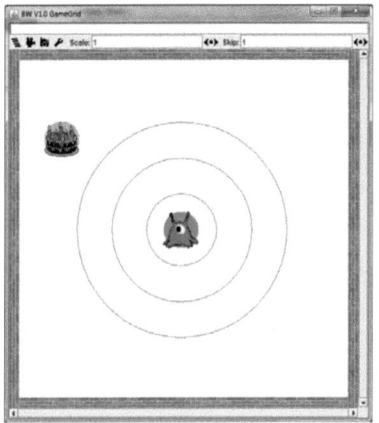
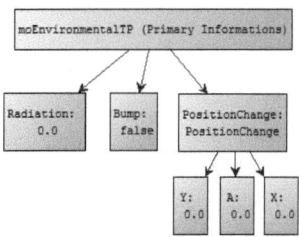
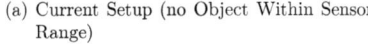

(a) Current Setup (no Object Within Sensor Range)

(b) Output of Corresponding Thing Presentations

Figure 6.9: Generated Perceptual Thing Presentations in an 'Empty' Environment (Screenshots of the Executed Simulation)

On the left hand side (Figure 6.9(a)), a screen-shot of the visualization of the agent is shown. The circles are indicating the three different vision ranges (far, medium, and near) of the agent. Since no object is within this range, the perception only consists of internal bodily sensors of the agent. This agent is equipped with three types of bodily sensors. The radiation sensor is able to detect nearby heat radiation and represents a way to simulate the humans sense to detect the temperature of the environment. The bump sensor is able to detect if the agent bumps into a physical object, an oversimplified form of the humans tactile sense. And the position change sensor detects positive and negative acceleration in any direction and the rotation. It can be compared to a simplified version of the human's vestibular system. In Figure 6.9(b), the generated thing presentations for each of these sensors are displayed. The associated values of sensors are '0.0' and 'false', because the agent is not moving at the moment. In Figure 6.10 the scenario has changed and the cake has been placed within the most distant vision range.

Results

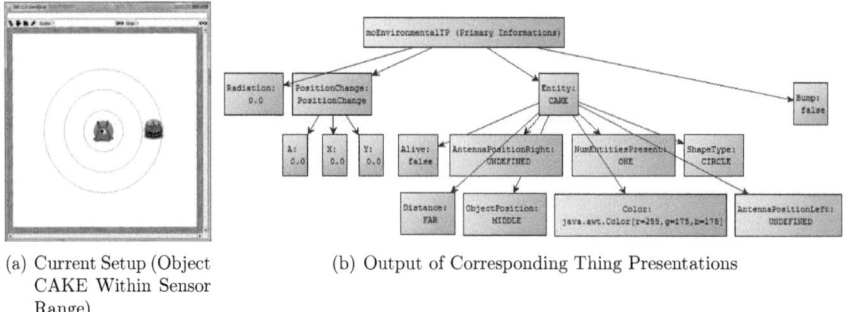

(a) Current Setup (Object CAKE Within Sensor Range)

(b) Output of Corresponding Thing Presentations

Figure 6.10: Generated Perceptual Thing Presentations in an Environment With one Object (Screen-shots of the Executed Simulation)

With the generated symbols corresponding thing presentations are produced. Figure 6.10(b) shows the output of the inspector of the module *Preliminary external perception* during this situation. Additionally to the thing presentations displayed in Figure 6.9, the symbols regarding the entity CAKE are also converted into thing presentations. The main thing presentation that is representing the perceived object CAKE, is associated to the additional perceivable properties of the object. The shape type has been assigned to be a circle. The object is in the outer most range and its distance is therefore far. The object position denotes whether the object is aligned to the left, center, or right of the agent's vision area. In this example, the agent detects the object CAKE at the object position MIDDLE, meaning straight ahead of his current heading direction.

It has been shown that the psychoanalytically inspired and implemented model is able to interpret the incoming symbolic data. Homeostatic values are transformed into the specified psychoanalytical data structures. The symbols of drives and the environment and additional bodily sensations are completely converted into thing presentations and associations of thing presentations. These resulting thing presentations and affects (included by drives) are the two main components of the primary information defined in Section 4.2.1. This data structure is the only one, processed within the modules of the primary process until it is converted into a secondary information. The following section shows the results for this primary process.

6.2.3 Search Parameters and Filtering Mechanisms

In the psychoanalytical model, displayed in Figure 3.14, the generated thing presentations of the external perception still have to be processed within the modules *Management of repressed content* and *Affect generator* until they can be evaluated within the module *Primary decision* and selected for a possible conversion to secondary organized information. The following section shows the output of these modules and discusses the respective functionality.

The first module *Management of repressed content* attaches additional data to certain selected environmental thing presentations. The basis for the following example output is the predefined content of the repressed content and the object semantic storage described in the previous Section 6.2.1 displayed in Figures 6.1 and 6.2. After a performed search within the object semantics storage, the unevaluated thing presentation of the object CAKE is associated with its corresponding drive content categories. Equipped with the ratios qualifying the oral, anal, phallic, and genital component (with respect to the current context), the drive content categories of the evaluated thing presentation are compared to each entry of the *Management of repressed content* (Figure 6.2). Table 6.1 shows the repressed contents (rc) with their corresponding context and their drive content category values.

Repressed content	Context		Category	Distance
GREEDY	rc: NOURISH ob: NOURISH	✓	rc: $0.8 \cdot o + 0.2 \cdot a + 0.0 \cdot p + 0.0 \cdot g$ ob: $0.7 \cdot o + 0.3 \cdot a + 0.0 \cdot p + 0.0 \cdot g$	0.2
DIRTY	rc: DEPOSIT ob: NOURISH	∅	rc: $0.0 \cdot o + 0.7 \cdot a + 0.3 \cdot p + 0.0 \cdot g$ ob: $0.7 \cdot o + 0.3 \cdot a + 0.0 \cdot p + 0.0 \cdot g$	1.4
PUNCH	rc: BITE ob: NOURISH	∅	rc: $0.0 \cdot o + 0.0 \cdot a + 0.8 \cdot p + 0.2 \cdot g$ ob: $0.7 \cdot o + 0.3 \cdot a + 0.0 \cdot p + 0.0 \cdot g$	2

Table 6.1: Table for Determining Best Match of Repressed Contents (rc) With External Object (ob).

Additionally, the rows are containing the context and the drive content categories of the object (ob) that has to be compared. The matching algorithm first searches for repressed content that is valid within the same context. In this example, only the repressed content GREEDY in the first row matches. In the simulation, several repressed contents can be available in the same context. Finally, the algorithm calculates the distance between the drive content category values of the repressed content and the object. The distance results from summing the differences between the category values. In the case of the repressed content GREEDY the distance is 0.2 and compared to the other distances it is the best match in the list.

Results

Figure 6.11 shows the output of the two modules *Management of repressed content* and *Affect generator* depicted in Figure 3.14. The situation is the same as described in the last chapter: the agent is in front of the object CAKE.

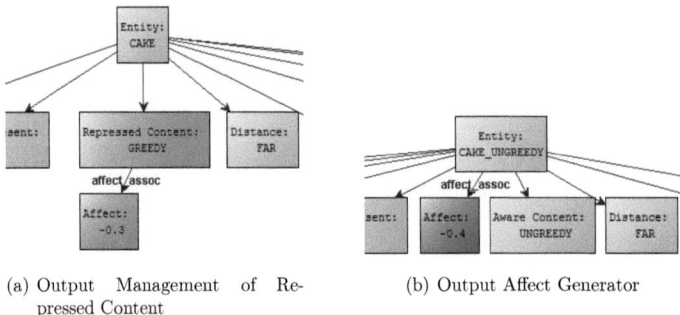

(a) Output Management of Repressed Content

(b) Output Affect Generator

Figure 6.11: Comparison Between Management of Repressed Content and Affect Generator (Screen-shots of the Executed Simulation)

As predicted in Table 6.1, the *Management of repressed content* attaches the repressed content GREEDY to object CAKE. It is shown in Figure 6.11(a) that the repressed content has also an assigned affect with the value -0.3, an association with displeasure. Although this content is not allowed to pass the *Primary to secondary interface*, it influences the search for objects that become associated with the incoming object cake. While the module *Primary content utilizer* performs this search, the module *Subjective perception* generates a single thing presentation out of the two presentations. The *Affect generator* adopts and attaches the affect of the result of the memory search to the new, subjective evaluated thing presentation perception. Figure 6.11(b) shows the output of the model.

The concept of comparing input data trees to templates in a possibly similar tree structure is applied to the defense mechanisms, the Super-Ego, and the knowledge-base functionalities in the same way. According to the input vector of data, all matching information is determined, evaluated, and the basis for further processing. In the Super-Ego the current perception is used as the search query for currently active Super-Ego rules. Within the different types of knowledge, a corresponding result set of associations with context specific information is the output parameter. The described methods are used to filter out unimportant information and focused on currently important information. The module *Decision making* and the successional processes, described in Section 3.2.3.3 are using this pre-evaluated information and perform the necessary steps to convert focused, evaluated secondary information into actions. The next section shows the outputs of this process.

6.2.4 Impacts on Decision Making and Information Flow

According to the input values from the homeostatic and external or bodily perception, the module *Decision making* selects the most urgent and – in the current situation – most reasonable wish that will be selected. In the current implementation, a predefined set of percepts (containing homeostatic, bodily and environmental) are assigned to the transition conditions of a plan. The first transition condition is representing the initial condition and is only executed, when a plan gets the corresponding priority. This priority results in a high drive tension, a high probability of success and a neglecting amount of Super-Ego and reality principle rules. The probability of success takes the available object perceptions into account. The generated list of Super-Ego and reality principle rules have to be considered.

The agent is equipped with a broad spectrum of predefined plans as described in Section 6.2.1. The initial conditions cover the functionality of plan selection. Figure 6.12 shows the timing diagram of the execution of one selected plan with the target to reach a visible object CAKE and interact with this object when reached. The example has already been used in the last Section 6.2.3.

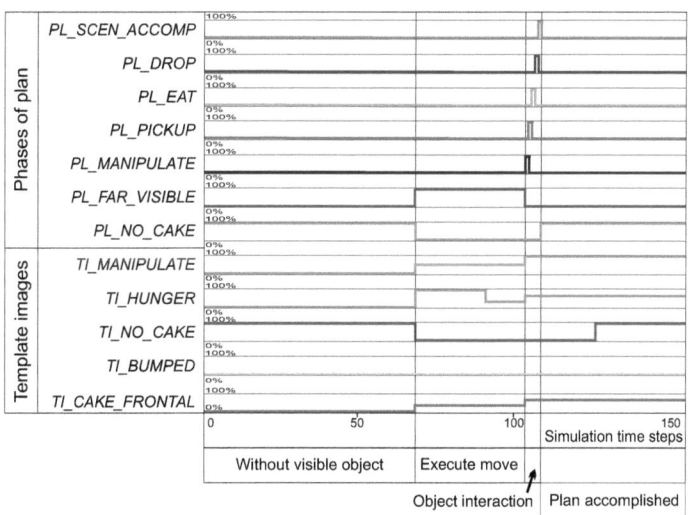

Figure 6.12: Timing Diagram of the Activated Template Images and Plan Phases

The diagram shows the matching ratio of defined template images in its lower part. According to the defined leaves of the rule tree described in detail in Section 4.1 and the

Results

current perception, the match can vary between zero percent for no match and hundred percent for a full match. On the upper part, the phases of the plan that will be executed are shown. For a phase, only two states are possible that denote wether the phase is active or not. Because there are no parallel phases defined in this plan, only one phase is active at one time. The first period up to step sixty-five is denoted as 'without visible object'. The agent does not have any visible object in range and its perception and internal states are not high enough to trigger any image except of the *TI_NO_CAKE* image that detects that no object CAKE is visible within the most distant vision area. When a plan with the target to reach this specific type of object is executed, this template image is used as an exit condition in each of the phases. In this case, a plan that searches for an object would be executed instead. As soon as the agent perceives the target object with its vision sensors, the template image *TI_NO_CAKE* is not active any longer. However, several other template images change their value, because they have the entity type *CAKE* defined as one of the conditions that have to match. *TI_HUNGER* returns a full match in the moment, the object CAKE appears in the vision area 'far'. This is the initial condition for executing the plan to consume the object CAKE as long as the decision has been made to satisfy the corresponding drive. It is shown that the initial plan phase *PL_NO_CAKE* has been changed its value and the next phase *PL_FAR_VISIBLE* is active now. The agent is now heading into the direction of the object CAKE and disappears from the most distant vision range (far). As soon as the object reaches the *manipulate area* of the agent (within this range, the agent is able to e.g. pick up objects), the template image *TI_MANIPULATE* completely matches and the plan phase switches from *PL_FAR_VISIBLE* to *PL_MANIPULATE*. In the following sequence of phases the agent first locks the object in its position to avoid a collision and accidentally add a force to the object. The template image *TI_BUMPED* shows that there was no collision with another object during the time of execution of the plan. Once the lock was successful, the agent consumes the cake by executing the action command 'BITE'. Finally, the position lock is removed (drop) and the plan has been accomplished. The plan phases return to their primary states because there is currently no need to execute the plan again. Changes of the template image matches have their origin in the changed position of the object CAKE that is now placed within the nearest vision area and the manipulate area as a subpart.

The state chart shows the close interrelationship between pre-evaluated abstract images as a part of the phases of a plan. The example only used template images as transition conditions for the plan phases. This means that only the current setting of sensations is relevant for the termination of a phase. Additionally, it is possible to include successfully detected template scenarios, representing a sequence of matching abstract images in time, as transition conditions for the plan. The output in picture 6.12 would be the same.

Using the implemented model introduced in Chapter 3 it has been shown that the agent is able to evaluate perceived data and searches for already experienced causalities and episodes. Together with a new model for the internal performance measure, the agent is able to select the most urgent variance from these internal measures with respect to social rules and semantic knowledge. With this information it searches for a corresponding plan and executes this plan that again contains a perceptual part for evaluation of the ongoing plan execution. The next section compares this performance with two selected architectures used in comparable agents. It further discusses the global output of the applied model and draws the conclusions from the presented simulation results.

6.3 Comparison to Classic AI Architectures and Conclusions Therefrom

The process that generates a reaction to a certain type or a sequence of stimuli can be achieved in different ways as discussed in Chapter 2. However, there are several criteria that have to be considered when evaluating the performance of an agent's reasoning architecture. The performance within a given test scenario is one of them. The following section compares the implemented and simulated agent architecture as introduced in the previous chapters with two architectures introduced in Section 2.1: The subsumption architecture ([Bro86]) and the BDI architecture (Belief, Desire, Intention – [GI89], [Bra87]). The possibilities of realizing a reactive, deliberative, or social controller are investigated for each of these architectures.

Reactive controller

In the first example, the agent is situated in a simulated, two-dimensional environment with the task of searching for and consuming energy sources in order to survive as long as possible. Each of the three architectures is supplied with sensory information through a predefined interface as described in Section 4.1. The agent is therefore able to move around (move forward/backward and turn left/right), avoid obstacles (when confronted with the borders of the environment) and to navigate to a recognized energy source to consume it. This 'job description' is exemplary for the subsumption architecture. The number of entity types that can be perceived is fixed (energy source, border) as well as the number of types of perceivable information (entities in visible range, energy level, bumped). The development process of the finite state machines of each layer follows a bottom-up approach. The program was hand-crafted and did not use an existing library or framework. Starting from the simple movement and obstacle avoiding routines, the higher layers of searching and object tracking can access these defined functionalities. Implemented in the described scenario, the system simply changes the states of its finite state machines and generates output actions according to the definitions in the activated state transitions. The system shows a good performance regarding processing power and output. The output depends on the efficiency of the random seeking algorithm. The agent using a BDI architecture is able to cope with the given demands as well. For the implementation, Jadex (described in Section 2.4) was used as the core processor for this task. With the already existing classification of data within the framework, the current perceptions were transferred to the system's beliefs. The goal of keeping the energy level optimal was formulated within the desires, and the possible action sequences and subsequences for searching, tracking, and obstacle avoidance were defined within the plan library that forms the intentions. Because of the overhead of the BDI frameworks, the execution of the control architecture became more complex compared with the subsumption architecture. However, the system design results in a clearly arranged knowledge-base of the dynamic world model (without any permanent memory in this case), an entry in the store of possible desires and a plan library including possible actions. The model introduced in Chapter 3 follows a comparable concept in its basic decision making and can be adapted to the example by using the XML-configuration files for a plan definition. Compared to the BDI implementation the model stringently distinguishes between different origins of its individual goals. For example, keeping the energy level within the optimal range is not the same type of goal as searching an energy source, although this is implicitly contained. Internal measurements are mandatory for this model and cannot be handled in the same manner as sensory data. Furthermore, the model provides an additional pre-evaluation for each perception that includes the subjective meaning of the kind of perception to the agent, i.e. an energy source is not just an energy source in the final decision process. Rather, it is classified as a positive object due to previously obtained satisfaction regarding internal measurement values. Together with further associations regarding the object's meaning to the system, a filtering mechanism is provided that suppresses unnecessary, irrelevant, or prohibited content within the base data used for deliberation. This concept is not relevant within the simple example but will be discussed in the following case.

Deliberative controller

The previous example scenario is changed by adding an additional object-type. This object is to be collected as efficiently as possible. In principle, the action-sequences to collect this new object-type are the same as searching and consuming energy but a new goal has been defined that makes planning necessary. The system's demands can no longer be met using only the data available at the time of the decision making [RN03, p. 932]. The decision must now be made on a more global layer using a model of the world. The subsumption architecture could still perform the tasks within tolerances, but it would not be able to determine a global performance measure like efficiency. Furthermore, the subsumption architecture described in the last example is only designed for the specific task of searching for energy sources. The modified setup merely requires an additional finite state machine on top of the old model. It extends the lower functionality, therefore the change in the implemented architecture would be acceptable. However, a larger change in the task specification would require a totally new design due to possible changes necessary in the lower level functionalities. In contrast to the subsumption architecture, the BDI framework offers an expandable plan library and a world model repository that is designed to store previously gained knowledge relevant for further planning. BDI implementations like Jadex offers a means-end reasoner, which is able to generate plans during runtime by using its assessment of the current situation, the desired situation, and a predefined or learned set of sub-plans including information on their impact on the world model. At the current implementation status, a means-end reasoner that uses methods of symbolic Artificial Intelligence for plan generation is more efficient than the static template-plan library in the introduced system. For the generation of possible plans, the model introduced in Chapter 3 is capable of such a means-end reasoner in the functional module *Decision making*, including a corresponding world model in the functional modules *Knowledge about reality* and *Knowledge base*. In addition to a means-end reasoner, the model is able to evaluate each plan not only in terms of efficiency (shortest path, lowest time cost, etc.) in terms of the internal impacts of each phase of a plan, each executed action and each perceived piece of information. The performance measurements represented by the homeostatic values (denominated under the umbrella term drive) are closely linked to each perception and influence the selection of plans by the design principle.

Social controller

Again, the above discussed example scenario is extended in its setup. In this iteration the setup is changed from a single agent to a multi agent simulation by adding two teams of agents. They have the same goal basis as the one defined in the scenario for the deliberative controller. Additionally, the agents are able to recognize team agents and opponent agents and possess a new performance measure, which represents the number of collected objects within a team. Because of the missing world model, the subsumption architecture is not discussed within this setup. The BDI framework is fully capable of this task and also able to determine cooperative plans that optimize the performance within a team, for example by communication. However, the controller becomes a social controller only if the behavior of an agent influences the future values of the performance measurements of another agent and if both are aware of the impact. With this added factor a new system dynamics arises and social rules have to be considered and observed (or violated). In the example scenario, the impact on the opposite team must be determined when harvesting their energy fields. These predicted impacts influence each individual agent's deliberation process and its resulting actions. The plain BDI framework does not give specific information on how to integrate such a socially influenced deliberation process, but at the same time it does not prevent a social decision approach. In the introduced model, decision making is socially influenced throughout a certain knowledge-base of social rules. An observing system awards the agent whenever these rules were observed and punishes the agent for their violation. Plans, actions as part of the plans, and their impact regarding the social environment are evaluated and stored. This can be seen as the basis for further implementations of social reinforcement-learning algorithms. The stored social impacts again influence the evaluation of generated action plans.

After the comparison of the introduced model with two different software architectures for embodied autonomous agents [RN03, p. 932], the strengths and weaknesses of the psychoanalytical model will be discussed based on the simulation results. The discussion will lead to a conclusion of the (in)consistency and (in)completeness of the psychoanalytical model defined in Chapter 3.

The system is highly adaptable to new sensor information and new sensor modalities thanks to its uniform data structures of primary and secondary information. Symbols and interconnected symbol meshes are converted into meshes of thing presentations representing the quality of a perception and corresponding affects representing the quantity of a sensation. With this conversion to a unified data structure, the functionality of further processing is decoupled from the underlying source structures and only the content is relevant. The advantage of the concept lies in the general possibility of applying concepts of data evaluation and association to any kind of information, independent from its structure. However, the model strictly distinguishes between the two data structures *primary information* for a preliminary data evaluation and reduction, and *secondary information* including additional concepts like causality and negation for higher deliberation processes like planning. The integration of internal performance measurements, originating in a necessary homeostatic system of the agent and manifesting in the psychoanalytical terms *drive* and *wish* is mandatory and predominant. Although the system is capable of suppressing individual needs within an introduced functional unit called *Ego* in psychoanalytical theory, any decision process becomes necessarily colored by the current internal states. The processes do not have a detailed knowledge of this circumstance during the higher processes of decision making. A drive is not grounded from the point of view of the decision-making process. It cannot be backtracked to its source of tension and becomes covered or partly disguised during a *primary decision process*. Another concept that is mandatory for implementation of the model is the evaluation of perceived sensory information of any kind. Sensory data alone, even after conversion into the systems predominant data structure of *primary information*, cannot be processed without further associations to individual meanings assigned through previous experience. The basis for these associations is the internal measurement system mentioned above. Each perceived sensation and each taken action is put in relation to the impact on the internal measurement system which reflects the positive or negative effect on the individual agent. Based upon this evaluation of perceived data, the model introduces a primary filtering process that diffuses or suppresses information. Information is refused when it is deemed not acceptable regarding the context of the current situation and related social rules and environmental demands. As presented in Section 4.2.3, the first implementation of applying social and environmental rules to perceptual information by the use of search algorithms is a minimal example that does not violate the requirements of the employed psychoanalytical theory. An extension of the implementation using theories of Artificial Intelligence in the future may increase the performance of the system. Finally, the model introduces a methodology of evaluating multiple sequential plans. This multi-dimensional evaluation also influences the abstracted internal performance measurements. This sets the model apart from the previously discussed architectures because the logically shortest path is not necessarily the best path. To realize an internally focused evaluation of plans, a BDI implementation or other architecture may be used or adapted.

Finally, the employed psychoanalytical theory that led to the model developed in this work can be regarded as sufficient to design a controlling unit for an autonomous agent. Perception, reaction, deliberation and execution layers as used in the theory of robotic software architectures according to [RN03] are included in the architecture. The possibilities for a memory system and an integration of reinforcement learning are also embedded. The integration of internal measurements into both, the knowledge-base and the decision-making process is described in the presented architecture. The data structures used and the methods of connecting them are specified in detail to realize them in a first implementation. However, the topic of different semantics between objects and the functionality of how this knowledge can be built is missing in the developed model. This includes the concept of applying causal rules to the process of plan generation. The main purpose of the introduced model therefore is to be seen in the evaluation and pre-processing of information for further

Results

planning algorithms. The current activity of the agent within the environment does not reflect the power of the data pre-evaluation process. The following chapter summarizes the results of the simulation and gives an overview of the three most important areas for further investigation: model refinement, knowledge representation, and planning.

7 Conclusion and Outlook

Applying logical rules is not enough to cope with the demands for an autonomous agent. Strengths and weaknesses of selected representatives of agent architectures available today were discussed and requirements for both model and architecture development were identified. The illustrated disadvantages of already existing, cognitive architectures were the motivation for formulating, modeling and implementing the introduced psychoanalytically inspired model for controlling an autonomous, embodied agent. For the formulation of this functional model a top-down design approach was applied to transfer the theory from psychoanalysis in a bionic approach to a controller on the one hand and to assure functional completeness and consistency on the other hand. According to the general requirements for an agent's controlling unit the following section gives a brief summary of the key components of the developed architecture and compares the requirements to the abilities the architecture is offering. Out of the insights based on the interpreted results, areas within the introduced model will be identified which will need to be further investigated in the future. From the current state of the art and the current state of the model, a short outlook on expected future trends in autonomous agent architectures and their modeling and implementation methods will be given.

7.1 Key Issues Regarding the Developed Agent Controller

The main focus of this work was to introduce an architecture for an agent's controlling unit that uses concepts of the human mind to cope with the rising demands on computer systems. They are expected to interpret situations in a real world environment and react to it in order to achieve certain user defined goals. To meet these requirements, the design of the model followed a bionic approach and used psychoanalytical theory in order to model the human decision-making process.

In a first intermediate step, the extracted psychoanalytical definitions of functionalities, sequences, and structures were transformed into a technical specification. With this knowledge-base, it became possible to define the functional units of the entire process according to the psychoanalytical theory. With the application of a top-down design approach, it was possible to investigate the theory regarding its distinct and complete description of functionality. This is necessary for the decision-making process and could be compared with the mandatory functions of the decision unit for an autonomous agent. Having developed a sequence for an information flow between the functional modules, the possibility of launching the psychoanalytically inspired model into an autonomous, embodied agent could be determined. The requirements discussed in Chapter 1.2 were included in the resulting functional modules.

The usage of the second topographical model (Id, Ego, Super-Ego) as the top level allowed a formulation and organization of specific data-types that every derived sub-functionality has in common. The resulting technical two-tier concept of primary and secondary information, representing the primary and secondary processes as defined in psychoanalysis, finally allowed the development of a definition for information containers within the model. It included the basic assembly of the data containers, but also the concepts of data processing that can be applied to the corresponding containers. The defined organization and handling of data was considered mandatory for each functional module. This data structure as the basic part of transfer parameters between the interconnected functional modules led to the described modular architecture.

When investigating the model's functional components, three main points turned out ti be predominant within the structure. First, the individual that hosts the developed decision unit – in this case the embodied agent – necessarily must possess an internal system reflecting positive or negative influences from the changing environment on the agent's body. Only with this concept of internalized and introspective performance measures can the psychoanalytical model be applied. Second, every single piece of perceived information is qualified in relation to the individual agent itself, including its meaning, past experiences, and evaluations. Although this concept is applied on each layer of the model, the associated information is not necessarily the same on each layer. Complying with the primary and secondary processes that handle primary or secondary information, a primary and a secondary association network also exists for the exclusive use of the corresponding processes.

Third, in contrast to the subjective associations of additional information from the perception, filtering and data condensation mechanisms are applied during the entire sequence of the process. Some information can be repressed and therefore does not exist in higher, secondary process layers of the model. Functions like the *Generation of imaginary actions* are therefore not influenced, whereas lower, primary process layers and their functionality are sustainably influenced. Additionally, information can be distorted and may appear in a different form than it was detected by the sensors. Especially in combination with the concept of individualizing data, the concept of symbol-grounding clearly gets extended in this two-tier architecture and can be described as a second, hidden symbol-grounding process.

When converting the model into a concrete implementation, the modular design can be realized within an object-oriented software design. This includes the defined data structures, interfaces, and functions. With several preconditions regarding data input and data output in the form of symbols, it has been shown how the model can be embedded into an embodied agent. This was done by way of a multi agent simulation platform. The implementation part of the agent controller that includes the psychoanalytically inspired model followed a modular design approach. The simulation was designed to contain the agent's controller, the agent's body, perceivable objects, and to handle the interrelationship between these objects. With this setup, the implemented controller could be provided with input data and had the capability to interact with its environment, including other agents, which is a precondition for proactive agents in general. The performed virtual field test allowed investigation the performance of each functional module and the performance of the agent within the virtual environment. From a technical point of view, the following can be concluded from the implementation's performance: Regarding the reduction of the search space due to applied filters while at the same time expanding information with associations to previous experiences, the model's advantage lies in the evaluation of perception regarding the agent's current and past internal performance measures. It therefore provides a model of focusing on relevant data and the functionality of determining relevant data with respect to a subsequent, causal planning. In the implemented version, the model does not give a specification on the content of the semantic web that arises with the association within primary and secondary information. Further, all plans necessary to reach arising goals are assumed as predefined and only vary in their context specific, associated evaluations. The following paragraphs compare the basic requirements for the controlling unit of an autonomous agent defined in Section 1.2 with the capabilities of the introduced model.

Perception

The developed model is designed to be embedded into a (neuro-)symbolic information process, converting raw sensor data into symbolic information as described in [Vel08]. With this form of information from the preceding perceptual data generation, the system uses the information contained in the symbols, and compares subsets of the symbolic stream to predefined memory traces of thing presentations. According to psychoanalytical theory, a thing presentation and a corresponding affect are generated when a memory trace contains a subset of the currently perceived symbols. Thing presentations represent symbolic data containers describing a certain quality of a specific sensation. The associated affect describes the corresponding quantity of this sensation. There is a distinction between homeostatic inputs (the origins of the internal measures called *drives*) and environmental and bodily inputs.

Evaluation

The evaluation of incoming sensory data follows two different concepts from psychoanalysis. The evaluation of homeostatic differences results in the drive, basically consisting of a thing presentation that holds the information of the quality and an associated affect that denotes the strength of the deviation. Drives reflect the systems current condition. The evaluation of environmental and bodily sensations is achieved with the use of previously experienced impacts of the perceived object on the individual and therefore on the homeostasis. Both types of evaluations together form the basis for further decision making.

Filter

There are two types of filters formulated in the described model. One is defined within the functionality of *defense mechanisms* as described in psychoanalytical theory. Influenced by individual needs originating in a deviation from homeostasis and social rules, a censoring mechanism only permits socially acceptable information to reach the higher cognitive processes. The second filter type directs the focus of attention of the system to currently important perceptions. They are closely related to the current context of the system and decrease or increase the affect (=quantity) associated with the perception.

World Model

Reliable and consistent models regarding knowledge about environmental and subjective object relations are stored in associated memory traces that are the patterns for thing presentations. However, no consistent model exists over the whole system, doe to the two different types of data representation and their correlation to the primary and secondary processes. The associations in the primary process are, according to psychoanalysis, highly inconsistent compared to their corresponding associations in the secondary process. The reason for this is the absence of the concepts of negation, causality and location within the primary process. Besides this differentiation, there is a distinction among previously experienced information regarding semantic, episodic, social, and repressed information. The former three are necessary for higher deliberation on realizing already formed intentions, whereas the repressed information influences the search results for the evaluation of externally perceived objects.

Intentions

A constant motivator for intentions is the drive system that represents the model's internal performance measure. The decision-making process depends also on the possibilities and impacts regarding the physical and social environment. Here, the often conflicting demands from the top level instances of the Id (including the generation of drives) and the Super-Ego (including social rules and a corresponding rewarding system) are evaluated and a single intention is formed.

Plans

Already experienced episodes are the basis for the system's planning. The best matching possibilities are evaluated imaginarily using the available knowledge about reality. Available knowledge regarding the current and the desired condition is also considered. However, the implementation showed a deficit in flexibility of the employed plan matching algorithm compared to other currently available planning models. As long as the already evaluated components of the plan phases are accordingly considered by the implementation, the usage of means-end reasoning with forward and backward chaining would be a promising next step within the implementation.

Efficiency and Finite Calculation Time

The amount of data necessary for the evaluation must not exceed a certain amount in order to achieve efficient decision making. The performance of the implemented algorithms was not explicitly considered during the design phase and plays a minor role in the simulation. An application to real world environments was outside the scope of this thesis. However, the current implementation uses pattern matching algorithms and a very reduced set of knowledge-base information. The realization of the described test case with e.g. a two wheeled robot would therefore be possible in principle, presuming pre-generated symbolic input data. Considerations regarding deadlocks and a possible handling within the sequential chain of function calls are not included within the model.

Evaluation of Outcomes

A positive or negative impact of a perception, an action, or an achieved goal results in the reduction or boost of tension and therefore pleasure or displeasure. The performance

Conclusion and Outlook

measures for this evaluation are defined within the model by the concept of drives. The impacts can be directly associated with the currently processed information. However the sample implementation used a static set of associations – learning algorithms were not implemented.

Reconsider Knowledge (Belief revision)
The implemented static knowledge-base including the plans of the agent do not perform a belief revision following an action or the execution of a plan. The application of semantic web technologies is necessary to improve the performance of the first test implementation and would give the agent the possibility to adapt its behavior in new, unknown situations.

Action
Using the predefined plans that include corresponding action sequences to execute these plans, the model provides the possibility of influencing the environment. The output data of the model is information in a symbolic form. A succeeding system is necessary which converts the symbols into actuator commands. Within the described test application, a distributed form of de-symbolization was realized. The employed virtual actuators can directly interpret symbols such as 'move forward' and convert them into corresponding physical actions such as moving one wheel of the motion unit of a robot.

Reactive / Deliberate
Currently, the model is restricted to producing an output when a corresponding sensory datum passes each functional module of the architecture. This can be seen as a deliberative approach. However, psychoanalytical theory includes concepts of 'short circuits' that are not caused by synaptic reasons, which would not be part of a psychoanalytical concept but rather a neurological one. These motor discharges can be one result of low level processes that are not censored by corresponding filter mechanisms.

Cooperation
The model allows cooperation between agents through additional plans and provides a knowledge container for social rules that describe socially acceptable interaction between agents. In principle, the cooperation between agents is not predefined within the model. Interaction can be performed through different sensor and actuator modalities attached to the agent. In contrast to a specified communication protocol regarding cooperation, the model provides a motivating system for cooperation with an independent and controlling instance following the concept of the psychoanalytical Super-Ego.

By applying the top-down design approach to the theory of psychoanalysis, a consistent model for an agent's control unit was defined. Consistency was proven regarding both functionality and the employed data structures. A two tier architecture was designed that applies the concepts of the primary and secondary process defined in psychoanalysis to the corresponding functional units of the model. The model was implemented and simulated in Java. Together with a physics engine, the multi agent simulation platform MASON provided a basic framework for the agent-environment interaction. The model proved capable of acting within a simulated environment by perceiving, evaluating and filtering current information from homeostatic, bodily, and environmental sensations. Based on the investigated impacts of primary evaluation and filtering functionality to the final information that is used as the basis for planning, the important issues of the bionic model are: The necessity of a permanent evaluation process based on object-related experiences, the achievement of data reduction with filtering mechanisms, and the new concepts of conflict resolution between homeostatic and environmental requirements.

During the process of designing, modeling, implementing, and testing the model, the insights gained into the employed psychoanalytical theory allowed certain conclusions about the completeness and consistency of the psychoanalytical model from a purely technical point of view. The following summarization gives an overview on the sufficiency of the employed psychoanalytical theory in terms of technical feasibility.

- The generation of drives regarding the values of homeostasis is firmly anchored in psychoanalytical theory and influences the functional behavior on almost every layer. The employed theory was sufficient for a technical implementation. However, pleasure may be achieved in many ways and not only by satisfying drives that originate in a homeostatic deviation. In this central issue, defense mechanisms seem to play a dominant role in psychoanalysis. Although several concepts for defense mechanisms are defined in psychoanalysis, these mechanisms are not limited to a certain context or a certain type of data. The manifold possibilities and exceptions make a transfer into a technical model difficult.

- The evaluation of perceived information according to individual past experiences follows different concepts regarding the two defined tiers of the primary and secondary process. The assembly of the different data structures in both processes is clearly specified but the functionality of how the data structures are organized will need to be investigated in more detail in a future step. The pleasure and reality principles seem to be the key topics of investigation.

- The introduced model did not consider learning and assumed a completely defined knowledge-base. Psychoanalysis does not offer an explicit learning concept but investigates the phases of human development from birth to adulthood. The importance of acquired experience is identified within the theory of depth psychology [SSK97]. However, the emerging object relationships described in depth psychology are just a part of the complete net of associations. The employed theory does not offer sufficient definitions to allow the realization of of a secondary process-organized ontology. Such definitions would influence the performance of the planning process dramatically, therefore additional psychological theories [Tul83] should be considered.

In summary, the psychoanalytical model showed great potential to be used as a global, modular framework for agent controllers. It offers a new concept for forming desires within an agent rather than relying on predefined lists of desires. This work is designed to allow different implementations of selected models that need not violate the model's conventions. This approach makes it possible to compare the performance of different implementation technologies and knowledge-bases. With the application of the model in agent based simulation and robots, a new concept for internal performance measurement and interpretation thereof is provided which supports planning processes and increases the efficiency of actions. Together with a developed simulation environment, the outcomes of the agent's can be tracked back to their origins. This makes the complex system transparent and efficient regarding the search for side effects. First approaches have been made to apply the perceptual parts of the model in building automation [LBVD09]. A possible application of the complete model will require a theory of mapping internal demands and bodily sensations of an embodied agent onto a building. Otherwise, a concept of learning drives and their relations to external perception during a learning phase would be necessary.

7.2 Hot Spots for Future Research

The main focus of this thesis was to develop a first architecture for the controller of an autonomous, embodied agent, following a bionic approach and therefore using concepts from psychoanalysis and the theory of metapsychology. In cooperation with psychoanalytical advisors, a number of necessary functions were defined that are mandatory for human-like decision making. These functionalities were technically specified and implemented in a first version to investigate the information flow and its effects on the decision-making process. During the modeling and implementation phase it was necessary to significantly reduce the complexity of the psychoanalytical theory and the employed software technologies in order to achieve a consistent model. However, future efforts in this area will have to reconsider some of the reductions made in order to refine and enhance the introduced model. The following paragraphs offer a brief overview of tasks which are to be considered long term goals and will require further interdisciplinary cooperation between specialists in the fields of neurology, psychology, psychoanalysis, artificial intelligence, cognitive science and computer engineering.

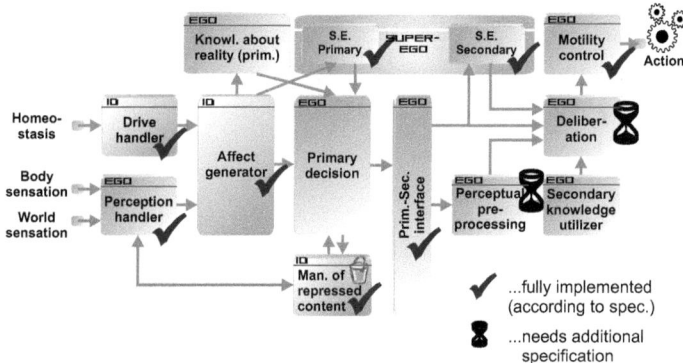

Figure 7.1: Road-map for Future Research Efforts to Refine the Introduced Model

Figure 7.1 shows the corresponding road-map of the model, where check marks indicate congruence between specification and implementation within this work. An hourglass denotes functional modules that are in need of refinement regarding specification or implementation, and modules without an additional sign are currently implemented with the most basic functionality possible.

Primary Decision
During data acquisition and associated discussions on psychoanalytical theory, it turned out that defense mechanisms, represented in the functional module *Primary decision* in Figure 7.1, are a central concept in human decision making processes. In contrast to the usage in one functional module located only within the primary process section of the developed model, psychoanalysis postulates the occurrence of various types of defense mechanisms on different levels of consciousness in the human psyche. According to [Fre38], the palette ranges from unconscious mechanisms like repression to (partly) conscious mechanisms like

humor. This thesis only considered the most basal defense mechanisms. In a further implementation, other defense mechanisms will need to be investigated with respect to their technical application. Although the various concepts are classified and defined in psychoanalysis, the way of applying these concepts is highly situation-dependent and cannot be described within a global equation. Together with knowledge representation techniques, new concepts for modeling and implementation will have to be introduced to cope with these demands.

Data Structures and Operators
The defined data structures and operators that can be applied to these structures follow the definitions given by psychoanalysis. These definitions can serve further research as a basic platform, but the concepts of assigning and associating information are scarcely defined in psychoanalysis. A detailed and interdisciplinary investigation into the psychoanalytical definition of the primary and secondary process and the way information is organized is mandatory for a more precise technical specification. It is the author's firm belief that the results of such investigation would increase the performance of a specific computational implementation on the one hand, while narrowing the gap that still exists between psychological, psychoanalytical, and neurological theory on the other hand.

Integration of Knowledge-Bases and Semantic Webs
The defined and implemented knowledge-bases used within the current implementation consist of several independent information stores that are not consistent as a whole. Figure 7.1 summarizes these knowledge-bases in the functional modules *Knowledge about reality*, *Management of repressed content*, and *Secondary knowledge utilizer*. Furthermore, the implementation assigned specific stores to certain functional modules within the model. From a bionic point of view, this assumption will have to be reconsidered. From the point of view of software development, integration of theories for semantic webs and ontologies may prove useful for narrowing the gap between information and semantics within the currently implemented knowledge-base. The necessary confinement to a primary or secondary process organization could be realized as an additional parameter within an ontology.

Integration of Symbol Based Planning and Reasoning
In symbolic Artificial Intelligence, a wide variety of planning algorithms exist. With the advent of the first declarative, high-level programming languages like Prolog, various problem solving methodologies (e.g. Newell's General Problem Solver, [New94]) using deductive and inductive reasoning were developed. Symbolic reasoning units for agents also implement planning algorithms following these concepts. Such concepts are to be seen as one part of the implementation in the functional module *Deliberation* depicted in Figure 7.1.

Integrating certain implemented concepts for causal planning and reasoning would improve the visible output of the agent due to the inherent possibility of describing actions and sub plans that can be used to create new plans by means-end reasoning, instead of pre-providing complete plans for each possible situation. Combined with complex event processing [PB09] and belief revision [GÖ8], the results would influence the agent's performance most positively.

Integration of Reinforcement Algorithms
With the realization of the concept of *drives* according to the psychoanalytical theory, the possibility is provided to directly associate events and actions with their impacts on the agent. Although learning was not within the focus of this thesis, this functionality is a vital step towards integrating reinforcement learning algorithms into the model. In conjunction with a tight connection to a mandatory knowledge-base, individual experiences with perceived objects or situations can be updated, which can be seen as the basic motivator for belief revision. The evaluation system of drives is only that efficient as the underlying, virtual 'organs' that produce the corresponding drive tensions. Current research efforts have already shown the importance of a complex body [PB07] and a complex internal system [DTM+09]. A combination with the results in this area will increase the possibilities for reinforcement learning within the introduced model.

Joining Connectionism and Cognitivism in Technology
The defined data structures *primary information* and *secondary information* can be described as symbolic information. The information processing used within the model therefore follows a purely cognitivistic schema. However, the complete model cannot be reduced to a cognitivistic approach, but combines concepts of both sides: The connectionistic approach is used to produce symbols from sensory data by applying concepts from neurology and artificial neural networks [LZD+08]. The cognitivistic side is represented by the basic theory described in the introduced model. Currently, the two parts communicate unidirectionally and do not influence each other. According to results of neuro-psychoanalysis [ST02], however, the two concepts are interrelated and cannot be separated. The fusion of both theories into one single concept would allow inter-modular communication.

Applying Concepts to Building Automation
In this work the agent-based model was applied to a robot-like, embodied, autonomous agent. The main goal of this research effort is to provide a general model for agents that is not limited to a specific kind of body. Human drives are closely related to very basic bodily functions that must be learned during our childhood and adolescence in order to survive within human's social and physical environment. Robotic drives cannot be identical to

human drives, due to their differing bodily functions and the different environments they are designed for. The introduced simulation used anthropomorphisms to enable efficient refinement of the psychoanalytical model during the discussions with the psychoanalytical advisors. In a further step, these anthropomorphisms will have to be rejected and new origins for robotic drives defined. This will be an important step towards an implementation in building automation.

7.3 Future Requirements to Decision Making Units

The project Artificial Recognition System (ARS) introduces and realizes new concepts in perceiving, processing, and interpreting data. Concepts that provide new dimensions in problem solving are urgently necessary considering the slow progress Artificial Intelligence has been making in the past decades. With the progressive integration of computer systems in everyday situations and rapidly increasing demands on existing computer systems, a transformation to a more efficient and flexible way of tackling the arising problems becomes mandatory. The psychoanalytically inspired framework introduced in this thesis could be a first step in transferring agent based development onto a higher level.

The integration of embodiment and the empowerment of agents to follow global goals without ignoring individual goals will be necessary in order to develop future computer systems. Computers have to be able to deal with the demands of ubiquitous computing, ambient intelligence, or pervasive computing. These demands will not affect high end computer machines only. Cheap and tiny computer nodes will find their way into different application areas where centralized computer systems cannot be applied. These 'smart dust' computer nodes will not be supplied with the same resources as centralized computers. The single node fulfills only a minuscule part of the functionality performed by the entire network of – for example wirelessly connected – agents. The full functionality emerges through cooperation within the society of agents. An agent is considered to be working properly when it fulfills the tasks required of it by the agent society. However, when the agent ignores or misinterprets its own demands it may stop working. Especially in areas of ultra-low power consumption nodes, like smart-dust objects, the loss of single agents can result in collapse of the entire network.

The author is certain that in future, agents will have to decide between collective and individual behavior. Psychoanalysis provides a framework for exactly this decision problem: following the urge to satisfy individual drives and wishes versus following social demands.

Despite the difficulty of this decision (we human beings know how hard it is) computer systems will require the capability to estimate the impact of their actions. Ethical reasoning will become a central topic that must be investigated. The actions taken by an agent may not influence a human being directly, but in ubiquitous computing, other agents are most likely involved – agents following other directives and realizing other goals, the goals given by other, human operators. The increasing possibilities of interaction within a society that contains agents of completely different types will make meta-deliberation such as ethical reasoning necessary. The model introduced in this thesis uses concepts of the human psyche, described by the theory of psychoanalysis, in order to realize human-like decision making in autonomous agents. To allow these agents to behave more like humans, the model provides a framework that handles the requirements of global, individual, social, and ethical decision making as described above. As long as current implementations of Artificial Intelligence merely integrate purely logical concepts or try to approach logical concepts as if they were human-like processes instead of identifying, modeling, and realizing the concepts of human decision making, the term 'intelligent system' will not refer to human like intelligence. Cooperations between scientists of various research areas, such as neurology, psychology, psychoanalysis, and engineering have already been started: www.simulatingthemind.info . It is to be hoped that they will herald a new generation of Artificial Intelligence.

Literature

[AA07]   Michael Anderson and Susan Leigh Anderson. Machine ethics: Creating an ethical intelligent agent. *AI Magazine*, 28 No. 4:4–15, 2007.

[ABB+04]   J. R. Anderson, D. Bothell, M. D. Byrne, S. Douglass, C. Lebiere, and Y. Qin. An integrated theory of the mind. *Psychological Review*, 111(4):1036–1060, 2004.

[Ari64]   Silvano Arieti. The rise of creativity: From primary to tertiary process. *Contemporary Psychoanalysis*, 1:51–68, 1964.

[AS05]   Virgil Andronache and Matthias Scheutz. Ade - an architecture development environment for virtual and robotic agents. *the International Journal of Artificial Intelligence Tools*, 15, 2005.

[Bad97]   Alan Baddeley. *Human Memory: Theory and Practice*. Psychology Press, 1997.

[BAE+04]   R. Brooks, L. Aryanada, A. Edsinger, P. Fitzpatrick, C. C. Kemp, U. O'Reilly, E. Torres-jara, P. Varshavskaya, and J. Weber. Sensing and manipulating built-for-human environments. *International Journal of Humanoid Robotics*, 1:1–28, 2004.

[BBF+99]   Kirill Bolshakov, Andrei Borshchev, Alex Filippoff, Yuri Karpov, and Victor Roudakov. Creating and running mobile agents with xj dome. *Proceedings of the 5th International Conference, PaCT-99*, pages 410–416, 1999.

[BBI+98]   Rodney A. Brooks, Cynthia Breazeal, Robert Irie, Charles C. Kemp, Matthew Marjanovic, Brian Scassellati, and Matthew M. Williamson. Alternative essences of intelligence. *Proceedings of the Fifteenth National Conference on Artificial Intelligence (AAAI-98)*, 1:961–969, 1998.

[Bes99] John B. Best. *Cognitive Psychology*. Wadsworth/Thomson Learning, 1999.

[BF04] Andrei Borshchev and Alexei Filippov. From system dynamics and discrete event to practical agent based modeling: Reasons, techniques, tools. Technical report, XJ Technologies and St. Petersburg Technical University, 2004.

[BGTB06] Matt Berlin, Jesse Gray, Andrea L. Thomaz, and Cynthia Breazeal. Perspective taking: An organizing principle for learning in human-robot interaction. *Proceedings of the Twenty-First National Conference on Artificial Intelligence (AAAI-06)*, pages 1444–1450, 2006.

[BHW07] R. H. Bordini, J. F. Hübner, and M Wooldridge. *Programming Multi-Agent Systems in AgentSpeak Using Jason.* ohn Wiley & Sons, Ltd., 2007.

[BLPV07] Wolfgang Burgstaller, Roland Lang, Patricia Pörscht, and Rosemarie Velik. Technical model for basic and complex emotions. *Proceedings of 2007 IEEE International Conference of Industrial Informatics*, pages 1033–1038, 2007.

[BR98a] Paolo Busetta and Kotagiri Ramamohanarao. An architecture for mobile bdi agents. In *Proceeding of the 1998 ACM Symposium on Applied Computing (SAC'98)*, pages 445–452, 1998.

[BR98b] Paolo Busetta and Kotagiri Ramamohanarao. The bdim agent toolkit design. Technical report, Department of Computer Science - The University of Melbourne, 1998.

[Bra87] Michael Bratman. *Intentions, Plans, and Practical Reason*. Harvard University Press, 1987.

[Bre01] Cynthia Breazeal. Affective interaction between humans and robots. *Proceedings of the Sixth European Conference on Artificial Life (ECAL2001), Prague, CZ*, 1:582–591, 2001.

[Bre02] Cynthia Breazeal. *Designing Sociable Robots*. MIT Press, Cambridge, MA, USA, 2002.

[Bre03] Cynthia Breazeal. Emotive qualities in lip-synchronized robot speech. *Advanced Robotics*, 17, No. 2:97–113, 2003.

[BRHL99] P. Busetta, R. Rönnquist, A. Hodgson, and A. Lucas. Jack intelligent agents - components for intelligent agents in java. *Agentlink News Letter*, 2(Jan), 1999.

[Bro86] Rodney A. Brooks. A robust layered control system for a mobile robot. *IEEE J. Robotics and Automation1*, pages 14–23, 1986.

[Bro90] Rodney A. Brooks. Elephants don't play chess. *Robotics and Autonomous Systems 6*, 1:3–15, 1990.

[Bro91] Rodney A. Brooks. Intelligence without representation. *Artificial Intelligence*, 47(47):139–159, 1991.

[Bro92] Rodney A. Brooks. Artificial life and real robots. In *Toward a Practice of Autonomous Systems: Proceedings of the First European Conference on Artificial Life*, 1992.

[Bru07] Dietmar Bruckner. *Probabilistic Models in Building Automation: Recognizing Scenarios with Statistical Methods*. PhD thesis, Vienna University of Technology, Institute of Computer Technology, 2007.

[BS93] Rodney A. Brooks and Lynn Andrea Stein. Building brains for bodies. *Technical Report MIT*, AI Memo No. 1439, 1993.

[BS02] Anrzej Buller and Katsunori Shimohara. On the dynamics of judgment: does the butterfly effect take place in human working memory? *Artificial Life and Robotics*, 5, Number 2:88–92, 2002.

[BSL07] Dietmar Bruckner, Brian Sallans, and Roland Lang. Behavior learning via state chains from motion detector sensors. *Proceedings of the 2nd International Conference on Bio-Inspired Models of Network, Information, and Computing Systems (BIONETICS 2007)*, 2007.

[Bul02] Andrzej Buller. Volitron: On a psychodynamic robot and its four realities. *Pro-ceedings Second International Workshop on Epigenetic Robotics: Modeling Cognitive Development in Robotic Systems*, 94:17–20, 2002.

[Bul05] Andrzej Buller. Building brains for robots: A psychodynamic approach. *Invited talk on the First International Conference on Pattern Recognition and Machine Intelligence, PReMIT'05*, pages 17–20, 2005.

[Bul08] Andrzej Buller. Toward machines that can daydream. *Proceedings of the Conference on Human System Interaction*, pages 609–614, 2008.

[Bul09]   Andrzej Buller. Four laws of machine psychodynamics. In Dietmar Dietrich, Georg Fodor, Gerhard Zucker, and Dietmar Bruckner, editors, *Simulating the Mind – A Technical Neuropsychoanalytical Approach*, pages 320 – 332. Springer, Wien, 1 edition, 2009.

[Bur07]   Wolfgang Burgstaller. *Interpretation of Situations in Buildings*. PhD thesis, Vienna University of Technology, Institute of Computer Technology, 2007.

[Byr01]   Mike D. Byrne. Act-r/pm and menu selection: Applying a cognitive architecture to hci. *International Journal of Human-Computer Studies*, 55:41–84, 2001.

[Che03]   Christopher Cheong. A comparison of jack intelligent agents and the open agent architecture. *RMIT University, School of Computer Science and Information Technology (This article has not been reviewed by a joiurnal)*, 2003.

[CMW06]   Nicholas Cassimatis, Erik T. Mueller, and Patrick Henry Winston. Achieving human-level intelligence through integrated systems and research: Introduction to this special issue. *AI magazine*, 27/2:12–14, 2006.

[Dam94]   Antonio Damasio. *Descartes' Error: Emotion, Reason, and the Human Brain*. Penguin, 1994. Published in Penguin Books 2005.

[Dam00]   Antonio Damasio. *The Feeling of What Happens: Body, Emotion and the Making of Consciousness*. Vintage, new ed edition, October 2000.

[Dam03]   Antonio Damasio. *Looking for Spinoza: Joy, Sorrow, and the Feeling Brain*. Harvest Books, 2003.

[Dan99]   M. Daniels. Integrating simulation technologies with swarm. *Agent Simulation: Applications, Models and Tools Conference*, 1999.

[DBG+07]   Shaul Druckmann, Yoav Banitt, Albert Gidon, Felix Schürmann, Henry Markram, and Idan Segev. A novel multiple objective optimization framework for constraining conductance-based neuron models by experimental data. *Frontiers in neuroscience*, 1:7–18, 2007.

[DBZ+09]   Dietmar Dietrich, Dietmar Bruckner, Gerhard Zucker, Brit Müller, and Anna Tmej. Psychoanalytical model for automation and robotics. *Proceedings of the 9th IEEE AFRICON 2009 (Technical keynote)*, 1, 2009.

[Den87]   Daniel C. Dennett. *The Intentional Stance*. The MIT Press, Cambridge, MA, 1987.

[DFR02]   Dietmar Dietrich, Clara Tamarit Fuertes, and Gerhard Russ. Bionische modellierung. *Elektronik Report*, 12:22–23, 2002.

[DFZ+09]   Dietmar Dietrich, Georg Fodor, Gerhard Zucker, Dietmar Bruckner, and et al. *Simulating the Mind - A Technical Neuropsychoanalytical Approach*. Springer, Wien, 2009.

[DGLV08]   Tobias Deutsch, Andreas Gruber, Roland Lang, and Rosemarie Velik. Episodic memory for autonomous agents. In *Proc. Conference on Human System Interactions*, pages 621–626, 25–27 May 2008.

[DGMM06]   Dietrich Dörner, Jürgen Gerdes, Monica Mayer, and Shalini Misra. A simulation of cognitive and emotional effects of overcrowding. *Proceedings of the Seventh International Conference on Cognitive Modeling (ICCM 2006).*, pages 92–99, 2006.

[Die00]   Dietmar Dietrich. Evolution potentials for fieldbus systems. *Proceedings of: IEEE International Workshop on Factory Communication Systems*, 1:145–146, 2000.

[DKM+04]   Dietmar Dietrich, Wolfgang Kastner, T. Maly, Charlotte Roesener, Gerhard Russ, and H. Schweinzer. Situation modeling. *Factory Communication Systems, 2004. Proceedings. 2004 IEEE International Workshop on*, pages 93–102, 2004.

[DLP+06]   T. Deutsch, R. Lang, G. Pratl, E. Brainin, and S. Teicher. Applying psychoanalytic and neuro-scientific models to automation. In *Proc. 2nd IET International Conference on Intelligent Environments IE 06*, volume 1, pages 111–118, 5–6 July 2006.

[Doo95]   Robert B. Doorenbos. *Production Matching for Large Learning System*. PhD thesis, Computer Science Department, Carnegie Mellon University, Pittsburgh, PA, 1995.

[Dor04]   Martin Dornes. *Der kompetente Säugling – Die präverbale Entwicklung des Menschen*. Fischer Taschenbuch Verlag GmbH, 2004.

[Dör02]   Dietrich Dörner. *Die Mechanik des Seelenwagens: Eine neuronale Theorie der Handlungsregulation (mechanics of the mindwaggon: a neuronal theory of actionregulation)*. Huber, Bern, 2002.

[Dör08]   Dietrich Dörner. Emotion und handeln. *Human Factors, Psychologie sicheren Handelns in Risikobranchen*, 1:94–113, 2008.

[DS03]   Chris Dobbyn and Susan Stuart. The self as an embedded agent. *Minds and Machines*, 13, No. 2:187–201, 2003.

[DTM+09]   Tobias Deutsch, Anna Tmej, Clemens Muchitsch, Gerhard Zucker, Christiane Riedinger, and Roland Lang. Failsafe aspects of a decision unit inspired by cognitive sciences - the id without ego and super-ego. *Proceedings of the 2nd International Conference on Human System Interaction*, Special Session 1 - 4th presentation, 2009.

[DZ08]   Dietmar Dietrich and Gerhard Zucker. New approach for controlling complex processes. an introduction to the 5th generation of AI. *Human System Interactions, 2008 Conference on*, pages 12–17, 2008. invited keynote speech.

[DZL07]   T. Deutsch, H. Zeilinger, and R. Lang. Simulation results for the ars-pa model. In *Proc. 5th IEEE International Conference on Industrial Informatics*, volume 2, pages 995–1000, 23–27 June 2007.

[DZLZ08]   T. Deutsch, Tehseen Zia, R. Lang, and H. Zeilinger. A simulation platform for cognitive agents. In *Proc. 6th IEEE International Conference on Industrial Informatics INDIN 2008*, pages 1086–1091, 13–16 July 2008.

[ERBB08]   Rick Evertsz, Frank E. Ritter, Paolo Busetta, and Jennifer L. Bittner. Cojack - achieving principled behaviour variation in a moderated cognitive architecture. *Proceedings of the Behavior Representation in Modeling and Simulation (BRIMS)*, 2008.

[FDDR01]   Clara Tamarit Fuertes, Dietmar Dietrich, Keith Dimond, and Gerhard Russ. A definition and a model of a perceptive awareness system (pas). *Proceedings of the IFAC International Conference on Fielbus Systems and their Applications FeT*, pages 1–7, 2001.

[Fod75]   J. Fodor. *The language of Thought*. Harvard University Press, 1975.

[For82]   C.L. Forgy. Rete: a fast algorithm for the many pattern/many object pattern match problem. *Artificial Intelligence*, 19(1):17–37, 1982.

[Fre91]   Sigmund Freud. *Zur Auffassung der Aphasien*. Fischer Taschenbuch, 1891.

[Fre00]   Sigmund Freud. The interpretation of dreams. *The Standard Edition of the Complete Psychological Works of Sigmund Freud*, Volume IV (1900): The Interpretation of Dreams (First Part):ix–627, 1900.

[Fre11]   Sigmund Freud. Formulations on the two principles of mental functioning. In James Strachey, editor, *The Standard Edition of the Complete Psychological Works of Sigmund Freud, Volume XII (1911-1913): The Case of Schreber, Papers on Technique and Other Works, 213-226*, volume 12, pages 218–226. London: Hogarth Press, 1911.

[Fre15a]   Sigmund Freud. Instincts and their vicissitudes. *The Standard Edition of the Complete Psychological Works of Sigmund Freud*, XIV (1914-1916): On the History of the Psycho-Analytic Movement, Papers on Metapsychology and Other Works:109–140, 1915.

[Fre15b]   Sigmund Freud. Repression. *The Standard Edition of the Complete Psychological Works of Sigmund Freud*, 14:146–158, 1915.

[Fre15c]   Sigmund Freud. *The Unconscious*, volume XIV (1914-1916) of *On the History of the Psycho-Analytic Movement, Papers on Metapsychology and Other Works*. 1915.

[Fre17]   Sigmund Freud. A difficulty in the path of psycho-analysis. *The Standard Edition of the Complete Psychological Works of Sigmund Freud*, Volume XVII (1917-1919): An Infantile Neurosis and Other Works:135–144, 1917.

[Fre23]   Sigmund Freud. The ego and the id. *The Standard Edition of the Complete Psychological Works of Sigmund Freud*, XIX (1923-1925):1–66, 1923.

[Fre25]   Sigmund Freud. Negation. *The Standard Edition of the Complete Psychological Works of Sigmund Freud*, Volume XIX (1923-1925): The Ego and the Id and Other Works:233–240, 1925.

[Fre33]   Sigmund Freud. *New Introductory Lectures On Psycho-Analysis.*, volume Volume XXII (1932-1936): New Introductory Lectures on Psycho-Analysis and Other Works, 1-182 of *The Standard Edition of the Complete Psychological*

Works of Sigmund Freud. Hogarth Press and Institute of Psych–Analysis, 1933.

[Fre38]   Anna Freud. The ego and the mechanisms of defence. *International Journal of Psycho-Analysis*, 19:115–146, 1938.

[Fre40]   Sigmund Freud. An outline of psycho-analysis. *International Journal of Psycho-Analysis*, 21:27–84, 1940.

[Fre72]   Sigmund Freud. Trieblehre. *Gesammelte Werke chronologisch geordnet*, XVII:70–73, 1972.

[Fue03]   Clara Tamarit Fuertes. *Automation System Perception - First Step towards Perceptive Awareness.* PhD thesis, Faculty of Electrical Engineering and Information Technology, Vienna University of Technology, 2003.

[Gö8]   Peter Gärdenfors. *Knowledge in Flux: Modeling the Dynamics of Epistemic States.* Kings College Pubn, 2008.

[GHLM01]   Paul R. Gray, Paul J. Hurst, Stephen H. Lewis, and Robert G. Meyer. *Analysis and Design of Analog Integrated Circuits.* Wiley, 4th edition, 2001.

[GI89]   Michael P. Georgeff and François Felix Ingrand. Decision-making in an embedded reasoning system. In *IJCAI*, pages 972–978, 1989.

[GLS99]   William Gropp, Ewing Lusk, and Anthony Skjellum. *Using MPI - 2nd Edition: Portable Parallel Programming with the Message Passing Interface (Scientific and Engineering Computation).* The MIT Press, 1999.

[GPP+99]   Mike Georgeff, Barney Pell, Martha Pollack, Milind Tambe, and Mike Wooldridge. The belief-desire-intention model of agency. *Proceedings of the 5th International Workshop on Intelligent Agents V: Agent Theories, Architectures, and Languages (ATAL-98)*, 1555:1–10, 1999.

[GVH03]   Brian Gerkey, Richard T. Vaughan, and Andrew Howard. The player/stage project: Tools for multi-robot and distributed sensor systems. *Proceedings of the 11th International Conference on Advanced Robotics*, 1:317–323, 2003.

[GW99]   et al. Gerhard Weiss. *Multiagent Systems: A Modern Approach to Distributed Artificial Intelligence.* The MIT Press, 1999.

[HC08] Antoine Hiolle and Lola Cañamero. Why should you care? an arousal-based model of exploratory behavior for autonomous robot. *Artificial Life XI: Proceedings of the Eleventh International Conference on the Simulation and Synthesis of Living Systems*, pages 242–248, 2008.

[HDN03] Wan Ching Ho, Kerstin Dautenhahn, and Chrystopher L. Nehaniv. Comparing different control architectures for autobiographic agents in static virtual environments. *Intelligent Agents, 4th International Workshop, IVA 2003, Kloster Irsee, Germany, September 15-17, 2003, Proceedings*, pages 182–191, 2003.

[HDN05] Wan Ching Ho, Kerstin Dautenhahn, and Chrystopher L. Nehaniv. Autobiographic agents in dynamic virtual environments - performance comparison for different memory control architectures. *Proceedings of IEEE Congress on Evolutionary Computation IEEE*, pages 573–580, 2005.

[HDNB04] Wan Ching Ho, Kerstin Dautenhahn, Chrystopher L. Nehaniv, and Rene Te Boekhorst. Sharing memories: An experimental investigation with multiple autonomous autobiographic agents. *IAS-8, 8th Conference on Intelligent Autonomous Systems*, pages 361–370, 2004.

[Hor00] Ian Horswill. A laboratory course in mobile robotics. *IEEE Intelligent Systems*, pages 16–21, 2000.

[Hsu02] Feng-hsiung Hsu. *Behind Deep Blue: Building the Computer that Defeated the World Chess Champion*. Princeton University Press, 2002.

[Hub99a] Marcus J. Huber. Considerations for flexible autonomy within bdi intelligent agent architectures. *Working Notes of the AAAI Spring Symposium on Agents with Adjustable Autonomy*, pages 65–72, 1999.

[Hub99b] Marcus J Huber. JAM: A BDI-theoretic mobile agent architecture. pages 236–243, 1999.

[IEE87] Ieee standard for software unit testing, 1987.

[JW06] Randolph M. Jones and Robert E. Wray. Comparative analysis of frameworks for knowledge-intensive intelligent agents. *AI magazine*, 27 No.2:57–70, 2006.

[KKSD08] Andrew Koster, Fernando Koch, Liz Sonenberg, and Frank Dignum. Augmenting bdi with relevance: supporting agent-based, pervasive applications.

In *Pervasive Mobile Interaction Devices (PERMID 2008) Workshop at Pervasive*, 2008.

[KM97]   David E. Kieras and David E. Meyer. An overview of the epic architecture for cognition and performance with application to human-computer interaction. *Human Computer Interaction 12*, 4:391–438, 1997.

[KSS00] K. Kaplan-Solms and M. Solms. *Clinical Studies in Neuro-Psychoanalysis*. International Universities Press, Inc.,Madison, CT,, 2000.

[LA08]   Juan Liu and Hiroshi Ando. Emotion eliciting and decision making by psychodynamic appraisal mechanism. *Proceedings of the Conference on Human System Interaction*, pages 645–650, 2008.

[Lan01] Roland Lang. A door control unit using the 42v board net within passenger cars. Master's thesis, University of Applied Sciences Technikum Wien, 2001.

[Lan06] Pat Langley. Cognitive architectures and general intelligent systems. *AI magazine*, 27 No.2:33–44, 2006.

[Lap73] J. Laplanche. *Das Vokabular der Psychoanalyse.* suhrkamp taschenbuch wissenschaft, Frankfurt am Main, 1973.

[LBG97] Liana M. Lorigo, Rodney A. Brooks, and W. E. L. Grimson. Visually-guided obstacle avoidance in unstructured environments. pages 373–379, 1997.

[LBP+03] Sean Luke, Gabriel Catalin Balan, Liviu Panait, Claudio Cioffi-Revilla, and Sean Paus. Mason: A java multi-agent simulation library. *Proceedings of the Agent 2003 Conference*, 2003.

[LBP06] Marianne Leuzinger-Bohleber and Rolf Pfeifer. Recollecting the past in the present: Memory in the dialogue between psychoanalysis and cognitive science. In Mauro Mancia, editor, *Psychoanalysis and Neuroscience*, pages 63–95. Springer Milan, 2006.

[LBP+07] Roland Lang, Dietmar Bruckner, Gerhard Pratl, Rosemarie Velik, and Tobias Deutsch. Scenario recognition in modern building automation. *Proceedings of the 7th IFAC International Conference on Fieldbuses & Networks in Industrial & Embedded Systems (FeT 2007)*, pages 305–312, 2007.

[LBSP92] Marianne Leuzinger-Bohleber, Henry Schneider, and Rolf Pfeifer. *Two Butterflies on My Head... - Psychoanalysis in the Interdisciplinary Scientific Dialog*. Springer, 1992.

[LBVD09] Roland Lang, Dietmar Bruckner, Rosemarie Velik, and Tobias Deutsch. Scenario recognition in modern building automation. *International Journal of Intelligent Systems and Technologies*, 4-1, No. 5:36–44, 2009.

[LC06] Pat Langley and Dongkyu Choi. Learning recursive control programs from problem solving. *Journal of Machine Learning Research*, 7:493–518, 2006.

[LCRPS04] Sean Luke, Claudio Cioffi-Revilla, Liviu Panait, and Keith Sullivan. Mason: A new multi-agent simulation toolkit. In *Proceedings of the 2004 Swarmfest Workshop*, 2004.

[LNR87] John E. Laird, Allen Newell, and P. S. Rosenbloom. Soar: An architecture for general intelligence. *Artificial Intelligence*, 33:1–64, 1987.

[Lor08] Emiliano Lorini. Agents with emotions: a logical perspective. *Association for Logic Programming Newsletter*, 21(2-3), 2008.

[LP73] J. Laplanche and J. B. Pontalis. *The Language of Psycho-Analysis: Translated by Donald Nicholson-Smith*. The Hogarth Press and the Institute of Psycho-Analysis, 1973.

[Lur73] Aleksandr Romanovich Luria. *The Working Brain - An Introduction in Neuropsychology*. Basic Books, 1973.

[LYHT91] John E. Laird, Eric S. Yager, Michael Hucka, and Christopher M. Tuck. Robo-soar: An integration of external interaction, planning, and learning using soar. *Robotics and Autonomous Systems*, 8(1-2):113–129, 1991.

[LZD+08] R. Lang, H. Zeilinger, T. Deutsch, R. Velik, and B. Muller. Perceptive learning - a psychoanalytical learning framework for autonomous agents. In *Proc. Conference on Human System Interactions*, pages 639–644, 25–27 May 2008.

[Mar06] H Markram. The blue brain project. *Nature Reviews, Neuroscience*, 7:153–160, Feb. 2006.

[MBLA96] Nelson Minar, Roger Burkhart, Chris Langton, and Manor Askenazi. The swarm simulation system: A toolkit for building multi-agent simulations -

report no.: 96-06-042. Technical report, Santa Fe (NM): Santa Fe Institute, 1996.

[MBV09] J. Mitterbauer, D. Bruckner, and R. Velik. Behavior recognition and prediction with hidden markov models for surveillance systems. *Proceedings of the IFAC FET*, 1:204–211, 2009.

[McC07] Lee McCauley. Demonstrating the benefit of computational consciousness. *AI and Consciousness: Theoretical Foundations and Current Approaches: Papers from the AAAI Fall Symposium*, FS-07-01:109–116, 2007.

[MDA05] Viviana Mascardi, Daniela Demergasso, and Davide Ancona. Languages for programming bdi-style agents: an overview. *Proceedings of the 6th WOA 2006 Workshop, From Objects to Agents (Dagli Oggetti Agli Agenti)*, pages 9–15, 2005.

[Min06] Marvin Minsky. *The Emotional Machine: Commonsense Thinking, Artificial Intelligence, and the Future of the Human Mind*. Simon & Schuster Paperbacks, 2006.

[MM07] Catherine Marcarelli and Jeffrey L. McKinstry. Testing for machine consciousness using insight learning. *AI and Consciousness: Theoretical Foundations and Current Approaches: Papers from the AAAI Fall Symposium*, FS-07-01:103–109, 2007.

[Moo65] Gordon E. Moore. Cramming more components onto integrated circuits. *Electronics*, 38-8, 1965.

[Nac98] Werner Nachtigall. *Bionik*. Springer, 1998.

[NCV06] Michael J. North, Nicholson T. Collier, and Jerry R. Vos. Experiences creating three implementations of the repast agent modeling toolkit. *ACM Trans. Model. Comput. Simul.*, 16(1):1–25, 2006.

[New94] Allen Newell. *Unified Theories of Cognition*. Harvard Univ Press, 1994.

[NTCJ07] M.J. North, E. Tatara, N.T. Collier, and Ozik J. Visual agent-based model development with repast simphony. *Proceedings of the Agent 2007 Conference on Complex Interaction and Social Emergence*, pages 173–192, 2007.

[OK98] William O'Donohue and Richard Kitchener. *Handbook of Behaviorism*. Academic Press Inc., 1998.

[Pal07]   Brigitte Palensky. *Introducing Neuro-Psychoanalysis towards the Design of Cognitive and Affective Automation Systems*. PhD thesis, Faculty of Electrical Engineering and Information Technology, Vienna University of Technology, 2007.

[Pan98]   Jaak Panksepp. *Affective Neuroscience, the Foundations of Human and Animal Emotions*. Oxford University Press, Inc. 198 Madison Avenue, New York, 1998.

[PB07]   Rolf Pfeifer and Josh Bongard. *How the body shapes the way we think*. MIT Press, 2007.

[PB09]   A. Paschke and H. Boley. Rules capturing events and reactivity. *Handbook of Research on Emerging Rule-Based Languages and Technologies: Open Solutions and Approaches*, page Section I, 2009.

[PBL03]   Alexander Pokahr, Lars Braubach, and Winfried Lamersdorf. Jadex: Implementing a bdi-infrastructure for jade agents. *EXP - in search of innovation (Special Issue on JADE)*, 3(3):76–85, 2003.

[PBL05]   Alexander Pokahr, Lars Braubach, and Winfried Lamersdorf. Jadex: A bdi reasoning engine. In *Multi-Agent Programming Languages, Platforms and Applications*. Springer US, 2005.

[Pic00]   Rosalind W. Picard. *Affective Computing*. MIT Press, 2000.

[PIG06]   Rolf Pfeifer, Fumiya Iida, and Gabriel Gómez. Designing intelligent robots – on the implications of embodiment. *Journal of Robotics Society of Japan*, 24(7):9–16, 2006.

[PKKK08]   Jong-Chan Park, Young-Min Kim, Hyoung-Rock Kim, and Dong-Soo Kwon. Robot's emotion generation model with personality and loyalty based on generalized context input variables. *39th International Symposium on Robotics*, pages 108–113, 2008.

[PL04]   Liviu Panait and Sean Luke. A pheromone-based utility model for collaborative foraging. *Proceedings of 2004 Conference on Autonomous Agents and Multiagent Systems*, pages 36–43, 2004.

[PP05]   G. Pratl and P. Palensky. Project ars - the next step towards an intelligent environment. *Proceedings of the IEE International Workshop on Intelligent Environments*, pages 55–62, 2005.

[PPDB05] Gerhard Pratl, Walter T. Penzhorn, Dietmar Dietrich, and Wolfgang Burgstaller. Perceptive awareness in building automation. *IEEE 3rd International Conference on Computational Cybernetics*, pages 259–264, 2005.

[Pra06] Gerhard Pratl. *Processing and Symbolization of Ambient Sensor Data*. PhD thesis, Faculty of Electrical Engineering and Information Technology, Vienna University of Technology, 2006.

[PS99] Rolf Pfeifer and Christian Scheier. *Understanding Intelligence*. MIT Press, 1999.

[Rie02] Alexander Riegler. When is a cognitive system embodied? *Cognitive Systems Research*, 3(3):339–348, September 2002.

[Rie09] Christiane Riediger. Psychoanalytical defense mechanisms applied to autonomous agents. Master's thesis, Vienna University of Technology, Faculty of Informatics, Institute of Computer Technology, 2009.

[RLD+07] C. Roesener, R. Lang, T. Deutsch, A. Gruber, and B. Palensky. Action planning model for autonomous mobile robots. In *Proc. 5th IEEE International Conference on Industrial Informatics*, volume 2, pages 983–988, 23–27 June 2007.

[RLJ06] Steven F. Railsback, Steven L. Lytinen, and Stephen K. Jackson. Agent-based simulation platforms: Review and development recommendations. *SIMULATION*, 82 No. 9:609–623, 2006.

[RN03] Stuart J. Russell and Peter Norvig. *Artificial Intelligence: A Modern Approach*. Pearson Education, 2003.

[Roe07] Charlotte Roesener. *Adaptive Behavior Arbitration for Mobile Service Robots in Building Automation*. PhD thesis, Vienna University of Technology, Institute of Computer Technology, 2007.

[Rus03] Gerhard Russ. *Situation-dependent Behavior in Building Automation*. PhD thesis, Vienna University of Technology, Institute of Computer Technology, 2003.

[SA04] Matthias Scheutz and Virgil Andronache. The apoc framework for the comparison of agent architectures. *Papers from the 2004 AAAI Workshop - Technical Report WS-04-07 published by The AAAI Pres*, 1:66–74, 2004.

[SC05]   Aaron Sloman and Ron Chrisley. More things than are dreamt of in your biology: Information-processing in biologically inspired robots. In Ron Sun, editor, *Cognitive Systems Reasearch*, volume 6, pages 145–174. Elsevier, 2005.

[SCS05]   Aaron Sloman, Ron Chrisley, and Matthias Scheutz. The architectural basis of affective states and processes. In M. Arbib and J-M. Fellous, editors, *Who Needs Emotions?: The Brain Meets the Robot*, pages 203–244. Oxford University Press, Oxford, New York, 2005.

[Sha09]   Michael John Shaffer. Decision theory, intelligent planning and counterfactuals. *Minds and Machines*, 19, No. 1:61–92, 2009.

[SLH07]   Ricardo Sanz, Ignacio López, and Carlos Hernández. Self-awareness in realtime cognitive control architectures. *AI and Consciousness: Theoretical Foundations and Current Approaches: Papers from the AAAI Fall Symposium*, FS-07-01:136–142, 2007.

[Slo04a] Aaron Sloman. Information-processing systems in nature. 2004.

[Slo04b] Aaron Sloman. What are emotion theories about? In *Symposium Technical Report*, pages 128–134. AAAI Spring, 2004.

[Slo09]   Aaron Sloman. Machines in the ghost. In Dietmar Dietrich, Georg Fodor, Gerhard Zucker, and Dietmar Bruckner, editors, *Simulating the Mind – A Technical Neuropsychoanalytical Approach*, pages 124 – 149. Springer, Wien, 1 edition, 2009. invited contribution for the 1st ENF - Emulating the Mind, 2007, Vienna.

[SM08]   Matthew Spackman and David Miller. Embodying emotions: What emotion theorists can learn from simulations of emotions. *Minds and Machines*, 18(3):357–372, 2008.

[SMFL06] Christian Scheve, Daniel Moldt, Julia Fix, and Rolf Lüde. My agents love to conform: Norms and emotion in the micro-macro link. *Computational and Mathematical Organization Theory (CMOT)*, 2006.

[SMP01]   R. Sun, E. Merrill, and T. Peterson. From implicit skills to explicit knowledge: A bottom-up model of skill learning. *Cognitive Science*, Vol.25, No.2:203–244, 2001.

[Sol96] Mark Solms. Was sind affekte (translated: What are affects). *Psyche*, 6:485–522, 1996.

[Sol06a] Philipp Soldt. The dialectics of affective and conceptual thought: Some general remarks on primary and secondary process functioning. *The Scandinavian Psychoanalytic Review*, 29:33–42, 2006.

[Sol06b] Mark Solms. Eine neurowissenschaftliche perspektive auf die psychoanalyse. In *Sigmund Freud - Zum Zeitgemäßen eines unzeitgemäßen Denkens oder: Wider das Veralten der Psychoanalyse*. Psyche, 2006.

[SRF00] C. Soucek, Gerhard Russ, and Clara Tamarit Fuertes. The smart kitchen project - an application on fieldbus technology to domotics. *Proceedings of the 2nd International Workshop on Networked Appliances (IWNA2000)*, page 1, 2000.

[SSK97] Peter Schuster and Marianne Springer-Kremser. *Bausteine der Psychoanalyse*. WUV-Universitätsverlag, 1997.

[ST94] Daniel L. Schacter and Endel Tulving. *Memory Systems*. The MIT Press, 1994.

[ST02] Mark Solms and Oliver Turnbull. *The Brain and the Inner World: An Introduction to the Neuroscience of Subjective Experience*. Karnac/Other Press, Cathy Miller Foreign Rights Agency, London, England, 2002.

[Str99a] Carol Strohecker. The chorus as internalized objects (working note). *AAAI-99 Fall Symposium on Narrative Intelligence*, 1999.

[Str99b] Carol Strohecker. The chorus as internalized objects (working paper). *AAAI Technical Report*, FS-99-01, 1999.

[TAA79] E. Tronick, H. Als, and L. Adamson. Structure of early face-to-face communicative interactions. In M. Bullowa, editor, *Before Speech: The Beginning of Interpersonal Communication*, pages 349–370. Cambridge University Press, Cambridge, UK, 1979.

[TB06] Andrea L. Thomaz and Cynthia Breazeal. Reinforcement learning with human teachers: Evidence of feedbackandguidance with implications for learning performance. *Proceedings of the Twenty-First National Conference on Artificial Intelligence (AAAI-06)*, pages 1000–1005, 2006.

[TNH+06]   E. Tatara, M.J. North, T.R. Howe, N.T. Collier, and J.R. Vos. An introduction to repast modeling by using a simple predator-prey example. *Proceedings of the Agent 2006 Conference on Social Agents: Results and Prospects*, 2006.

[Tod82]   Masanao Toda. *Man, Robot and Society*. Martinus Nijhoff Publishing, 1982.

[Tul83]   Endel Tulving. *Elements of Episodic Memory*. Oxford: Clarendon Press, 1983.

[Tur89]   Sherry Turkle. Artificial intelligence and psychoanalysis: A new alliance. In S. R. Graubard, editor, *The Artificial Intelligence Debate: False Starts, Real Foundations*, pages 241–268. MIT Press, Cambridge, MA, 1989.

[Tur04]   Sherry Turkle. Whither psychoanalysis in computer culture? *Psychoanalytic Psychology*, 21:16–30, 2004.

[Tur06]   Sherry Turkle. A nascent robotics culture: New complicities for companionship. *AAAI Technical Report Series*, WS-06-09:51–61, 2006.

[Tur07]   Sherry Turkle. Authenticity in the age of digital companions. *Interaction Studies - Social Behaviour and Communication in Biological and Artificial Systems*, 8 Issue 3:503–517, 2007.

[UML09a]   Omg unified modeling language (omg uml), infrastructure; version 2.2, 02 2009.

[UML09b]   Omg unified modeling language (omg uml), superstructure; version 2.2, 2 2009.

[Vel94]   Manuela M. Veloso. *Planning and Learning by Analogical Reasoning*. Springer; 1 edition (December 27, 1994), 1994.

[Vel08]   Rosemarie Velik. *A Bionic Model for Human-like Machine Perception*. PhD thesis, Vienna University of Technology, Institute of Computer Technology, 2008.

[VLBD08]   R. Velik, R. Lang, D. Bruckner, and T. Deutsch. Emulating the perceptual system of the brain for the purpose of sensor fusion. In *Proc. Conference on Human System Interactions*, pages 657–662, 25–27 May 2008.

[VTR93]   Francisco J. Varela, Evan Thompson, and Eleanor Rosch. *The Embodied Mind: Cognitive Science and Human Experience*. The MIT Press, 1993.

[Wei66]   Joseph Weizenbaum. Eliza: A computer program for the study of natural language communication between man and machine. *Communications of the ACM*, 9(1):36–45, 1966.

[Wie65]   Norbert Wiener. *Cybernetics - 2nd Edition: Or the Control and Communication in the Animal and the Machine: Or Control and Communication in the Animal and the Machine*. MIT Press, 1965.

[WL07]   Yongjia Wang and John E. Laird. The importance of action history in decision making and reinforcement learning. *Proceedings of the Eighth International Conference on Cognitive Modeling*, 2007.

[Woo00]   Michael J. Wooldridge. *Reasoning about Rational Agents (Intelligent Robotics and Autonomous Agents)*. MIT Press, 2000.

[ZLM09]   Heimo Zeilinger, Roland Lang, and Brit Müller. Bionic inspired information representation for autonomous agents. In *in press*, 2009.

[ZMD08]   Gerhard Zucker, Brit Mueller, and Tobias Deutsch. Way to go for AI. *Proceedings of IT Revolutions 2008, Venice*, 2008.

A Abbreviations and Formalisms

A.1 Abbreviations

AI	Artificial Intelligence
ANN	Artificial Neural Networks
ARS	Artificial Recognition System
ARS-PA	Artificial Recognition System - Psychoanalysis
ARS-PC	Artificial Recognition System - Perception
ARSi09/Lang	Artificial Recognition System Implementation 2009 / Lang
BFG	Bubble Family Game
BWv1	Bubble World Version 1
GNU LGPL	The GNU Lesser General Public License
HTML	Hyper Text Markup Language
MASON	Multi-Agent Simulator Of Neighborhoods... or Networks... or something...
UML	Unified Modeling Language
XML	Extensible Markup Language

A.2 Usage of Mathematical Formalisms

Example equation 1:

$$M = \{m_i \mid 1 \leq i \leq n \text{ and } i,\, n \,\epsilon\, \mathbb{N}\}$$

M	A capital letter denotes a set as a collection of distinct objets.
m_i	A lower case letter is an element of the corresponding set. The subscript qualifies the ith element in the set.

Abbreviations and Formalisms

	Start of the qualification of the objects within the set.
$\leq$ and geq	The 'lower or equal than' and 'greater or equal than' operator is used for either solely natural or real numbers.
$\mathbb{N}$	Natural numbers
$\mathbb{R}$	Real numbers

Example equation 2:

$$IT_1 = \{w_3 \otimes s_3 \wedge w_{17} \otimes s_{17}\}$$

$w_3 \otimes s_3$	The used operator $\otimes$ returns the real number of its left operand if the right operand is defined in a predefined set, or '0' if this is not the case.
$\wedge$ and $\vee$	The used logical operands only depict the dependency within the corresponding, logical relationship. An $\wedge$-relationship requires both terms to be greater than '0' to return an overall weight greater than '0'. An $\vee$-relationship requires only one term.

A.3 Utilized Unified Modeling Language (UML) Version 2.2 Notations

The following Figure A.1 shows the usage according to the UML 2.2 standard that is used for the description of the class diagrams according to [UML09a, p. 129 ff] within this work.

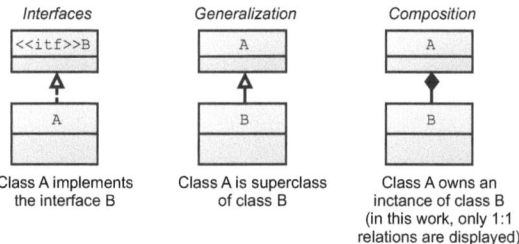

Figure A.1: UML-Elements Used for Class Diagrams

Figure A.2 shows an example for the used UML-notation within sequence diagrams according to [UML09b, p. 459 ff]. Within this example, a function of the instance of class A calls a function of the instantiated class B. After the response (it can include return information) was returned to the function of class A, another external function call of a third class is executed. The white bars are indicating the sequential activities of of the class instances.

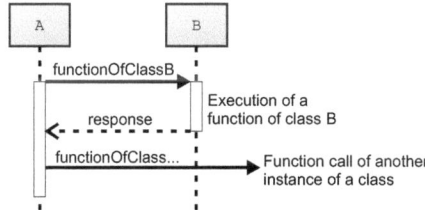

Figure A.2: UML-Elements Used for Sequence Diagrams

Die VDM Verlagsservicegesellschaft sucht für wissenschaftliche Verlage abgeschlossene und herausragende

Dissertationen, Habilitationen, Diplomarbeiten, Master Theses, Magisterarbeiten usw.

für die kostenlose Publikation als Fachbuch.

Sie verfügen über eine Arbeit, die hohen inhaltlichen und formalen Ansprüchen genügt, und haben Interesse an einer honorarvergüteten Publikation?

Dann senden Sie bitte erste Informationen über sich und Ihre Arbeit per Email an *info@vdm-vsg.de*.

Sie erhalten kurzfristig unser Feedback!

VDM Verlagsservicegesellschaft mbH
Dudweiler Landstr. 99　　　　　Telefon +49 681 3720 174
D - 66123 Saarbrücken　　　　　Fax　　　+49 681 3720 1749
www.vdm-vsg.de

Die VDM Verlagsservicegesellschaft mbH vertritt

Printed by Books on Demand GmbH, Norderstedt / Germany